Drinking and Driving Offences

DRINKING AND DRIVING OFFENCES

Law and Practice

Second edition

Jonathan Black

The Law Society

Crown copyright material is reproduced with the permission of the Controller of Her Majesty's Stationery Office

Tables 12.1(a) and (b) are reproduced with the permission of the Magistrates' Association.

ISBN-10: 1-85328-559-5
ISBN-13: 978-1-85328-559-1

Published in 2006 by the Law Society
113 Chancery Lane, London WC2A 1PL

Typeset by J&L Composition, Filey, North Yorkshire
Printed by MPG Books Ltd, Bodmin, Cornwall

Contents

Preface   *viii*
Table of cases   *xi*
Table of statutes   *xix*
Table of statutory instruments   *xxii*

1   An overview of the procedure   **1**

1.1   Introduction   1
1.2   Preliminary test   2
1.3   Providing a specimen at the police station or hospital   2

2   Power to require preliminary tests   **5**

2.1   The legislation   5
2.2   Preliminary breath test device   8
2.3   Constable in uniform   11
2.4   Reasonably suspects   12
2.5   Reasonably believes   17
2.6   Accident   19
2.7   Place for administering the preliminary test   20
2.8   Failing to provide the specimen   20
2.9   Reasonable excuse   22
2.10 Impairment tests   23

3   The arrest   **27**

3.1   The legislation   27
3.2   Arrest   29
3.3   Trespass   31
3.4   Entry by implied licence   35
3.5   Detention of persons affected by alcohol or a drug   36
3.6   Hospital patients   37

4   Protection for hospital patients and testing of incapacitated drivers   39

4.1   The legislation   39
4.2   Definitions   41
4.3   Treatment   43
4.4   Preliminary breath test   44
4.5   Providing the specimen   44
4.6   Specimen of blood taken from persons incapable of consenting   45

5   Driving or in charge whilst unfit   49

5.1   The legislation   49
5.2   Definitions   49
5.3   Blood/urine option where evidence of drug impairment   58
5.4   Arrest provisions   61

6   The 'in charge' statutory defence   63

6.1   The legislation   63
6.2   Applying the defence   63

7   Driving whilst over the prescribed limit   67

7.1   The legislation   67
7.2   Prescribed limit   67
7.3   Provision of specimens for analysis   68
7.4   Approval of devices   83
7.5   Challenges to approved devices   84
7.6   Driver's obligation and option to provide blood or urine   95

8   Evidence of analysis   111

8.1   The legislation   111
8.2   Status of the statement   112
8.3   Requirement to serve the statement   113
8.4   Errors on the face of the statement   117
8.5   Requirement to sign the statement   118
8.6   Authorised analyst   119

9   Using specimen evidence, post-accident consumption and back-calculation   121

9.1   The legislation   121
9.2   European Convention issues   122

9.3   Methods of analysis   125
9.4   Dividing the specimen   127
9.5   Evidence of the proportion of alcohol   130
9.6   Back-calculation   135

10 Failure to provide a specimen   **139**

10.1 The legislation   139
10.2 Comparison between section 7(3) and   140
      section 7(6)/section 7A(6)
10.3 Warning of the consequences of failure   141
10.4 Effect of an unlawful arrest   142
10.5 'Fails' and 'refuses'   143
10.6 Consulting a doctor or solicitor   143
10.7 Making every effort   147
10.8 Reasonable excuse   151
10.9 'Driving' or 'in charge': effect on sentence   157

11 Causing death whilst under the influence of drink or drugs **161**

11.1 The legislation   161
11.2 The offence   161

12 Sentencing   **167**

12.1 Penalties for the offences   167
12.2 Interim disqualification   170
12.3 Maximum penalties   171
12.4 Special reasons   172
12.5 Alternative verdicts   184
12.6 Drink-drive rehabilitation courses   184
12.7 High risk offenders   186
12.8 Sentencing guideline tables   187

13 Road Safety Act 2006   **191**

13.1 Background   191
13.2 Sections   191

Index   *197*

Preface

Since the first edition of this book was published in 2003, there have been numerous significant changes to the legislation contained in sections 3A to 11 of the Road Traffic Act 1988, most notably those introduced by the Railways and Transport Safety Act 2003 and the Serious Organised Crime and Police Act 2005. The effect of these changes has been to expand the range of preliminary testing available to a police officer who reasonably suspects a person to be driving whilst above the prescribed limit and to tighten up procedures at the police station and in hospitals to ensure that evidential specimens can be obtained in all appropriate cases.

These provisions are not the end of the proposed changes. The Road Safety Act 2006 received Royal Assent on 8 November 2006 and contains a number of provisions designed to enhance road safety which will have an impact on the drinking driver. It is, therefore, timely to produce a second, updated edition of the book.

Legislation governing the drinking driver was first passed in 1925 and since that time, the procedural and evidential requirements of the legislation have provided a rich harvest of legal points for those wishing to challenge the provisions.

Prior to 1962, it was an offence to drive whilst unfit through drink or drugs; the evidence necessary to prove this being obtained either by reference to the way in which the vehicle had been driven or to the physical appearance or behaviour of the driver. In 1962, the offence became one of driving whilst impaired, but unfortunately, no definition of impairment was provided by statute. At the same time provision was made for courts to take account of blood–alcohol levels in determining the extent and nature of the impairment, although in practice, most police forces continued to rely upon evidence of bad driving or behaviour rather than on scientific proof.

The Road Safety Act 1967 was to prove a landmark in providing an evidential basis upon which to found what previously were mere suspicions. The Act, which came into force on 9 October 1967, created three new offences:

(a) driving or being in charge of a vehicle having consumed a quantity of alcohol over the prescribed limit;

(b) refusing to take a screening breath test; and

(c) refusing to provide a blood or urine specimen for a laboratory test.

The 1967 Act also introduced a new word into the English language: the breathalyser, a device designed to give an indication at the roadside that a driver was driving or in charge of a vehicle after consuming so much alcohol that he was over a prescribed limit – defined as being more than 80 milligrammes (mg) of alcohol in 100 ml of blood, or more than 107 mg in the case of a sample of urine.

The latter provisions aroused strong feelings in Parliament, especially during the Committee stages of the Bill where Mr Gresham Cooke maintained that 'the prohibited level could be reached after three or four drinks at a cocktail party'.

The Times of 25 November 1966 also quoted Mr David Mitchell as claiming that the average guest at a civic function would consume two cocktails, a third of a bottle of wine and a glass of port. This, it was asserted, would take him over the limit so that:

> When the Prime Minister stands up at the Lord Mayor's Banquet and talks, are we suggesting that he is drunk in charge of the Nation's affairs and impaired in his judgement because he has gone to such a dinner and had the normal things?

The provisions of the Act were introduced by the then Minister of Transport, Mrs Barbara Castle MP as a 'tough law for a tough problem'. Certainly, the police reacted with gusto, carrying out 2,791 roadside breath tests in England and Wales between 9 and 13 October, of which 1,029 were positive (*Hansard*, 23 November 1967). However, a comparison of successful drink-driving related prosecutions before and after the Act tended to show only a slight increase in the number of successful prosecutions after the implementation date.

Implementation of the Act also opened up new pastures for those concerned with defending drivers alleged to be over the limit. The *Justice of the Peace* newspaper reported in its 23 December 1967 edition that:

> . . . innumerable tips, none effective, on how a drinking motorist could avoid the consequences of his folly, having circulated in the temporarily diminished bars of the country reached the pages of the newspapers (a motorist who followed one of those tips had a conviction for failing to supply a specimen of breath added to his conviction of exceeding the statutory limit) while the President of the National Federation of Licensed Victuallers tested, to his apparent satisfaction, 'anti-breathalyser tablets'.

In addition, tests on the effect of certain popular brands of aftershave were extensively carried out to ensure that drivers were not prejudiced by a form of intoxication by osmosis!

Subsequent changes in drink-driving law and procedure were brought about by the Transport Act 1981, which came into force on 6 May 1983. The 1981 Act replaced what were, by then, the provisions of the Road Traffic Act 1972 with new provisions of driving, attempting to drive or being in charge of a motor vehicle with excess alcohol levels, together with offences of failing to provide a specimen of breath for a roadside test or for laboratory analysis.

Most importantly, the 1981 Act replaced, to a large extent, the messy and time-consuming requirements to provide specimens of blood or urine, with a new procedure which analysed at the police station the proportion of alcohol in the offender's breath (subject to the option to supply blood or urine in limited cases). Again, the new procedures created a catalogue of case law as defendants tested first the wording of the statute, then the reliability of the new devices and finally the procedures themselves.

A final consolidation of the various statutory provisions and penalties was brought about by the Road Traffic Act 1988 and the Road Traffic Offenders Act 1988. Subject to certain amendments contained in various statutes since that time, the law in this book refers to those enactments unless otherwise stated.

This book examines the effect of Divisional Court (and other) judgments relative to the main provisions of the Road Traffic Acts of 1988. The book looks at the extent to which these judgments have impinged upon that area of the law since major changes in the law were introduced on 6 May 1983 and consolidated in the Road Traffic Acts of 1988. It provides a logical route for practitioners through the maze of legislation, practice and case law that has developed around the subject of drink-driving. The book concentrates mainly on case law since 1988, although previous case law is referred to either where new developments have superseded that case law or where it is necessary to refer to the old in order to understand the new.

Thanks, as always, to my wife, Helen and to Will and Dom for their encouragement and support.

The law is stated as at 8 November 2006.

Jonathan S W Black LLM, Solicitor
Petersfield

Table of cases

Anderton v. Kinnard [1986] RTR 11, DC 116–17
Anderton v. Lythgoe [1985] 1 WLR 222; [1985] RTR 395, DC 98–9
Anderton v. Royle [1985] RTR 91, DC 30
Anderton v. Waring [1986] RTR 74, DC 148
Arnold v. Kingston-upon-Hull Chief Constable [1969] 1 WLR 1499, DC 20
Ashton v. DPP [1998] RTR 45, DC 79
Askew v. DPP [1988] RTR 303, DC 42–3
Associated Provincial Picture Houses Ltd v. Wednesbury Corp [1948] 1 KB
  223, CA 94
Attorney-General's Reference (No.1 of 1976), Re [1977] 1 WLR 646, CA 42–3
Attorney-General's Reference (Nos.14 & 24 of 1993), Re [1994] 1 WLR
  530, CA 163
Attorney-General's Reference (No.1 of 2004), Re [2004] EWCA Crim 1025;
  [2004] 1 WLR 2111; [2004] 2 Cr App R 424, CA 22
Badkin v. Chief Constable of South Yorkshire [1988] RTR 401, DC 88, 130–1
Baker v. Oxford [1980] RTR 315, DC 18
Baldwin v. DPP [1996] RTR 238, DC 104
Beard v. Wood [1980] RTR 454, DC 12–13
Beauchamp-Thompson v. DPP [1989] RTR 54, DC 122
Beck v. Scammell [1986] RTR 162, DC 117
Bell v. DPP (1998) WRTLB 92, DC 60
Bentley v. Chief Constable of Northumbria [1984] RTR 276, DC 9
Blake v. Pope [1986] 1 WLR 1152; [1987] RTR 77, DC 17
Bobin v. DPP [1999] RTR 375, DC 174
Bowman v. DPP (1990) 154 JP 524; [1991] RTR 263, DC 55
Bradford v. Wilson [1984] RTR 116, DC 50
Braham v. DPP (1995) 159 JP 527; [1996] RTR 30, DC 34–5
Brewer v. DPP [2004] EWHC Admin 355; [2005] RTR 5, QBD 55–6
Brown (Gary) v. Procurator Fiscal, Falkirk 2002 SLT 756; [2003] RTR 17, HCJ
  Appeal 94
Butler v. DPP [1990] RTR 377, DC 128–9
Butler v. DPP [2001] RTR 28, DC 45
Causey v. DPP [2004] EWHC Admin 3164; (2005) 169 JP 331, QBD 146–7
Chatters v. Burke [1986] 1 WLR 1321; [1986] RTR 396, DC 177, 179
Chief Constable of Avon and Somerset v. Fleming [1987] 1 All ER 318; [1987]
  RTR 378, DC 56

Chief Constable of Avon and Somerset v. Kelliher [1987] RTR 305, DC 77–8
Chief Constable of Avon and Somerset v. Singh [1988] RTR 107, DC 23, 141
Chief Constable of Gwent v. Dash [1986] RTR 41, DC 13–14
Chief Constable of Kent v. Berry [1985] RTR 321, DC 73
Chief Constable of Northumbria v. Browne [1986] RTR 113, DC 83
Chief Constable of Surrey v. Wickens (1985) 149 JP 333; [1985] RTR
    277, CA 119
Chief Constable of West Midlands Police v. Billingham [1979] 1 WLR 747;
    [1979] RTR 446, DC 19
Clowser v. Chaplin [1981] 1 WLR 837; [1981] RTR 317, HL 31
Cole v. DPP [1988] RTR 224, DC 60
Collins v. Lucking [1983] RTR 312, CA 125–6
Corner v. Southend Crown Court [2005] EWHC Admin 2334; (2006) 170 JP
    6, QBD 170
Cosgrove v. DPP [1997] RTR 153, DC..................................151
Cotgrove v. Cooney (1987) 151 JP 736; [1987] RTR 124, DC 148–9
Cracknell v. Willis [1988] AC 450; [1988] RTR 1, HL 89–91, 133
Crampsie v. DPP [1993] RTR 383, DC 158
Cutter v. Eagle Star Insurance Co Ltd [1998] 1 WLR 1647; [1998] RTR
    309, CA 54
Davies v. DPP [1989] RTR 391, DC 75–6
Davis v. DPP [1988] RTR 156, DC 74
Dawes v. Taylor [1986] RTR 81, DC 21
De Freitas v. DPP [1992] Crim LR 894; [1993] RTR 98, DC 155
De Munthe v. Stewart [1982] RTR 27, DC 178–9
Dear v. DPP [1988] RTR 148, DC 129
Dempsey v. Catton [1986] RTR 194, DC 74
Denny v. DPP (1990) 154 JP 461; [1990] RTR 417, DC 72
Dhillon (Surinder Singh) v. DPP (1993) 157 JP 420, DC 101
DPP v. Alderton [2003] EWHC Admin 2917; [2004] RTR 23, QBD 50–1
DPP v. Ambrose [1992] RTR 285, DC 155
DPP v. Anderson (1991) 155 JP 157; [1990] RTR 269, DC 52
DPP v. Barber (1999) 163 JP 457, DC 79
DPP v. Barker [1990] RTR 1, DC 181
DPP v. Beech [1992] RTR 239, DC 155
DPP v. Bell [1992] RTR 335; [1992] Crim LR 176, DC 177
DPP v. Billington [1988] 1 WLR 535; [1988] RTR 231; (1988) 152 JP 1, QBD ...144
DPP v. Boden [1988] RTR 188, DC 75
DPP v. Bristow [1998] RTR 100, DC 177
DPP v. Brown; DPP v. Teixeira [2001] EWHC Admin 931; (2002) 166 JP 1;
    [2002] RTR 23, QBD 80, 92–4, 135
DPP v. Butterworth [1995] 1 AC 381; [1994] RTR 330, HL 158–9
DPP v. Byrne (1991) 155 JP 601; [1991] RTR 119, DC 101–2
DPP v. Carey [1970] AC 1072; [1970] RTR 14, HL 9–10
DPP v. Chambers [2003] EWHC Admin 2142; (2004) 168 JP 231, QBD 135
DPP v. Charles [1996] RTR 247 (Note), DC 103
DPP v. Conroy [2003] EWHC Admin 1674; (2003) 167 JP 418, QBD 180
DPP v. Corcoran (Joseph Patrick) (1991) 155 JP 597; [1991] RTR 329, DC 180

DPP v. Corcoran (Terence) [1993] 1 All ER 912; [1992] RTR 289, DC 157–9
DPP v. Coyle [1996] RTR 287, DC 151
DPP v. Crofton [1994] RTR 279, DC 156
DPP v. Curtis [1993] RTR 72, DC 153
DPP v. Donnelly [1998] RTR 188, DC 107
DPP v. Eddowes [1991] RTR 35, DC 149
DPP v. Elstob [1992] RTR 45, DC 130
DPP v. Falzarano (2001) 165 JP 201; [2001] RTR 14, DC 156–7
DPP v. Fearnley [2005] EWHC Admin 1393; (2005) 169 JP 450, QBD 94
DPP v. Fountain [1988] RTR 385, DC 154–5
DPP v. Frost [1989] RTR 11, DC 61, 64–5
DPP v. Furby [2000] RTR 181, DC 153–4
DPP v. Goddard [1998] RTR 463, DC 178
DPP v. Godwin [1991] RTR 303, DC 14–15
DPP v. Hastings [1993] RTR 205, DC 51
DPP v. Heywood [1998] RTR 1, DC 11, 21–2
DPP v. Hicks [2002] EWHC Admin 1638; (2002) 166 JPN 594, QBD 178
DPP v. Hill [1991] RTR 351, DC 88–9, 91
DPP v. Humphreys (2000) 164 JP 502 180
DPP v. Hutchings [1991] RTR 380, DC 113
DPP v. Jackson; Stanley v. DPP [1999] 1 AC 406; [1998] RTR 397, HL . . .45, 104–8
DPP v. Janman [2004] EWHC Admin 101; [2004] RTR 31, QBD 52–3
DPP v. Jowle (1999) 163 JP 85, DC 176
DPP v. Kay [1999] RTR 109, DC 9–10
DPP v. Kennedy [2003] EWHC Admin 2583; (2004) 168 JP 185, QBD 10
DPP v. Kinnersley [1993] RTR 105, DC 174
DPP v. Lonsdale [2001] EWHC Admin 95; [2001] RTR 29, QBD 154
DPP v. McGladrigan [1991] RTR 297, DC .14–15, 33, 35
DPP v. McKeown; DPP v. Jones [1997] 1 WLR 295; [1997] RTR 162, HL . . .79, 118
DPP v. Memery [2002] EWHC Admin 1720; [2003] RTR 18, QBD 94
DPP v. Mukandiwa [2005] EWHC Admin 2977; (2006) 170 JP 17; [2006]
    RTR 24, QBD 151–2
DPP v. Neville (1996) 160 JP 758, DC 56
DPP v. Noe [2000] RTR 351, DC 147
DPP v. O'Connor (1992) 13 Cr App R (S) 189; [1992] RTR 66, DC 182–3
DPP v. O'Meara [1989] RTR 24, DC 175–6
DPP v. Ormsby [1997] RTR 394 (Note), DC 103–4
DPP v. Pearman (1993) 157 JP 883; [1992] RTR 407, DC 156
DPP v. Radford [1995] RTR 86 151
DPP v. Robertson [2002] EWHC Admin 542; (2002) 166 JP 649; [2002] RTR
    22, QBD 30
DPP v. Rous [1992] RTR 246 98
DPP v. Saddington [2001] RTR 15, DC 56–7
DPP v. Sharma [2005] EWHC Admin 879; [2005] RTR 27, QBD 182
DPP v. Short [2001] EWHC Admin 885; (2002) 166 JP 474, QBD 67
DPP v. Singh [1988] RTR 209, DC 132–3
DPP v. Smith [2000] RTR 341, DC 84
DPP v. Spurrier [2000] RTR 60; (2000) 164 JP 369, DC 91, 133–4

DPP v. Stephens [2006] EWHC Admin 1860, DC 116
DPP v. Thomas (Elwyn Kenneth) (1993) 157 JP 480; [1996] RTR 293, DC 150
DPP v. Varley [1999] Crim LR 753, DC 22
DPP v. Vivier [1991] 4 All ER 18; (1991) 155 JP 970; [1991] RTR 205, DC 54–5
DPP v. Waller [1989] RTR 112, DC 176
DPP v. Warren [1993] AC 319; [1993] RTR 58, HL 45, 101–8
DPP v. Watkins [1989] QB 821; [1989] RTR 324, DC 53
DPP v. White [1988] RTR 267, DC 175
DPP v. Wilson [1991] RTR 284, DC 15–16
DPP v. Wood; DPP v. McGillicuddy [2006] EWHC Admin 32; (2006) 170
    JP 177, QBD 85–6
Drake v. DPP [1994] Crim LR 855; [1994] RTR 411, DC .65
Edmond v. DPP [2006] EWHC Admin 463; [2006] RTR 18, QBD 82
Elkins v. Cartlidge [1947] 1 All ER 829, KBD 55
Fawcett v. Gasparics [1987] Crim LR 53; [1986] RTR 375, DC 88, 118
Fraser v. DPP [1997] RTR 373, DC 102–4, 107
Gage v. Jones [1983] RTR 508, DC 12
Gaimster v. Marlow [1984] QB 218; [1984] RTR 49, DC 112
Gardner v. DPP (1989) 153 JP 357; [1989] RTR 384, DC 157
Garner v. DPP [1990] RTR 208, DC 119
George v. DPP [1989] RTR 217, DC 157
Gilham v. Breidenbach [1982] RTR 328, DC 36
Gould v. Castle [1988] RTR 57 See Gumbley v. Cunningham
Grady v. Pollard [1988] RTR 316, DC 148–9
Graham v. Albert [1985] RTR 352, DC 70–1
Grant v. DPP [2003] EWHC Admin 130; (2003) 167 JP 459, QBD 10
Greenaway v. DPP (1994) 158 JP 27; [1994] RTR 17, DC 115
Griffiths v. DPP [2002] EWHC Admin 792; (2002) 166 JP 629, QBD 125
Grix v. Chief Constable of Kent [1987] RTR 193, DC 76
Gull v. Scarborough [1987] RTR 261, DC 142
Gumbley v. Cunningham; Gould v. Castle [1989] AC 281; [1989] RTR 49,
    HL; affirming [1988] QB 170; [1988] RTR 57, DC 135–7
Haghigat-Khou v. Chambers [1988] RTR 95, DC 78
Harper v. DPP [2001] EWHC Admin 1071, QBD 35
Hartland v. Alden [1987] RTR 253, DC 142–3
Hasler v. DPP [1989] RTR 148, DC 114–15
Hawes v. DPP [1993] RTR 116, DC 71, 142
Hawkins v. DPP [1988] 1 WLR 1166; [1988] RTR 380, DC 117
Hayes v. DPP [1994] RTR 163; [1993] Crim LR 966, DC 103
Hayward v. Eames [1985] RTR 12, DC 83
Hobbs v. Clark [1988] RTR 36, DC 101–2
Hollingsworth v. Howard [1974] RTR 58, DC 42
Horrocks v. Binns [1986] RTR 202 (Note), DC 73
Howard v. Hallett [1984] Crim LR 565; [1984] RTR 353, DC 72, 98, 141
Howell v. DPP (1994) 158 JP 680, DC 55
Hughes v. McConnell [1986] 1 All ER 268; [1985] RTR 244, DC 89–90
Jarvis v. DPP (2001) 165 JP 15, DC 172–4
Johnson v. West Yorkshire Metropolitan Police [1986] RTR 167, DC 99

Johnson v. Whitehouse [1984] RTR 38, DC 18
Jones v. Crown Prosecution Service [2003] EWHC Admin 1729; (2003) 167
    JP 481, QBD 127
Jones (Vivian) v. DPP [2004] EWHC Admin 3165; [2005] RTR 15, QBD 41
Joseph v. DPP [2003] EWHC Admin 3078; [2004] RTR 21, QBD 100
Jubb v. DPP [2002] EWHC Admin 2317; (2003) 167 JP 50; [2003] RTR
    19, QBD...82
Kelly v. Hogan [1982] RTR 352, DC 52
Kemp v. Chief Constable of Kent [1987] RTR 65, DC 154
Kennedy v. DPP [2002] EWHC Admin 2297; [2004] RTR 6, QBD 144–5
Khatibi v. DPP [2004] EWHC Admin 83; (2004) 168 JP 361, QBD 120
Kirkup v. DPP [2003] EWHC Admin 2354; (2004) 168 JP 255, QBD 145
Leeson v. DPP [2000] RTR 385, DC 89
Leetham v. DPP [1999] RTR 29, DC 60
Lodwick v. Brow [1984] RTR 394, DC....................................174
Lodwick v. Saunders [1985] 1 WLR 382; [1985] RTR 385; [1985] Crim LR 210,
    DC 13
Lonergan v. DPP [2002] EWHC Admin 1263; [2003] RTR 12, QBD 135
Louis v. DPP (1998) 162 JP 287; [1998] RTR 354, DC 79, 116
Lunt v. DPP [1993] Crim LR 534, DC....................................33
McClenaghan v. McKenna [2001] NIECA June 19, CA (NI) 125
McCormack v. DPP [2002] EWHC Admin 173; [2002] RTR 20, QBD 115–16
McCormick v. Hitchins [1988] RTR 182, DC 183–4
MacDonald v. Skelt [1985] RTR 321, DC 128
McGarry v. Chief Constable of Bedfordshire [1983] RTR 172, DC 68
McGrath v. Vipas [1984] RTR 58, DC 23, 142
McKoen v. Ellis (1987) 151 JP 60; [1987] RTR 26, DC 51
Matto v. Wolverhampton Crown Court [1987] RTR 337, DC 9, 34
May v. DPP [2000] RTR 7, DC 150
Mayon v. DPP [1988] RTR 281, DC 78, 89
Mercer v. DPP [2003] EWHC Admin 225; [2004] RTR 8, QBD 81
Millard v. DPP (1990) 154 JP 626; [1990] RTR 201, DC 122–4
Morgan v. Lee [1985] RTR 409, DC 114
Morris v. Beardmore [1981] AC 446; [1980] RTR 321, HL 31
Murray v. DPP [1993] RTR 209; (1994) 158 JP 261, DC 98, 103, 141
Myles v. DPP [2004] EWHC Admin 594; [2004] 2 All ER 902; [2005] RTR 1,
    QBD...146
O'Connell v. DPP [2006] EWHC Admin 1419; [2006] All ER (D) 260, QBD 127
Ogburn v. DPP [1994] 1 WLR 1107; [1994] RTR 241, DC 45, 104
Oswald v. DPP [1989] RTR 360, DC 68, 126
Owen v. Chesters [1985] RTR 191, DC 114
Owen v. Morgan [1986] RTR 151, DC 72
Palmer v. Killion [1983] RTR 138, DC 152
Parker v. DPP (1993) 157 JP 218; [1993] RTR 283; DC 87
Parker v. DPP [2001] RTR 16, DC 123
Patterson v. Charlton DC [1986] RTR 18, DC 132
Pearson v. Metropolitan Police Commissioner [1988] RTR 276, DC 71
Penman v. Parker [1986] 1 WLR 882; [1986] RTR 403, DC 116

Perry v. McGovern [1986] RTR 240, DC 128
Planton v. DPP [2001] EWHC Admin 450; [2002] RTR 9, QBD 56
Price v. Nicholls [1986] RTR 155, DC 89–90
Pridige v. Grant [1985] RTR 196, DC 180
Pugh v. Knipe [1972] RTR 286, DC 56
R v. Bolton Magistrates' Court, ex parte Scally [1991] 1 QB 537; [1991] RTR 84,
    DC 131
R v. Boyd [2002] EWCA Crim 2836; [2004] RTR 2, CA 162
R v. Brentford Magistrates' Court, ex parte Clarke [1987] RTR 205, DC 118
R v. Burton on Trent Justices, ex parte Woolley [1995] RTR 139, DC 45, 104
R v. Cook [1996] RTR 304, CA 168
R v. Cooksley [2004] 1 Cr App R (S) 1 164–6
R v. Coventry Magistrates' Court, ex parte Perks [1985] RTR 74, DC 84
R v. Downey [1970] RTR 257; [1970] Crim LR 287, CA 23
R v. Drummond [2002] EWCA Crim 527; [2002] RTR 21; [2002] Crim LR 666,
    CA 124
R v. Ealing Magistrates' Court, ex parte Woodman (1994) 158 JP 997; [1994]
    RTR 189, DC 49–50
R v. Fox [1986] AC 281; [1985] RTR 337, HL 31–4
R v. Gravesend Magistrates' Court, ex parte Baker (1997) 161 JP 765; [1998]
    RTR 451, DC 183
R v. Gray [2006] 1 Cr App R (S) 126, CA 166
R v. Grimwood [2005] EWCA Crim 1411; (2005) 169 JP 373, CA 46–7
R v. Jackson; R v. Hart [1970] 1 QB 647; (1970) 53 Cr App R 341; [1970]
    RTR 165, CA 172–3
R v. Kingston upon Thames Justices, ex parte Khanna [1986] RTR 364, DC 91
R v. Lennard [1973] 1 WLR 483; [1973] RTR 252, CA 22, 147–9, 151
R v. Millington (1996) 160 JP 39; [1996] RTR 80, CA 162
R v. Newton (1983) 77 Cr App R 13, CA 159
R v. Noble [2002] EWCA Crim 1713; [2003] RTR 6, CA 166
R v. Rivano (1994) 158 JP 288, CA 169
R v. Samuel [1988] QB 615, CA 35
R v. Sang [1980] AC 402, HL 32, 34
R v. Shoult [1996] RTR 298, CA 168
R v. Skegness Magistrates' Court, ex parte Cardy; R v. Manchester Crown
    Court, ex parte Williams [1985] RTR 49, DC 84–5
R v. Spence [1999] RTR 353, CA 55
R v. Tower Bridge Magistrates' Court, ex parte DPP [1989] RTR 118, DC ..85, 113
R v. Wagner [1970] Crim LR 535; [1970] RTR 422, CA 21
R v. Wickens (1958) 42 Cr App R 236 172–5
R v. Willer [1987] RTR 22, CA 177
R (on the application of Cunliffe) v. West London Magistrates' Court [2006]
    EWHC Admin 2081, DC 86
Redmond v. Parry [1986] RTR 146, DC 179
Revel v. Jordan: Hillis v. Nicholson [1983] RTR 497, DC 30
Robinson v. DPP [2003] EWHC Admin 2718; (2004) 168 JP 522, QBD 183
Robinson (Dena) v. DPP [1997] RTR 403 (Note), DC 104

Russell v. Devine [2001] NIECA 28, CA (NI); affirmed [2003] UKHL 24;
  [2003] 1 WLR 1187, HL 42
Salabiaku v. France (1988) 3 EHRR CD 379, ECHR 123
Sandy v. Martin [1974] RTR 263; (1974) 139 JP 241, DC 55
Scheiner v. DPP [2006] EWHC 1516; [2006] All ER (D) 110, DC 79
Scott v. Baker [1969] 1 QB 659, DC 29
Sharpe v. DPP (1994) 158 JP 595; [1993] RTR 392, DC 34–5
Shaw v. DPP [1993] 1 All ER 918; [1993] RTR 45, DC 158–9
Sheldrake v. DPP [2004] UKHL 43; [2005] 1 AC 264; [2005] RTR 2, HL 64
Simpson v. Spalding [1987] RTR 221 141
Skinner v. DPP [2004] EWHC Admin 2914; [2005] RTR 17, QBD 94
Slasor v. DPP [1999] RTR 432, DC 129–30
Slender v. Boothby [1986] RTR 385, DC 87–8
Smith v. DPP [1990] RTR 17; (1990) 154 JP 205, DC 100, 181–2
Smith v. Geraghty [1986] RTR 222, DC...............................136, 181
Smyth v. DPP [1996] RTR 59, DC 143
Snelson v. Thompson [1985] RTR 220, DC 9
Snook v. Mannion [1982] RTR 321, DC 35
Sparrow v. Bradley [1985] RTR 122, DC 72
Steadman v. DPP [2002] EWHC Admin 810; [2003] RTR 2, QBD 75
Steel v. Goacher [1983] RTR 98, DC 13
Stephenson v. Clift [1988] RTR 171, DC 126
Stepniewski v. Commissioner of Police for the Metropolis [1985] RTR 330,
  DC 149–50
Steward v. DPP [2003] EWHC Admin 2251; [2004] 1 WLR 592; (2004) 168
  JP 146; [2004] RTR 16, QBD 113
Stewart v. Crowe 1999 SLT 899, HCJ Appeal 15
Stewart v. DPP [2003] EWHC Admin 1323; (2004) 168 JP 82; [2003] RTR 35,
  QBD 82
Stokes v. Sayers [1988] RTR 89, DC 78
Swales v. Cox [1981] 1 QB 849, QBD 33
Sykes v. White [1983] RTR 419, DC....................................152
Teape v. Godfrey [1986] RTR 213, DC 152–3
Thom v. DPP [1994] RTR 11; (1994) 158 JP 414, DC 78–9, 115
Thomas v. DPP [1991] RTR 292, DC 143
Thomson v. Ritchie 2000 SLT 734, HCJ Appeal 16
Tobi v. Nicholas (1987) 86 Cr App R 323; [1988] RTR 343, DC 116
Tomkinson v. DPP [2001] EWHC Admin 182; [2001] RTR 38, DC 178
Townson v. DPP [2006] EWHC 2007 (13 June 2006, unreported), DC 75
Walton v. Rimmer [1986] RTR 31, DC 115
Watt v. MacNeill 1980 SLT 178; [1988] RTR 310 (Note), HCJ 43
Webb v. DPP [1992] RTR 299, DC 77
Webber v. DPP [1998] RTR 111, DC 44
Whelehan v. DPP [1995] RTR 177, DC 52
White v. Proudlock [1988] RTR 163, DC 73–4
Whitley v. DPP [2003] EWHC Admin 2512; (2004) 168 JP 350, QBD 145–6
Whittal v. Kirby [1947] 1 KB 194, KBD 173

Williams *v.* DPP [1991] 1 WLR 1160; [1991] 3 All ER 651; [1991] RTR 214,
   DC 115
Williams *v.* Osborne [1975] RTR 181, DC 22
Woolfe *v.* DPP [2006] EWHC 1497; [2006] All ER (D) 261, DC 81, 175
Woon *v.* Maskell [1985] RTR 289, DC 10–11
Yhnell *v.* DPP [1989] Crim LR 384; [1989] RTR 256, DC 100–1
Young *v.* Flint [1987] RTR 300, DC 85
Young (Paula Anne) *v.* DPP (1993) 157 JP 606; [1992] RTR 328; [1992]
   Crim LR 893, DC 76, 155
Zafar *v.* DPP [2004] EWHC Admin 2468; [2005] RTR 18, QBD 80–1

Table of statutes

Criminal Attempts Act 1981
 s.1(4)..52
Criminal Justice Act 1967
 s.10 116
Criminal Justice Act 2003
 s.143(2) 168
 s.144 168
 s.164(1), (2).............................167
 s.172 168
 s.285 163
Criminal Procedure and Investigations
 Act 1996
 s.8..86
  (3)(a).......................................86
  (4)..86
 s.63..83
Food Safety Act 1990........................119
 s.27 112
Health Act 1999
 s.60(2)...97
Human Rights Act 1998.........32, 35, 64,
  122–3
 s.3 123
 Sched., Art. 6...................145, 147
  (2).....64, 122–5, 131
Magistrates' Courts Act 1980
 s.97..86
Police and Criminal Evidence Act
 1984..98
 s.24 28
 s.25 28
  (6)..28
 s.58 ....144–5, 147
 s.66 144
 s.69 118
 s.78.................10, 14–15, 30, 32–6,

  38, 98, 127, 143, 145, 147, 159
  (1) 33
 Sched.2.......................................28
Police Reform Act 2002 ....140, 192
 s.56..19
  (1) 39
Powers of Criminal Courts (Sentencing)
 Act 2000
 s.1 171
 s.6(4)..170
 s.10 170
Public Passenger Vehicles Act 1981
 Pt II....................................6, 17
Railways and Transport Safety Act
 2003 ....5, 37, 59, 82
 s.107 41
 Sched.7...................................7, 41
Road Safety Act 1967........................173
Road Safety Act 2006
 s.13 191
 s.14 192
 s.15...192–3
 s.16 193
 s.31...193–4
 s.35 194
Road Traffic Act 1962 57
Road Traffic Act 1972 ....29, 31
 s.7(4)...21
Road Traffic Act 1988.........3, 24, 32, 42,
  47, 51–2, 55, 74, 80, 83, 99, 143–5
 Pt V 6, 17
 s.3 162
 s.3A..............23, 29, 44, 59, 68, 70,
  95–6, 112, 121, 139, 161–3,
  167, 171–2, 184, 189, 193–4
  (3) 194

Road Traffic Act 1988—*cont.*
  s.4 .....1–2, 4, 23, 29, 31, 35, 37, 44,
        49–50, 54, 57, 59–66, 68, 70–1,
        95–6, 112, 121, 139, 142,
        158–9, 162, 167, 184
    (1) 168, 172, 189
    (2)...............................63, 189
    (3) 57, 63
    (4) 63
    (6) 61
    (7) 33, 61
    (8) 61
  s.5 .....1, 4, 29, 35, 37, 44, 50, 54–6,
        60–8, 70–1, 95, 112, 121, 139,
        142, 145, 158–9, 162, 167, 184
    (1) 64, 67–8, 168
    (a) 172, 187, 189
    (b) 63, 67, 189
    (2)...............................63–4, 67
    (3) 63, 67
  s.6 ....1, 5–7, 15, 17, 27, 30–1, 50,
        112, 121, 167
    (1) 14
    (2)..............................17–18, 41
    (3)..17
    (4) 17, 189
    (5) 17, 19, 28, 69, 95
    (b) 44
    (6) 20, 22
    (7)..11
    (8)(b) 17
  s.6A 5–8, 11, 20, 28, 44
    (3) 20
  s.6B...................5–8, 11, 20, 23, 44
    (2) 57
    (4) 20
  s.6C.............5–8, 11, 20, 23, 44, 82
    (2) 20
  s.6D 5, 7, 27–9, 31, 61
    (1A), (2A) 27
    (3) 37, 41
  s.6E 5, 7, 28, 32–3, 36, 38
    (1) 35
  s.7 ....1, 27, 37, 39, 42, 44–5, 58,
        68–72, 95–8, 112, 118, 121,
        125, 127, 139–40, 146, 152,
        161–2, 167, 184, 186, 192

    (1)(a)....................................94
    (b) 82
    (2)....................................41, 72
    (c) 97
    (3) 59, 76–7, 98, 101–2, 105–8,
        153, 155
    (a) 75–6, 140, 155
    (b) 87
    (bb) 82–3
    (bc)................................59, 82
    (c)................................59–60
    (4) 97–9, 101–2, 105, 108
    (6) 45, 75–6, 102, 107, 140,
        150, 153, 155, 158–9, 168,
        172, 183, 188–9
    (7) 40, 82, 106, 141
  s.7A..................1–2, 19, 37, 39–40,
        45, 47, 122, 125, 127, 192–4
    (4) 46
    (5)...............................40, 140
    (6) 46, 140, 172, 189, 192, 194
  s.8 ....1, 27, 96–8, 101, 112, 121
    (2)..............................98, 101–8
  s.9 .1–2, 27, 39–43, 45, 68, 95, 112,
        121, 139
  s.10 ....1, 27, 36–7, 41, 112, 121
    (2A) 41
  s.11....................................1, 41, 149
    (2) 20, 49, 61, 67–8, 83, 97, 143
    (3) 11, 21, 97, 147–8
    (b) 82
    (4) 97
  s.88....................................191–2
  s.94(4) 186, 192
  s.163....................................12–13
  s.185 56
  s.189 56
  s.192 54
Road Traffic Act 1991 ....1, 161, 184
Road Traffic (New Drivers) Act
  1995...194
Road Traffic Offenders Act 1988..........6,
    17, 178
  Pt III 6, 17
  s.15................4, 121–5, 127–9, 135
    (1) 112
    (2) ...87, 90, 93, 98, 122–3, 125,
        133, 135, 141

(3).........................87, 123, 135
(5) 42, 111, 125, 127
   (a)..................................130
(5A) 111
s.16 ....4, 111–13, 116–19, 121
   (1)(a) 112
   (2) 113
   (3)(a) 115–16
   (6) 116
s.24 184
   (1) 194
s.26.......................................170–1
s.30A 194
s.34 184
   (1) 172
   (3)...............................169, 172
s.34A 184–5, 192, c194–5
ss.34B, 34BA, 34C 194

ss.34D–34G, 41B 192
s.42.......................................169–70
s.45(7) 192
Sched.2 158
Road Traffic Regulation Act
   1984...6, 17
Serious Organised Crime and Police
   Act 2005 37
   s.110 28
   s.111..49, 61
   s.154..27, 71
      (4)–(6) 70
   Sched.7, para.27(2)..............49, 61
   Sched.17, Pt 2......................49, 61
Summer Time Act 1972 87
Transport Act 1981 31
Vehicle Excise and Registration Act
   1994...54, 56

Table of statutory instruments

Courses for Drink-Drive Offenders (Experimental Period) (Termination of
    Restrictions) Order 1999, SI 1999/3130 185
Driving Licences (Disqualification until Test Passed) (Prescribed Offence) Order
    2001, SI 2001/4051 163
Magistrates' Courts Rules 1981, SI 1981/552
        r.12 159
            (1) 158–9
        r.67(2) 117
        r.100 159
Motor Vehicles (Driving Licences) Regulations 1999, SI 1999/2864
        reg.74 . . . . .186, 192

CHAPTER 1

An overview of the procedure

1.1 INTRODUCTION

The procedure for detecting and processing the drinking driver, whether actually driving or merely in charge of the vehicle, is now contained in the Road Traffic Act 1988 (RTA 1988), ss.4–11. The Road Traffic Act 1991 (RTA 1991) introduced a new offence of driving carelessly and causing death whilst under the influence of drink or drugs.

The way in which evidence leading to a conviction is obtained has changed substantially since the first edition of this book was published in 2003. Amendments to RTA 1988, s.6 to allow for preliminary testing of various kinds for alcohol or drugs, rather than just a screening test for alcohol, have provided police forces with a more flexible procedure for determining whether or not a driver may have been drinking or taking drugs. Additionally, there have been subtle changes to processes and procedures as technology has developed and this has led to improvements, notably in the speed with which cases are brought before courts and the manner in which evidence is obtained.

Initially, a police constable in uniform must reasonably suspect that a person who is driving, attempting to drive or who is in charge of a motor vehicle whilst the vehicle is on a road or other public place, has alcohol in his body or has committed what is termed a 'moving traffic offence'. In some circumstances driving may have ceased, but the constable may still reasonably suspect that the person concerned has been driving or attempting to drive, or has been in charge of a motor vehicle on a road with alcohol in his body and that alcohol is still present in his body.

Similarly, although driving may have ceased, a traffic offence may have been committed whilst the vehicle was being used. Again, a police constable may reasonably suspect the person driving, or attempting to drive, or in charge of the vehicle, to have been the person driving or in charge at the time of the commission of the traffic offence.

1

1.2 PRELIMINARY TEST

In each of the above circumstances, and subject to the provisions of the
RTA1988, s.9 (which give some protection to a motorist whilst at a hospital),
a constable may require the driver to co-operate with a preliminary test.
Usually, this will consist of a 'roadside breath test' although the circumstances of the request may be such that it is actually required at some distance
from the roadside. It is, essentially, a screening procedure.

A similar procedure applies where there has been an accident owing to the
presence of a motor vehicle on a road or other public place, which allows a
constable to require a specimen for a breath test from any person who he
reasonably believes was driving or attempting to drive or in charge of a
vehicle at the time of the accident. Again, RTA 1988, s.9 gives limited protection to those who are hospital patients although RTA 1988, s.7A now
provides a procedure whereby a blood sample can be taken even where the
driver is unconscious, provided he is subsequently given the opportunity to
consent to its taking.

Whilst in the vast majority of circumstances the preliminary test signals
the start of the procedure, RTA 1988, s.4 reflects the original intention of the
legislation whereby a police constable may arrest without warrant any person
who he reasonably suspects is driving or attempting to drive a mechanically
propelled vehicle on a road or other public place whilst unfit to do so through
drink or drugs.

1.3 PROVIDING A SPECIMEN AT THE POLICE STATION OR HOSPITAL

Notwithstanding the various reasons that might lead to a request to co-
operate with a preliminary test, a positive test or failure to provide the specimen allows a police constable to arrest without warrant, unless the motorist
is then at a hospital as a patient.

Following arrest, a police constable at a police station may require the
detained motorist to provide two specimens of breath for analysis by means
of a device approved by the Secretary of State. In certain prescribed circumstances, a constable may alternatively require the provision of a specimen of
blood or urine for a laboratory test. Such a requirement can only be made at
a police station or at a hospital. It can only be made at a police station for
five reasons where:

(a)   the constable has reasonable cause to believe that, for medical reasons,
      a specimen of breath cannot be provided or should not be required;

(b) at the time of the requirement, the machine used to test the breath spec-
     imen is not available at the police station or it is not practicable for it to
     be used;
(c) there is reasonable cause to believe that the device has not produced a
     reliable indication of the proportion of alcohol in breath;
(d) following a preliminary test the constable reasonably believes there is
     some drug in the driver's body; or
(e) a constable has been advised by a medical practitioner that the condition
     of the person providing the specimen is due to some drug.

Where a request is made for the provision of blood or urine, the question
of which it is to be is a matter to be decided by the constable making the
requirement, although RTA 1988 contains a saving provision where a medical
practitioner is of the opinion that, for medical reasons, a specimen of blood
cannot or should not be taken. In these circumstances, the specimen required
has to be a specimen of urine.

Whatever requirement is made as to the type of specimen, a person who,
without reasonable excuse, fails to provide a specimen when so required is
guilty of an offence, provided a warning has been given that failure or refusal
to provide could lead to a prosecution.

Where an accident has occurred and a constable wishes to require the
provision of a specimen of blood, but the person to whom the request is to
be made is incapable through medical reasons of giving any consent to blood
being taken, a police medical practitioner can be requested to take the sample
and the motorist be required to give consent to its being taken at a later stage.
Such a sample can then be analysed in the normal way.

Over the years, national pro forma documents have evolved that should
enable a police constable to concentrate on the procedure and the results
without having to pay undue attention to the actual words used. However,
failure to fully inform the motorist of all the options available at each stage
may render the procedure invalid.

Where a motorist has been required to provide two specimens of breath
for analysis, the result of the test is immediately provided by the breathalyser
machine. The specimen with the lower proportion of alcohol in breath is the
one used in any subsequent prosecution, whilst the other is disregarded.
Where the specimen with the lower proportion of alcohol contains no more
than 50 µg (microgrammes) of alcohol in 100 ml of breath, the person who
provided it may request that it be replaced by a specimen of blood or urine
although, again, the decision as to which this is to be is one for the constable
who made the initial requirement for breath, subject to any medical advice he
may receive.

Where the specimen to be relied on is one of blood or urine, the sample is divided; one part being sent by the police for forensic analysis and one being provided to the motorist to allow independent analysis of the specimen if so required.

Sections 15 and 16 of the Road Traffic Offenders Act 1988 (RTOA 1988) provide for the use of specimens in proceedings for an offence under RTA 1988, s.4 or s.5 and for the use of documentary evidence to prove the proportion of alcohol or existence of a drug in a specimen of breath, blood or urine.

CHAPTER 2

Power to require preliminary tests

2.1 THE LEGISLATION

Relevant legislation is provided in RTA 1988, ss.6–6E (as amended by the Railway and Transport Safety Act 2003). Section 6 is headed 'Power to administer preliminary tests' and provides:

(1) If any of subsections (2) to (5) applies, a constable may require a person to co-operate with any one or more preliminary tests administered to the person by that constable or another constable.

(2) This subsection applies if a constable reasonably suspects that the person –

    (a) is driving, is attempting to drive or in charge of a motor vehicle on a road or other public place, and

    (b) has alcohol or a drug in his body or is under the influence of a drug.

(3) This subsection applies if a constable reasonably suspects that the person –

    (a) has been driving, attempting to drive or in charge of a motor vehicle on a road or other public place while having alcohol or a drug in his body or while unfit to drive because of a drug, and

    (b) still has alcohol or a drug in his body or is still under the influence of a drug.

(4) This subsection applies if a constable reasonably suspects that the person –

    (a) is, or has been driving, attempting to drive or in charge of a motor vehicle on a road or other public place, and

    (b) has committed a traffic offence while the vehicle was in motion.

(5) This subsection applies if –

    (a) an accident occurs owing to the presence of a motor vehicle on a road or other public place, and

    (b) a constable reasonably believes that the person was driving, attempting to drive or in charge of the vehicle at the time of the accident.

(6) A person commits an offence if, without reasonable excuse he fails to co-operate with a preliminary test in pursuance of a requirement imposed under this section.

(7)   A constable may administer a preliminary test by virtue of any of subsections (2) to (4) only if he is in uniform.

(8)   In this section –

(a)   a reference to a preliminary test is to any of the tests described in sections 6A to 6C, and

(b)   'traffic offence' means an offence under –

(i)   a provision of Part II of the Public Passenger Vehicles Act 1981 (c.41),

(ii)   a provision of the Road Traffic Regulation Act 1984 (c.27),

(iii) a provision of the Road Traffic Offenders Act 1988 (c.53) other than a provision of Part III, or

(iv)   a provision of this Act other than a provision of Part V.

Section 6A of RTA 1988 is headed 'Preliminary breath test' and provides:

(1)   A preliminary breath test is a procedure whereby the person to whom the test is administered provides a specimen of breath to be used for the purpose of obtaining, by means of a device of a type approved by the Secretary of State, an indication whether the proportion of alcohol in the person's breath or blood is likely to exceed the prescribed limit.

(2)   A preliminary breath test administered in reliance on section 6(2) to (4) may be administered at or near the place where the requirement to co-operate with the test is imposed.

(3)   A preliminary breath test administered in reliance on section 6(5) may be administered –

(a)   at or near the place where the requirement to co-operate with the test is imposed, or

(b)   if the constable who imposes the requirement thinks it expedient, at a police station specified by him.

Section 6B is headed 'Preliminary impairment test' and provides:

(1)   A preliminary impairment test is a procedure whereby the constable administering the test –

(a)   observes the person to whom the test is administered in his performance of tasks specified by the constable, and

(b)   makes such other observations of the person's physical state as the constable thinks expedient.

(2)   The Secretary of State shall issue (and may from time to time revise) a code of practice about –

(a)   the kind of task that may be specified for the purpose of a preliminary impairment test,

(b)   the kind of observation of physical state that may be made in the course of a preliminary impairment test,

(c)   the manner in which a preliminary impairment test should be administered, and

(d)   the inferences that may be drawn from observations made in the course of a preliminary impairment test.

6

(3)   In issuing or revising the code of practice the Secretary of State shall aim to ensure that a preliminary impairment test is designed to indicate –

(a)   whether a person is unfit to drive, and
(b)   if he is, whether or not his unfitness is likely to be due to drink or drugs.

(4)   A preliminary impairment test may be administered –

(a)   at or near the place where the requirement to co-operate with the test is imposed, or
(b)   if the constable who imposes the requirement thinks it expedient, at a police station specified by him.

(5)   A constable administering a preliminary impairment test shall have regard to the code of practice under this section.

(6)   A constable may administer a preliminary impairment test only if he is approved for that purpose by the chief officer of the police force to which he belongs.

(7)   A code of practice under this section may include provision about –

(a)   the giving of approval under subsection (6), and
(b)   in particular, the kind of training that a constable should have undergone, or the kind of qualification that a constable should possess, before being approved under that subsection.

Section 6C is headed 'Preliminary drug test' and provides:

(1)   A preliminary drug test is a procedure by which a specimen of sweat or saliva is –

(a)   obtained, and
(b)   used for the purpose of obtaining, by means of a device of a type approved by the Secreatry of State, an indication whether the person to whom the test is administered has a drug in his body.

(2)   A preliminary drug test may be administered –

(a)   at or near the place where the requirement to co-operate with the test is imposed, or
(b)   if the constable who imposes the requirement thinks it expedient, at a police station specified by him.

Sections 6D and 6E of RTA 1988, which deal with a police constable's power to arrest following a preliminary breath test or a failure to co-operate with a preliminary test and the concurrent power of entry by force if necessary, are dealt with in **Chapter 3**.

The amended provisions to require preliminary tests under the substituted s.6 and ss.6A–6E were contained in Sched.7 to the Railways and Transport Safety Act 2003 and were implemented on 30 March 2004. Whilst the scope for preliminary testing has been greatly widened by implementation of these provisions, many of the cases decided under the law in force before 30 March 2004 continue to be of relevance to these new provisions.

There are now three different specific kinds of preliminary tests available:

- a preliminary breath test under s.6A;
- a preliminary impairment test under s.6B; or
- a preliminary drug test under s.6C.

A preliminary impairment test under s.6B is designed to indicate to a police officer that the person being tested is unfit to drive through drink or drugs. The test prescribed under s.6C will, once an appropriate device has been approved by the Secretary of State, apply only to tests to ascertain whether a driver has ingested a drug.

2.2 PRELIMINARY BREATH TEST DEVICE

Approved devices

Since 1968 there have been a number of roadside screening devices approved for use by police forces in Great Britain starting with the Alcotest 80 which was approved in 1968. Any 'type approval' requires approval by the Secretary of State from a date specified by Order. The following list shows those devices approved in recent years and which are still regularly used by police forces in Great Britain when carrying out preliminary breath tests under s.6A. In some cases, the specified approval relates to an upgraded software version of an earlier device:

- Draeger Alcotest 7410 (approved 1993)
- Lion Alcolmeter SL 400 (UK) (approved 1993)
- Alcosensor IV UK (approved 1999)
- Lion Alcolmeter SL 400A (approved 2000)
- Lion Alcolmeter SL 400B (approved 2002)
- Lion Alcolmeter SL 400AM (approved 2003)
- Lion Alcolmeter SL 500 (approved 2004)
- Intoximeter Alco-sensor FST (approved 2005)
- Draegar Alcotest 6510 (approved 2005).

A full list of device approval orders can be viewed on the Home Office website (see **www.police.homeoffice.gov.uk/operational-policing/road-traffic.html**).

Sections 6A, 6B and 6C each contains a statutory definition of the term 'preliminary test' insofar as it applies to the particular test to be carried out. It follows, therefore, that whichever of the three sections the test is being carried out under, any device which has not been so approved, but which is used to obtain such a preliminary indication, renders the evidence of the preliminary indication illegal. However, providing the police have acted without *mala fides* in so obtaining the evidence, it would appear that any subsequent arrest and any evidence obtained later at the police station is admissible (*Matto* v. *Wolverhampton Crown Court* [1987] RTR 337).

Judicial notice may be taken of the fact that a device had been approved by the Secretary of State, despite the fact that the relevant Breath Test Device Approval Order has not been produced in court and cannot be cited (*Bentley* v. *Chief Constable of Northumbria* [1984] RTR 276).

In *Snelson* v. *Thompson* [1985] RTR 220 the defendant provided two specimens of breath for analysis at a police station where the lower reading showed 56 µg of alcohol in 100 ml of breath. One hour later, he supplied a screening sample in order to ascertain his fitness to leave the police station. The screening sample, supplied on a Lion Alcolmeter S-L2, indicated that his breath did not contain alcohol above the prescribed limit. At his trial an expert, who had not examined either of the two devices used, gave evidence that the results were inconsistent with the average rate at which a normal person would eliminate alcohol from his body. The justices found that the screening device was merely a device to provide an indication and was not as accurate as any device used in the police station and convicted the defendant. On the defendant's appeal against conviction, the Divisional Court agreed with the decision of the justices. The Lion Alcolmeter S-L2 was designed to provide a general indication without any degree of precision whether alcohol had been consumed. The Lion Intoximeter 3000, however, was designed to produce, with little or no error, an accurate calculation of the amount of alcohol in a person's breath.

Manufacturer's instructions

In *DPP* v. *Carey* [1970] AC 1072 the House of Lords considered a number of cases dealing with the manner in which such preliminary devices should be used. It was held that whilst the manufacturer's instructions supplied with the device (in this case an Alcotest) did not form a part of the device, as approved by the Secretary of State, the device had to be correctly assembled in accordance with the manufacturer's instructions, otherwise the test would be invalidated. In addition, provided that it could be proved that there had been a *bona fide* use of the device by the constable, subsequent proof of noncompliance with the other instructions would not invalidate the breath test. This was expressly taken to include the requirement that 20 minutes should elapse between consumption of alcohol and the breath test and the requirement that the bag should be inflated in not less than 10 seconds and not more than 20 seconds.

This decision was followed in *DPP* v. *Kay* [1999] RTR 109 where the respondent was requested to provide a screening breath test and produced a positive sample. The police officer was unaware that the manufacturers of the device stated in the instructions for use that there should be a time interval of at least 20 minutes between the motorist's last drink and the administration of the test. In this case, the last drink had been only five minutes before the test.

At trial, the magistrates concluded that the police officer's lack of knowledge of the instructions rendered the breath test so unreliable that it would be unfair to allow the prosecution to rely on it. That evidence, and subsequent evidence obtained at the police station, was excluded under the Police and Criminal Evidence Act 1984 (PACE 1984), s.78.

The prosecutor's appeal was successful. In the absence of a finding of bad faith on the part of the officer, there were no circumstances justifying the decision to exclude his evidence. Courts should be slow to exclude evidence of the taking of a specimen because of a technical shortcoming in the procedure carried out at the roadside. The officer was under no duty to ask when the respondent had taken his last drink and a failure to ask the question did not invalidate the roadside breath test or subsequent arrest.

The rationale of the decision in *Carey* was quoted with approval by the Divisional Court in *Grant* v. *DPP* (2003) 167 JP 459 where a defendant who had been followed for a considerable distance by the police, but then claimed to have had a drink in the five minutes before being stopped by them was found to be clearly lying; accordingly, there was no need for the officer to wait a further 15 minutes before administering the preliminary breath test.

It would appear that only evidence of *mala fides* on the part of the constable administering the breath test would be sufficient to have the evidence of the breath test excluded and vitiate any subsequent arrest.

In *DPP* v. *Kennedy* (2004) 168 JP 185 the appellant submitted before justices that as the police officer administering the roadside breath sample had not followed the manufacturer's instructions with regard to changing the mouthpiece of the device, any subsequent evidence should be disregarded under PACE 1984, s.78.

The Divisional Court said there was no sound basis for the conclusion that the device had not been properly assembled and the roadside test not properly carried out. The justices should have considered whether the failure to change the device could have had any significant effect upon the test result. The failure to comply with the manufacturer's instructions was not of such significance as to render the test invalid.

If effect was to be given to the change in the law which made proof of lawful arrest no longer a condition precedent to the admission of evidence as to tests administered at the police station, there must be something more than simple proof of unlawful arrest before a court was entitled to rely on s.78 to exclude the evidence.

In *Woon* v. *Maskell* [1985] RTR 289 the defendant was requested to supply a sample of breath on a Lion Alcometer S-L2 device. Upon the defendant's blowing into it, the constable observed that both lights A and B illuminated, whereupon the constable depressed the 'Read' button following which a red light signified a positive reading. The manufacturer's instructions required that the 'Read' button be depressed for at least 40 seconds, and it was argued for the defendant that the purported positive reading was unreliable and that the subsequent arrest was unlawful. Rejecting this argument, the Divisional Court held that there had been a breach of the manufacturer's instructions, but only as to process and not as to assembly and that the arrest was therefore lawful.

Where, however, a police officer has followed the manufacturer's instructions and refused to illuminate the 'Read' button in circumstances where the motorist has failed to supply sufficient breath for the machine to work, he cannot be criticised for that refusal, even where illuminating the button would have given either a reliably positive or unreliably negative result (*DPP* v. *Heywood* [1998] RTR 1).

Achieving the objective of the test

Breath supplied for a preliminary breath test must be both sufficient to enable the test to be carried out and provided in such a way as to enable the objective of the test to be satisfactorily achieved. Section 11(3) of RTA 1988 is specific in that it states that a person does not co-operate with a preliminary test or provide a specimen of breath for analysis unless his co-operation or the specimen:

(a)   is sufficient to enable the test or the analysis to be carried out; and
(b)   is provided in such a way as to enable the objective of the test or analysis to be satisfactorily achieved.

2.3   CONSTABLE IN UNIFORM

Other than where the test is required to be carried out because there has been an accident owing to the presence of a motor vehicle on a road (s.6(7)) a prerequisite to the carrying out of any test under ss.6A–6C is that the constable is a constable in uniform. The use of the word 'constable' in this context is not used in terms of police force rank, but to refer to any member of an officially recognised police force within the jurisdiction. Thus, for example, members of the British Transport police or the Ministry of Defence police could lawfully require a motorist to undertake preliminary testing.

The requirement that the constable be in uniform ensures public confidence that a preliminary test is required by someone who is immediately recognisable as a police officer. Thus, where a requirement for a breath test was made by a police officer who was driving his own car and who was wearing an overcoat over his uniform, it was held that this did not vitiate the procedure, a finding having been made that the motorist was aware that the person requiring the specimen of breath was a police officer.

In *Gage* v. *Jones* [1983] RTR 508 the defendant collided with the car of an off-duty police officer and did not stop. The off-duty officer obtained the assistance of a passing police sergeant who was on duty. The sergeant drove to the defendant's house and asked him to supply a specimen of breath. This request was refused and the defendant was arrested. No evidence was given before the justices that the sergeant who required the breath test was or was not in uniform, and on a submission of no case to answer the case was dismissed.

The Divisional Court, in allowing the appeal by the prosecutor, said that a presumption that a police officer was in uniform was raised if he was on duty in the street and if a member of the public was able to recognise him as a police officer. It was a well-known fact that a breath test had to be obtained by a police officer in uniform and it was improbable that the police would visit a motorist with breathalyser equipment unless they were in uniform.

2.4   REASONABLY SUSPECTS

Under the law that applied prior to 30 March 2004, there was a requirement for a police officer to have 'reasonable cause to suspect' that a person was or had been driving whilst over the prescribed limit or had committed a moving traffic offence. The amended legislation requires the officer to 'reasonably suspect' the same. In practice the two phrases are almost interchangeable and case law under the old provisions would seem to be just as relevant to the amended legislation.

The Act permits a requirement to be made for a preliminary test where a constable reasonably suspects a person to be driving, or attempting to drive, or in charge of a motor vehicle with alcohol or drugs in the body, or to have committed a moving traffic offence. The prosecution must prove that the constable had a reasonable suspicion, which of itself is a matter of fact, and will depend on the circumstances of each individual case. The fact that no alcohol was consumed is not a defence to any subsequent prosecution for failing to supply a specimen (although it may be relevant as to sentence).

Section 163 and 'random' testing

The requirement for the officer to 'reasonably suspect' does not give an officer the power to effect random stopping of motor vehicles in order to inquire into whether the driver has been drinking. Section 163 of RTA 1988 provides that a person driving a motor vehicle on a road must stop the vehicle on being required to do so by a constable in uniform and that a person who fails to do so is guilty of an offence. In *Beard* v. *Wood* [1980] RTR 454 it was held that it was possible for a constable to require a vehicle to stop under the statutory provisions of s.163 and thereafter to form a reasonable suspicion (now to reasonably suspect) that consumption of alcohol had taken place. This decision, however, was based on an acceptance that the interval between the stopping of the vehicle and the constable forming a suspicion was not so great that it could no longer be said that the motorist was driving or attempting to drive.

The power under s.163 was further considered in *Lodwick* v. *Saunders* [1985] Crim LR 210, in which a police constable's power to require a vehicle to stop under the section was held to extend to allow him to detain the vehicle in order to exercise any other powers he might have in those circumstances, e.g. to require the driver to supply a specimen of breath where, subsequently, the constable reasonably suspected him to have consumed alcohol.

In *Steel* v. *Goacher* [1983] RTR 98 the defendant was stopped by police officers carrying out a random crime check. The vehicle, which contained two male occupants, was being driven in a residential area shortly after midnight and bore a registration mark that was not local to the area. There were no concerns over the manner in which the car was being driven. After the vehicle was stopped and the police constable had had an opportunity to speak to the occupants, he formed a suspicion that there had been consumption of alcohol by the driver, who was later convicted of an offence of driving whilst over the limit.

His appeal against conviction on the grounds that the police had not been acting in the execution of their duty was dismissed. The inquiry had been a reasonable one and it had been reasonable to ask the defendants to stop. Accordingly, when alcohol was smelt on the defendant's breath, the police officer, acting in the execution of his duty, had reasonable cause to suspect the defendant of having alcohol in his body and thus to require him to provide a specimen.

The legal position of 'random' testing was considered further by the Divisional Court in *Gwent* v. *Dash* [1986] RTR 41. In this case, motor vehicles were being stopped randomly by police officers in order to ascertain whether the drivers had alcohol in their bodies. The defendant was stopped by a police officer under training designed to familiarise her with the basic procedure for carrying out breath tests. It was accepted in evidence that there was nothing in either the defendant's driving or in the condition of his vehicle that would normally attract the attention of the police.

Following the stopping of the vehicle, alcohol was smelt on the breath of the defendant and he was subsequently convicted by justices of the offence of driving with excess alcohol in his blood. His appeal to the Crown Court was upheld on the grounds that random stopping of motor vehicles by police officers amounted to malpractice thus rendering any subsequent procedures unlawful.

The prosecutor appealed against this decision. The Divisional Court held that, in the absence of malpractice or oppressive, capricious or opprobrious behaviour, there was no restriction on the stopping of motorists by a police officer in the execution of his duty and the subsequent administration of a breath test if the officer then and there genuinely suspected the ingestion of alcohol. Since the police officers were making genuine inquiries by stopping vehicles in order to detect whether or not the drivers had, or could reasonably be suspected of having, alcohol in their bodies, the officers were acting in the course of their duties and were neither oppressive nor capricious in their behaviour.

After vehicle stopped

The suspicion that the defendant has alcohol in his body need not be restricted to the officer's observations of the vehicle whilst it is being driven. In *DPP* v. *McGladrigan* [1991] RTR 297 a motorist who was manoeuvring out of a car park stalled the engine, restarted it and drove on a road for some 40–50 feet. A uniformed constable stopped the defendant, who confirmed that he had previously consumed alcohol. On providing a positive breath test, the defendant was arrested and subsequently charged with an offence of driving with excess alcohol in his breath.

The justices found that the constable did not have reasonable grounds to suspect that the defendant had alcohol in his body at the time when he was seen driving, as a result of which he had been unlawfully arrested. They therefore held that the unlawful arrest vitiated any subsequent procedures and excluded that evidence under their discretionary power in PACE 1984, s.78.

The prosecutor's appeal was allowed by the Divisional Court. As the defendant had confirmed to the police officer after being stopped that he had previously consumed alcohol, the court held that the constable had reasonable cause, within s.6(1), to suspect that the defendant had alcohol in his body and a complete basis therefore for requiring him to provide a specimen for a breath test and then, accordingly, to arrest him when that test proved positive. The justices had erred in restricting their consideration to the reasonable cause the constable had whilst the car was being driven, and on that basis the case was remitted to the justices with a direction to convict.

The decision in *DPP* v. *McGladrigan* was followed by *DPP* v. *Godwin* [1991] RTR 303 in which the defendant was stopped by a police constable carrying out traffic stop checks and was instructed to pull in to a lay-by. The constable asked the defendant if he had been drinking and he replied that he had not. He then failed a screening breath test, was arrested and subsequently provided breath specimens for analysis that were over the prescribed limit. The justices were of the opinion that the constable had no reasonable cause to suspect alcohol in the defendant's body and that therefore his arrest was unlawful. They therefore excluded the evidence of the police station procedure and, in their discretion, the breath analysis evidence.

The prosecutor appealed, arguing that in the absence of bad faith by the police or oppressive conduct on the part of the prosecuting authorities, the justices should not have exercised their discretion under PACE 1984, s.78. The Divisional Court dismissed the appeal, saying that the discretion in s.78 did not require oppression or bad faith in order for it to be exercised. The defendant had been denied the protection of RTA 1988, s.6 and the prosecutor had thereby obtained evidence that he otherwise would not have obtained. In order to redress the prejudice to the defendant, the justices had been right to exclude the evidence.

The two cases are distinguishable in that, in *McGladrigan*, the police constable formed his reasonable suspicion after the vehicle had been stopped and after an opportunity to talk to the defendant (and smell alcohol on the defendant's breath), whereas in *Godwin* the constable did not form a reasonable suspicion until after the screening breath test had been applied. In the latter instance, it was the subsequent evidence of the breath test that provided reasonable suspicion; in the former, it was the admission of the motorist.

Proper campaign

In *Stewart* v. *Crowe* 1999 SLT 899 motorists were stopped and breathalysed as part of a police campaign against drinking and driving, designed to warn and educate about the 'morning after effect'. This was held to be a perfectly proper campaign with no evidence that the police were acting capriciously or oppressively. The general nature of the campaign ruled out any question of randomness.

It would appear, therefore, that there is no bar to the police operating a policy of random stopping of motorists, although there is such a bar to subsequent random breath testing. Whilst the distinction between the two would appear to be minimal, it is nevertheless an important one when considering the question of the basis on which a police constable forms a reasonable suspicion in such cases.

Information provided by another

Can a successful prosecution be mounted on the back of evidence that has resulted from the constable forming a reasonable suspicion from information provided to him by another person (whether a police officer or not) or, indeed, anonymously? This particular issue has been of more importance in recent years, especially in those areas where the police have operated a well-publicised campaign in which members of the public are encouraged to provide information where they feel that drink-driving laws are being or are about to be transgressed.

In *DPP* v. *Wilson* [1991] RTR 284 the Divisional Court held that a constable was entitled to act on anonymously provided information and that

15

an acceptable basis for forming a reasonable suspicion existed where a constable then smelt alcohol on the breath of a driver who had been stopped in the course of driving. In addition, a police constable had a duty to act on information passed to him and to act appropriately when an offence was committed.

In *Thomson* v. *Ritchie* 2000 SLT 734 an anonymous phone call was made to the police at 7.10 a.m. to the effect that a specified vehicle had left an address and was being driven by a person who was under the influence of alcohol. The message was relayed to officers in a police car in the area. They arrived at the address stated within four minutes of the original message. They spotted the vehicle that had been specified, but it was unoccupied. After a short interval, two persons approached the vehicle and got in. The vehicle was driven for a short distance before it was stopped by the police who, on the strength of the anonymous phone call, required the driver to take a breath test. The test was positive and the driver was charged. At his trial, after the close of the prosecution case, the driver submitted that there was no case to answer; there was insufficient evidence to establish that the police officers had reasonable cause to suspect that the driver was under the influence of alcohol. The submission was dismissed and the driver was convicted. The driver's appeal by way of case stated was dismissed. The sole issue was whether or not the anonymous phone call relayed to the police officers who stopped the driver was sufficient to give them reasonable cause to suspect that the driver was driving under the influence of alcohol. The driver had drawn attention to the absence of any evidence to indicate that the police had formed an opinion for themselves; their suspicion was based entirely on information supplied by an anonymous person and relayed to them via a civilian clerk. It was argued that there had been a material break between the event referred to in the original call and what the police had themselves observed; it was suggested that it was necessary for there to be some independent circumstance (e.g. the smell of alcohol on the breath) to enable the police to form the view that a road traffic offence was being committed by the driver. (It was not suggested that the anonymity of the original caller in some way vitiated the basis on which the police relied.) Lord McCluskey said that the court did not feel that there had been any real, significant and material break in the continuity between the original phone call and the administration of the breath test. It had been conceded that the police had reasonable cause to stop the vehicle, namely information that it was being driven by a person who was under the influence of alcohol; accordingly, there had been no break in the circumstances that gave reasonable cause for stopping the vehicle and the circumstances in which the police concluded that they had reasonable cause to suspect that the driver was then committing the offence of driving with alcohol in his body.

Offence committed whilst vehicle in motion

Suspicion can also arise where a traffic offence has been committed whilst the vehicle was in motion.

Section 6(8)(b) of RTA 1988 defines traffic offence as an offence under:

- a provision of Part II of the Public Passenger Vehicles Act 1981;
- a provision of the Road Traffic Regulation Act 1984;
- any provision of the Road Traffic Offenders Act 1988 except Part III; or
- any provision of RTA 1988 except Part V.

Whilst traffic offences are usually non-recordable for the purposes of national police records, offences of failing to co-operate with a preliminary test under RTA 1988, s.6 (and offences where convictions are recorded in the same proceedings) may be recorded.

It should be noted that the offence must have been committed whilst the vehicle was in motion and must, of course, have been an offence contrary to one of the specified statutory provisions. It is unusual for the fact of a moving traffic offence of itself to be used as a means of founding a requirement to supply a specimen of breath. In cases decided some years ago, making a U turn in the road, using a wrong indicator and speeding were held not of themselves to indicate a reasonable suspicion of consumption of alcohol and the courts held that as these were the only facts adverse to the driver, they were insufficient to constitute a suspicion of alcohol. Practice shows that the majority of police constables would tend to use the moving traffic offence as a reason for stopping the vehicle in the first place, but would then rely on the evidence of their subsequent conversation with the driver and their sensory observations in order to acquire any reasonable suspicion.

Provided that it is made clear that the reasonable suspicion was formed on one ground or the other, there can be no challenge to the validity of any conviction if the prosecution proceeds on that ground.

Finally, it should be noted that there is no need for there to be a nexus between the driving and a police constable's arrival and suspicion of consumption of alcohol. Thus, in *Blake* v. *Pope* [1986] 1 WLR 1152 where a motorist was restrained by another motorist pending arrival of the police, justices were directed to convict, even though there had been a gap of some 10 minutes between the end of the driving and the appearance of the police officer who then formed his suspicion as to the defendant's consumption of alcohol.

2.5   REASONABLY BELIEVES

The requirement in s.6(2)–(4) that the police constable should reasonably suspect is replaced in s.6(5) by the words 'reasonably believes'. There is an obvious and intended difference between the two: a constable requiring a driver to undergo a preliminary test on the grounds of suspected alcohol consumption or commission of a moving traffic offence need not be as definite as regards the circumstances that lead him to decide to administer a preliminary test as he needs to be where an accident has occurred owing to the presence of a motor vehicle on a road and he believes a person to be the driver of one of the vehicles involved.

The requirement to co-operate in a preliminary test under this subsection does not depend upon consumption of alcohol or on the fact that the driver has fallen below the standard of a normal prudent motorist in his driving. It is common practice for the police to administer a preliminary test under the section – usually a screening breath test – to all drivers involved in an accident (and, in some cases, to anyone they believe to have been in charge of the vehicle at the time of the accident). There have been, and no doubt will be, many motorists whose culpability for a road traffic accident has been minimal, but who have been convicted of offences under the relevant legislation and have lost their driving licences under the mandatory disqualification provisions of that legislation. Additionally, such a test can be required, provided the police constable has reasonably formed his belief, in circumstances where there has been no accusation levied against the driver of having committed a traffic offence and where the driving has been finished for some time.

In *Baker* v. *Oxford* [1980] RTR 315 the distinction between the words 'suspect' and 'believe' was emphasised and justices were warned of the need to be sure not only of the distinction, but also of the circumstances in which the difference might arise.

In *Johnson* v. *Whitehouse* [1984] RTR 38 a police constable attended the scene of a road traffic accident where he found an abandoned vehicle with blood on the steering wheel and front seats. Documents in the car bore the defendant's name and address, and consequently the police officer went to that address. On arrival, he saw the defendant enter the garden, fall over in a drunken state and noticed that he was bleeding from cuts to his hands and face. The constable then required him to provide a specimen of breath on the grounds that he suspected the defendant of driving the vehicle when it had been involved in the accident. The defendant refused.

He was convicted of failing to provide the necessary specimens and appealed to the Divisional Court. He argued that the use by the police constable of the word 'suspect' instead of 'believe' invalidated any request for a breath test, as the constable's state of mind was not sufficiently made up so as to found a reasonable belief. Dismissing the appeal, the Divisional Court held that the word 'believe' having greater force than 'suspect' was an essential part of the law that a requirement for a breath test (under the then s.6(2)) could be justified only if there were reasonable grounds for believing that the person concerned was driving at the time of the accident and that the constable, in having said 'suspect' rather than 'believe', was merely using inaccurate language when accurate language was not essential. There was therefore no ground upon which the defendant's conviction could be faulted.

There may be occasions where the police are called to an accident and are unable to administer a preliminary test (or require the provision of a specimen for analysis) because the driver of the vehicle has been rendered incapable of providing such by the accident. In these circumstances, RTA 1988, s.7A (added by Police Reform Act 2002, s.56 and implemented on 1 October 2002) empowers a police constable at the scene who has reasonable cause to believe that the driver has been involved in the accident to request a police medical practitioner to take a specimen of blood from the person concerned. Thereafter, that specimen can only be subjected to a laboratory test if the person from whom it was taken has been required by a constable to give his permission for a laboratory test of the specimen and has given that permission.

2.6 ACCIDENT

Section 6(5) requires that there has been an accident and it is not sufficient that a constable has formed an honest and reasonable belief that an accident has taken place.

There is no definition of the word 'accident' in the legislation for these purposes, and it is wrong to seek to construe the word in like manner to other attempts at construction in other areas of the law. In *Chief Constable of the West Midlands Police* v. *Billingham* [1979] 1 WLR 747 it was held that the test to be applied when deciding whether or not there had been an accident was to ask: 'Would an ordinary person conclude on the facts of the particular case that there had been an accident?' In other words, would the archetypal 'man in the street' see the event or the aftermath of the event and return home and report to his family that there had been 'an accident'?

The subsection also requires that the accident must have occurred 'owing to the presence of a motor vehicle on a road'. Whether or not the accident can be directly linked to the presence of a motor vehicle on the road is a question of fact in each particular case. Nonetheless, it is submitted that there must be some sufficient link between the presence of the vehicle and the cause of the accident, thus covering the case of the parked vehicle in an unlit road that is not displaying lights, but not the case of the parked vehicle that is itself damaged as a result of a collision between two other vehicles.

2.7 PLACE FOR ADMINISTERING THE PRELIMINARY TEST

Sections 6A(3), 6B(4) and 6C(2) all allow the preliminary test to be administered at or near the place where the requirement to co-operate with the test is imposed or, at the police officer's discretion for reasons of expediency, at a police station. These provisions substantially mirror the previous legislation which allowed a constable to carry out a screening breath test at or near where the requirement was made or, if he saw fit, at a police station.

Not surprisingly, the Divisional Court has not been particularly troubled by having been asked to construe this subsection. The requirement that the specimen be taken 'at or near the place' is similar to the requirement in the original legislation that it be made 'there or nearby'. Those particular words had been construed as having their ordinary common sense meaning, and the Divisional Court in *Arnold* v. *Kingston-upon-Hull Chief Constable* [1969] 1 WLR 1499 said that it would not act to overturn a decision of justices as to whether the requirement had been made 'there or nearby', unless the decision had been so perverse that no reasonable tribunal could possibly have come to that conclusion.

2.8 FAILING TO PROVIDE THE SPECIMEN

By virtue of s.6(6) a person commits an offence if, without reasonable excuse, he fails to co-operate with a preliminary test in pursuance of a requirement imposed under the section.

Section 11(2) of RTA 1988 – the interpretation section – defines 'fail' as including 'refuse'. Thus, the offence is committed not only by failing under ss.6A, 6B or 6C to co-operate with the specified preliminary test, but also by the driver who refuses, without reasonable excuse, to provide any required specimen, be it of breath, saliva or sweat. Once a person has been given an opportunity to do something and does not do it, there is a failure to comply with the request. The majority of pre-amendment cases on this particular point concerned the situation where the motorist, having been stopped by the police, was then requested to wait either for the necessary screening equipment to arrive or for a period of 20 minutes to elapse between the last consumption of alcohol and the provision of the sample. The operating instructions for many types of screening device approved by the Secretary of State require that a period of 20 minutes should elapse following consumption of alcohol. This is to ensure that any residual alcohol in the mouth or airways has dissipated prior to providing the breath sample so that a proper indication can be obtained.

Thus, in a number of cases, drivers have been detained and there has been a time interval prior to the screening test being taken, during which the driver has decided to absent himself from the scene. In these circumstances the

Divisional Court has adopted the consistent approach that once a person has been requested to do something, has had an opportunity to do it and has not done it, there is a *prima facie* failure to do it. See, for example, *R* v. *Wagner* [1970] Crim LR 535.

Section 11(3) of RTA 1988 provides that a person does not co-operate with a preliminary test or provide a specimen of breath for analysis unless his co-operation or the specimen:

(a)   is sufficient to enable the test or the analysis to be carried out, and
(b)   is provided in such a way as to enable the objective of the test or analysis to be satisfactorily achieved.

In *Dawes* v. *Taylor* [1986] RTR 81 police discovered the defendant asleep at night in his car in a public car park. He had removed his trousers and shoes and was in a sleeping bag in the rear of the car. Having been spoken to by the police, he was required to provide a screening breath test on a Lion Alcometer S-L2 device. This machine operates by means of two lights that are capable of being illuminated by breath pressure. One police constable sat in the front seat of the police vehicle and held the Alcometer; the defendant was required to blow into it from his position in the rear of the vehicle. He was instructed to 'blow long enough and hard enough so that the lights come on and stay on'. He blew into the device, could not observe the lights and did not blow at sufficient pressure or for sufficient time to illuminate either of the lights.

He was charged and convicted by justices of failing without reasonable excuse to provide a specimen of breath contrary to RTA 1972, s.7(4). He appealed to the Crown Court, which found that whilst he had not been deliberately obstructive during the test, there was no reasonable excuse for failing to provide the sample on the grounds that the device was either difficult to operate at first attempt or the defendant's position in the car made it impossible, or because the defendant had difficulty in following the instructions. His appeal to the Divisional Court was dismissed. For a person to provide a specimen of breath when required to do so, the information had to be properly given to him so that he was capable of understanding it and he had to be capable of performing the physical act. As he had understood what was required of him and had no physical problems in providing the specimen, his appeal failed.

In *DPP* v. *Heywood* [1998] RTR 1 the defendant blew into an Alcolmeter device on two occasions, but was unable to illuminate both the 'A' and 'B' lights. The justices accepted the defence submission that, even though insufficient breath had been supplied to the device for a proper reading to be obtained, nevertheless the constable administering the test should have illuminated the 'Read' button to see if a 'reliably positive' or 'unreliably negative' result appeared.

The prosecutor's appeal was allowed. There was a failure to provide a specimen of breath for a roadside breath test if the testing device was blown into in such a way as to illuminate light 'A' but not light 'B', when the device so operated that if in such circumstances, the 'Read' button was pressed, a positive result might be given that (if given) would be reliable, but a negative result might be given and (if given) might be false. The objective of carrying out the test was to obtain a reliable positive or negative reading, not to obtain a reading that was reliable in some circumstances and not in others.

2.9 REASONABLE EXCUSE

Section 6(6) provides that a person does not commit the offence of failing to co-operate with a preliminary test in pursuance of a requirement imposed under that section if he has a reasonable excuse for failing or refusing to do so.

Once a driver puts forward the defence of reasonable excuse, it is for the prosecution to negate it. Given that the driver will, in all probability, be fully aware of the facts and circumstances which give rise to the reasonable excuse, it is probable that the burden on the driver of proving the reasonable excuse will require him to prove the matter on the balance of probabilities rather than just to lay an evidential basis (see *Attorney-General's Reference No.1 of 2004* [2004] 2 Cr App Rep 424).

Even where a motorist has done all that he is able to do in attempting to co-operate with the test, but for some inexplicable reason is unable to provide one, he may still be convicted of a failure to co-operate. This would appear to be a proportionate response to the balancing exercise required whereby the legislation makes inroads into individual freedoms in order to try to prevent those who have consumed too much alcohol from driving on the roads and causing danger to the public.

In *R* v. *Lennard* [1973] 1 WLR 483 it was held by the Court of Appeal that a reasonable excuse must arise out of a physical or mental inability to provide a specimen or a substantial risk in its provision. However, in *DPP* v. *Varley* [1999] Crim LR 753 the Divisional Court held that the test in *Lennard* was 'for guidance only and not to be treated as part of the statute'.

Once the defendant has sought to rely on a reasonable excuse for failing to provide a specimen of breath, it falls to the prosecution to negate that defence. As such, whilst the defendant need only show on the balance of probabilities that he had a reasonable excuse, the prosecution must show beyond reasonable doubt that the defendant had no reasonable excuse.

In *Williams* v. *Osborne* [1975] RTR 181 it was held that it was not a reasonable excuse for the defendant to believe that he was not in charge of a motor vehicle when the allegation against him was that he was, and similarly where the defendant did not accept that he had committed a moving traffic offence

(*R* v. *Downey* [1970] Crim LR 287) and where he did not believe that he had consumed alcohol or was not the driver at the time of the accident (*McGrath* v. *Vipas* [1984] RTR 58).

A failure to understand a requirement to co-operate with a preliminary test may amount to a reasonable excuse although this would have to be determined on a case-by-case basis. It cannot do so, however, where the defendant's refusal is based upon a false assertion that he was not the driver of the vehicle at the time (*Chief Constable of Avon & Somerset* v. *Singh* [1988] RTR 107).

2.10 IMPAIRMENT TESTS

Whilst there are, as yet, no approved devices generally available to allow police forces to carry out preliminary drug testing under RTA 1988, s.6C, police forces have developed procedures which enable them to observe individual drivers carrying out certain tasks and make observations as to that person's physical state which will be of use in determining whether the driver has driven whilst unfit through drink or drugs. These field impairment tests are carried out under RTA 1988, s.6B.

The Secretary of State for Transport has issued a Code of Practice (the Code) dated December 2004 which covers the use of such tests. The aim of the Code is to ensure that a preliminary impairment test is designed to indicate:

• whether a person is unfit to drive; and
• if he is, whether or not the unfitness is likely to be due to drink or drugs.

The Code states that a preliminary impairment test may be a test of any type provided that it meets the requirements and objectives of RTA 1988 and is administered in accordance with the Code of Practice issued by the Secretary of State for the purpose.

The Code further states that 'it is not possible to pass or fail all or any one of the tests. There is no benchmark for pass or failure, nor is there any scoring system to indicate relative success.' It is the intention that, at the conclusion of the tests, the constable should be able to form an overall opinion, considering what they know of the subject's driving, their demeanour and anything learned in general observation, together with the subject's performance during the tests and the observation of the pupillary examination, whether the person is impaired to drive a motor vehicle through drink or drugs. The constable may then decide whether or not there is sufficient evidence to effect an arrest under RTA 1988, ss.3A or 4.

The Code makes it clear that prior to requiring a preliminary impairment test it is vital that there must be a suspicion that the driver is impaired to drive and that the manner of driving and/or the signs and symptoms of drug use are of importance in arriving at that conclusion.

The approved tests consist firstly of a pupillary examination of the driver's eyes – looking for over-large pupil size (brown-eyed people have a distinct advantage because of the difficulty of distinguishing between pupil and iris at night) and other signs such as reddening or watering of the eyes and drooping or tremulous eyelids.

The second series of tests comprise 'tests of divided attention'. The Romberg Test looks at an individual's ability to measure the passage of time by asking him to assess the passage of a period of 30 seconds – with eyes closed. Estimations of less than 22 or in excess of more than 30 actual seconds might suggest impairment. Other tests which might be used include the 'one-legged stand' (the ability to stand on one leg with eyes closed for a short period); the 'walk and turn' test (which requires an ability to walk along a defined line, turn correctly as instructed with one heel fixed to the ground and then reverse the procedure); and the 'finger to nose' test (where the hand is brought round in a wide arc from the side to make the index finger touch the tip of the nose – again with eyes closed).

The Code requires that all information obtained during a preliminary impairment test is recorded on Form MG DD/F. It is intended that the evidence obtained from field impairment tests is used to enhance the information available to a court about the physical state of a suspect at the time of testing.

CHECKLIST   The preliminary screening test

1. Was the police constable in uniform?
2. Was the driving – or the attempt to drive – on a road or other public place?
3. What are the circumstances giving rise to the constable's request to the driver to co-operate with a preliminary test?
4. Was this a random check by the police or was it a random stopping in order to administer a preliminary test?
5. Does the reason given require the constable to reasonably suspect driving or a moving traffic offence or to reasonably believe that the person concerned has been involved in an accident?
6. If the driver was stopped for a moving traffic offence, was the alleged offence one that is defined as such for the purposes of RTA 1988?
7. If the constable is alleging that he reasonably believed that an accident had taken place and that the motorist was the driver (or in charge), what was the information that led the police constable to believe that this was the case?
8. Was the language used by the constable requiring the motorist to co-operate with a preliminary test such as to make it clear what was required of him?
9. What type of device was used to analyse either a breath or other screening specimen?
10. Has the device used received the approval of the Secretary of State?
11. How should the device be assembled? Was it properly assembled on this occasion?
12. Where appropriate, was there a gap of 20 minutes between the last consumption of alcohol and the provision of the specimen?

13. If less than 20 minutes, was the officer acting *mala fides* in making the request during this lesser timescale?
14. Was the motorist required to co-operate with the preliminary test at or near the place where it was requested?
15. Was there a gap in time between the motorist being stopped and any screening device becoming available? If so, was it reasonable in all the circumstances for the motorist to be required to wait for that period of time?
16. Does the motorist have a reasonable excuse for failing or refusing to provide the specimen of breath?
17. Does it arise out of a physical or mental inability to provide a specimen?
18. Is evidence of a medical nature required to prove this?
19. Was any test of unfitness to drive conducted in accordance with the relevant Code of Practice? Is a copy of Form MG DD/F available as part of prosecution disclosure?
20. Were the police officer's observations appropriate in light of the driver's responses to the tests of 'divided attention'?

CHAPTER 3

The arrest

3.1 THE LEGISLATION

Section 6D of RTA 1988 (as amended) is headed 'Arrest' and provides:

(1) A constable may arrest a person without warrant if as a result of a preliminary breath test the constable reasonably suspects that the proportion of alcohol in the person's breath or blood exceeds the prescribed limit.

(1A) The fact that specimens of breath have been provided under section 7 of this Act by the person concerned does not prevent subsection (1) above having effect if the constable who imposed on him the requirement to provide the specimens has reasonable cause to believe that the device used to analyse the specimens has not produced a reliable indication of the proportion of alcohol in the breath of the person.

(2) A constable may arrest a person without warrant if –

   (a) the person fails to co-operate with a preliminary test in pursuance of a requirement imposed under section 6, and
   (b) the constable reasonably suspects that the person has alcohol or a drug in his body or is under the influence of a drug.

(2A) A person arrested under this section may, instead of being taken to a police station, be detained at or near the place where the preliminary test was, or would have been, administered, with a view to imposing on him there a requirement under section 7 of this Act.

(3) A person may not be arrested under this section while at a hospital as a patient.

Subsections (1A) and (2A) were added by the Serious Organised Crime and Police Act 2005, s.154 which was implemented from 1 July 2005. The amendments, taken together with other amendments to ss.7, 8, 9 and 10 will permit police to carry out an evidential breath test not only at a police station, but also at a hospital, or at or near the place (such as the roadside) where a preliminary breath test has been administered. The results of the evidential breath test will be admissible as evidence in court. Under pre-amendment law an evidential breath test could only be administered at a police station.

The preliminary test will continue to be available under s.6A for the police to screen suspects. The option of taking a person to a police station for an evidential test remains.

In the event of a positive result or a refusal, or if the police officer believes the equipment not to be working properly, the person may be arrested and taken to a police station. If a person is unable to provide breath he may be required to provide a specimen of blood or urine, which must be taken at a police station. If the breath reading is no more than 50 µg of alcohol per 100 ml of breath, the person who provided it may ask for it to be replaced by a specimen of blood or urine which must be taken at a police station.

Although the police may complete the evidential breath testing procedure satisfactorily at the roadside they may need in some circumstances to arrest the person and detain him at a police station until he is fit to drive.

Section 6E of RTA 1988 is headed 'Power of entry' and provides:

(1)   A constable may enter any place (using reasonable force if necessary) for the purpose of –

(a)   imposing a requirement by virtue of section 6(5) following an accident in a case where the constable reasonably suspects that the accident involved injury of any person, or

(b)   arresting a person under section 6D following an accident in a case where the constable reasonably suspects that the accident involved injury of any person.

Prior to 31 December 2005, the arrest provisions in s.6D relied for their validity on PACE 1984, s.25(6) (which stated that the general arrest provisions outlined in s.25 do not prejudice any other power of arrest conferred in any other enactment) rather than, as previously, on any specific provision contained in PACE 1984, Schedule 2. However, PACE 1984, ss.24 and 25 were specifically repealed with effect from 1 January 2006 by the Serious Organised Crime and Police Act 2005, s.110 and replaced by a new s.24 which provides a constable with a general power of arrest without warrant. The power of summary arrest conferred by (the new) s.24 is exercisable only if a constable has reasonable grounds for believing that, for any of the following reasons, it is necessary to arrest the person in question:

- to enable the name of that person to be ascertained (in the case where the constable does not know, and cannot reasonably ascertain, the person's name, or has reasonable grounds for doubting whether a name given by the person is his real name);
- correspondingly as regards that person's address;
- to prevent that person:

  - causing physical injury to himself or any other person;
  - suffering physical injury;
  - causing loss or damage to property;

- – committing an offence against public decency;
- – causing an unlawful obstruction of the highway;
- to protect a child or other vulnerable person from that person;
- to allow the prompt and effective investigation of the offence or of the conduct of that person;
- to prevent any prosecution for the offence from being hindered by the disappearance of that person.

It should be noted that s.6D confers a discretion on a police officer as to whether an arrest is necessary or not. However, practice suggests that the majority of police officers tend to arrest rather than deal with the matter in any other way. In theory, however, an arrest should only take place where the officer has reasonable grounds for believing that one of the above criteria apply and that an arrest is a proportionate method of ensuring that a driver can be taken to a police station or elsewhere in order to carry out further investigation of the suspected offence.

3.2 ARREST

In effect, s.6D provides that a constable may arrest:

(a) where, as a result of the preliminary breath test the constable reasonably suspects that the motorist has a quantity of alcohol above the prescribed limit in his body, or

(b) where the motorist fails (or refuses) to co-operate with any of the preliminary tests available and the constable reasonably suspects that the person has alcohol or a drug in his body or is under the influence of a drug, or

(c) where the officer believes that the device used to analyse the specimens has not produced a reliable indication of the amount of alcohol in the driver's breath.

Under RTA 1972, before a certificate of analysis could be admitted in the proceedings, the defendant had to be proved to have been arrested. In *Scott* v. *Baker* [1969] 1 QB 659 it was held that this meant 'lawfully arrested'. In order to prove a lawful arrest, the prosecution had to prove either that there had been strict compliance with the procedure for obtaining the breath test or that there had been a lawful arrest because the defendant was driving whilst unfit.

By contrast, RTA 1988 entitles a constable to require specimens of blood, breath or urine 'in the course of an investigation into whether a person has committed an offence under section 3A, 4 or 5'. As a result, the unlawfulness of an arrest or the fact that the prosecution has failed to prove a valid arrest is irrelevant provided that the subsequent specimen for analysis was obtained without inducement, threat, coercion, trick or other impropriety.

The requirement on the constable under s.6 is that he should reasonably suspect, not believe, the consumption and presence of alcohol. This is important, requiring that the constable's state of mind, provided it is reasonably formed, operates not to the level of belief, but to the lesser level of suspicion.

In *Anderton* v. *Royle* [1985] RTR 91 the defendant was stopped by two police officers whilst driving his car on a road. One of the officers smelt alcohol on the motorist's breath and asked him to accompany them to a police station to provide a breath test there. At the police station he provided two positive specimens of breath on a Lion Intoximeter 3000, following which he was arrested and charged.

The justices found that the defendant had not been required to provide a roadside test, that the officers had been acting *bona fide* but that as the prosecutor had failed to prove a valid arrest, the evidence of the breath specimen analysis was inadmissible. Accordingly, they dismissed the charge.

The prosecutor's appeal was upheld by the Divisional Court. The justices had erred in concluding that the defendant had been unlawfully arrested and were wrong in law to dismiss the charge on the basis of the 'unlawful arrest'. The procedure for requiring the breath specimens had been correctly carried out, the analysis result was admissible and the case was remitted to the justices with a direction to convict.

It would appear from the authority of *DPP* v. *Robertson* [2002] RTR 383 that even if the preliminary breath test proves to be a negative one, an arrest would not be unlawful if based on other evidence upon which the officer reasonably suspects the person to be over the prescribed limit, nor would it engage the provisions of PACE 1984, s.78 so as to allow the justices subsequently to exercise their discretion to exclude evidence of the analysis of any breath specimen at the police station. In this case, although the preliminary breath test was negative, the officer arrested the driver after hearing him slur the name of his solicitor when spoken to at the roadside.

Similarly, there is nothing in the procedure laid down by s.6 to prevent a constable from exercising his discretion to require the motorist to provide a second screening sample following failure or refusal to provide a first sample and then to effect an arrest either on the result of the second screening test or on a second failure or refusal to supply one (*Revel* v. *Jordan*; *Hillis* v. *Nicholson* [1983] RTR 497). Nor would it appear that such a requirement will afford a defence to a motorist that, because of the time factor involved in making a second discretionary requirement, the motorist is no longer driving or attempting to drive (see *Hillis* v. *Nicholson*).

3.3 TRESPASS

In deciding the lawfulness or otherwise of an arrest in order to at least raise the possibility of exclusion of subsequently obtained analysis evidence at trial, the Divisional Court was regularly required in the past to determine whether an arrest was a lawful one where there had been either a pursuit by a constable of a motorist, or where there had been a traffic accident and, in each case, an attempted arrest of the motorist had taken place off the road and on the private property of the motorist.

In order to fully understand the position of a potentially trespassing police officer and the provisions of what is now RTA 1988, s.6D it is necessary to compare previous legislation as interpreted by the courts and, in particular, the House of Lords' decision in *Morris* v. *Beardmore* [1981] AC 446. In this case an accident had occurred owing to the presence of a motor vehicle on a road. Acting on information received, two police officers went to the defendant's house where they were let in by his son. Following a conversation with his son, the defendant indicated that he did not wish to discuss the matter and that the officers were to leave his premises. The officers went to his bedroom and requested the defendant to supply a specimen of breath. He again told them to leave, indicating to them at this stage that they were trespassers. He was arrested under the provisions of the then existing RTA 1972.

It was held by the House of Lords that the arrest was unlawful as the constables were trespassers at the time that the arrest had been made. In subsequent cases it was held that even where there had been a lawful requirement for a breath test, subsequent refusal to supply a specimen could not lead to a lawful arrest where the police were trespassers on the defendant's land and where it had been made clear to them that they were no longer welcome (*Clowser* v. *Chaplin* [1981] 1 WLR 837).

In view of these inherent difficulties, Parliament, when enacting the Transport Act 1981, made express provision enabling a police constable to enter any premises, if need be by force, to require a person to provide a breath specimen, but only in the circumstances where, following an accident, injury had been caused to another person, or where there had been a failure or refusal to provide a requested specimen. This express provision applied only to offences under RTA 1988, s.4 or s.6 and left a potential lacuna as regards the position of the trespassing police officer who cannot fulfil the preconditions for a valid arrest under the aforementioned sections.

That lacuna was dealt with by the House of Lords in *R* v. *Fox* [1986] AC 281. In this case the defendant who was driving with a passenger was involved in an accident. No other person or vehicle was involved. The driver and his passenger left the scene before the police arrived. After tracing the vehicle, the police, who had no knowledge at this time of the physical condition of either the driver or his passenger, went to the defendant's house where they attempted to gain entry by knocking on the door. They received no

31

response and, finding the door to be unlocked, entered the house. They found the defendant inside and requested him to provide a screening sample, which was refused. The defendant was then arrested and taken to a police station, where he supplied specimens of breath that were over the prescribed limit.

He was subsequently convicted of failing to provide a specimen of breath for a breath test and of driving whilst over the prescribed limit. The Divisional Court initially quashed his conviction for failing to provide the specimen of breath on the grounds that the constables had been trespassers when they had required the breath specimen, but upheld his conviction for driving with excess alcohol.

The defendant appealed to the House of Lords. His appeal was dismissed on the grounds that a successful conviction for driving whilst over the prescribed limit was not dependent on the accused having been lawfully arrested in the first place. Furthermore, as statute vested a discretion in police officers to decide whether or not to effect an arrest following provision of a positive screening sample, there was no longer a requirement for there to have been an arrest in order for a prosecution under the RTA 1988 for driving whilst over the limit to be successful.

It was further held in this case that there was no general principle that evidence obtained unlawfully was inadmissible if relied upon to prove the prosecution case (*R v. Sang* [1980] AC 402). There was a discretion to exclude evidence where it had been obtained by trick or deception or by oppressive behaviour on the part of the police, but there was no evidence of such in this case and therefore the discretion did not fall to be exercised. (The provisions of PACE 1984, s.78 had not been implemented at this time and were not considered.) The defendant had supplied positive breath specimens at the police station in accordance with approved procedures even though he had been unlawfully arrested and had therefore been properly convicted of the offence of driving whilst over the prescribed limit.

In reaching its decision the House of Lords made it clear that in cases of this nature at least, the interests of the State in ensuring that evidence that bore upon the commission of crime and which was necessary to enable justice to be done should not be withheld from courts of law. Such a principle took precedence over the conflicting, but just as important, interest of the citizen to be protected from illegal or irregular invasions of his liberty by the authorities. Whilst this principle still holds good, any further reconsideration of the issues raised would now additionally have to be subject to the balancing exercises required by the Human Rights Act 1998 in determining proportionality.

It is now abundantly clear that, apart from the exception contained in RTA 1988, s.6E, a police constable has no express power to enter a driver's property and that a motorist who is being pursued for a reason other than that set out in the exception can require the police to leave on the basis that they are trespassers. Thereafter, however, whilst any arrest for failing or refusing to provide a specimen will be unlawful and cannot lead to a successful prosecution for the offence of failing to provide a preliminary test, it would not impact on any evidence obtained at the police station unless, as is considered below, PACE 1984, s.78 can be said to be engaged.

The extent to which the power under RTA 1988, s.6E may be used was considered by the Divisional Court in *Lunt* v. *DPP* [1993] Crim LR 534 (a case which depended on a similar power to enter premises then contained in RTA 1988, s.4(7)) where the appellant appealed against his conviction for wilfully obstructing a police officer in the execution of his duty. He was seen to alight from a vehicle involved in an accident and refused to open his door to the police when they arrived at his house. He was informed that if he did not open his door, entry would be forced. However, the police officers did not give their authority or their reasons for seeking to enter the premises. Entry was eventually forced and the appellant arrested on suspicion of driving whilst unfit through drink.

In the Divisional Court, Waller J emphasised the warning given by Donaldson LJ in *Swales* v. *Cox* [1981] 1 QB 849 that the use of force must only be resorted to 'if need be' and that those words carry 'immense weight and importance'. A constable must take all reasonable steps to obtain permission from the occupier to enter, because there should be no entry by force if consent to enter can be obtained. The court was not prepared to say that the police officer should state the precise legal authority under which he intended to act, although it would seem that he must, at least, inform the occupant of the reasonable belief that had led him to the defendant's house. If such information is not given, is it then open to a police officer to enter by force on the basis that he has taken all reasonable steps to obtain entry without the use of force?

The decision in *R* v. *Fox* pre-dated the coming into force of PACE 1984, s.78 which states:

(1) In any proceedings the court may refuse to allow evidence on which the prosecution proposes to rely to be given if it appears to the court that, having regard to all the circumstances, including the circumstances in which the evidence was obtained, the admission of the evidence would have such an adverse effect on the fairness of the proceedings that the court ought not to admit it.

In *DPP* v. *McGladrigan* [1991] RTR 297 the Divisional Court said that *R* v. *Fox* had been decided on the basis that if *mala fides* existed on the part of the police in that they had operated a trick or deception in order to obtain the evidence or had behaved oppressively, the evidence of the arrest could be excluded. However, the court noted that *R* v. *Fox* had been decided prior to the implementation of s.78, which gave the court a new and considerably wider discretion to exclude evidence without any need to show *mala fides* or impropriety.

An example of the use to which courts have been prepared to put s.78 can be seen in *Matto* v. *Wolverhampton Crown Court* [1987] RTR 337. In this case the defendant drove his car from a road on to private property and was followed by a police car. He was informed by the police officers that he had been speeding and that they were concerned over the manner of his driving. The defendant told the police officers that the property was private and that they were unable to act. The police were therefore aware at this time that any implied licence to be on the property had been revoked. The defendant was told that the police officers knew what they were doing and that he could sue them if he felt that he had been unlawfully arrested.

Following his conviction, the defendant appealed to the Crown Court and subsequently to the Divisional Court, which allowed his appeal. The court held that circumstances existed for the exercise of discretion to refuse to admit the breath–alcohol analysis in evidence, namely the presence of *mala fides* in that the police officers were acting in excess of their powers, which they were aware of, whilst on private property. It had therefore been open to the Crown Court to conclude that the fairness of the breath-analysis procedure at the police station was so affected by the previous oppressive behaviour of the police that the matter should have been considered in the light of the provisions in s.78. In that the Crown Court had adopted the wrong approach by considering the exclusion requirements in *R* v. *Sang*, the appeal would succeed.

Similarly, in *Braham* v. *DPP* (1995) 159 JP 527, the Divisional Court held that magistrates had a discretion to exclude evidence obtained from breath tests if the behaviour of the prosecution had been oppressive. In this case magistrates found that the police had reasonable grounds to suspect the commission of an offence and were, therefore, justified in entering the appellant's flat. They were not referred to their power to exclude evidence under s.78. The Divisional Court agreed with the decision, but left open the question of whether the evidence would have been admissible had s.78 been raised.

In *Sharpe* v. *DPP* (1994) 158 JP 595 police officers followed the appellant, who was driving erratically, to his home and into his driveway. From there he was then taken back to the road where he refused to take a screening breath test. The appellant had made it clear to the officers that they were trespassers and that their presence was unwelcome. An application was refused at the start of trial for witness summonses for two of his neighbours in order that they could give evidence of the constable's oppressive behaviour and thus open the way for the defendant to exclude evidence of the subsequent breath specimen analysis under s.78.

The appellant's subsequent appeal against conviction was upheld. A discretion remained, post-*R* v. *Fox*, to exclude the evidence in a breathalyser case under s.78 where criticism was made of the conduct of police officers prior to arrest. The magistrates had declined to consider applying this discretion because they had refused to issue witness summonses relevant to the matter and the conviction could not stand.

It was further argued that where the defence established *mala fides* on the part of the police, the discretion under s.78 could only be exercised by excluding the evidence of the breath analysis. The Divisional Court refused to accept this somewhat 'extreme submission' making the point that the decision in *DPP* v. *McGladrigan* [1991] RTR 297 which had followed that in *R* v. *Samuel* [1988] QB 615 expressly took the opposing view.

An appeal based on a refusal to exercise any discretion under s.78 can only proceed if it can be shown that the matter was first raised before the justices (*Braham* v. *DPP* [1996] RTR 30).

More recently, in *Harper* v. *DPP* [2001] EWHC Admin 1071 the Administrative Court refused to exclude subsequent breathalyser evidence in a case where the unlawfulness of the arrest had been caused by a slip of the tongue, the police officer having cited s.5 instead of s.4 which did not provide him with a power of arrest in the circumstances of the case. While it was plain from the authorities that a technical error would not avail a person who was charged with wrongfully arresting a citizen, the situation was quite different when it came to the exercise of discretion as to the admission of evidence under s.78 where the court was concerned with substantive issues of fairness and unfairness. The position was no different under the Human Rights Act 1998, which was concerned with matters of substance rather than of form. The unlawfulness of the arrest of the driver in this case had been a matter of form, not substance and it was fair to admit the evidence of what happened at the police station.

3.4 ENTRY BY IMPLIED LICENCE

Where there has not been an accident causing injury to another person, so that the provisions of s.6E(1) are not engaged, a police officer who follows an errant motorist on to his private property must rely on a general implied licence to be there rather than on any power conferred by statute. In *Snook* v. *Mannion* [1982] RTR 321 police officers followed the defendant into the driveway of his house, told him that they suspected him of having alcohol in his body and that they required a breath sample. The defendant's response was to tell the officers to 'fuck off'. It was held by the justices that the use of this expletive did not revoke the implied licence that the officers had, but was merely vulgar abuse. On appeal against conviction, the Divisional Court held that police officers had an implied right to enter the driveway of a house in order to transact lawful business with the occupier until such time as that right was expressly withdrawn. It was for the justices to decide whether the expression used had been mere vulgar abuse or did operate to withdraw the licence.

Similarly, in *Gilham* v. *Breidenbach* [1982] RTR 328 the Divisional Court expressed astonishment that the justices had been treated to a lengthy exposition of the meaning of the phrase 'fuck off you planks' to show that it had been said in order to terminate a police officer's licence to enter private property. Justices were perfectly capable of deciding from their own local knowledge whether the words were used as mere vulgar abuse or had some meaning of another kind.

The present position would appear to be:

- an arrest is not a prerequisite for the admission in evidence of the result of an analysis of blood, breath or urine taken at a police station;
- the police cannot act *mala fides* and PACE 1984, s.78 may apply to exclude unfairly obtained evidence in the event of an arrest;
- a police constable has no express power to enter a defendant's property unless pursuant to the exceptions in RTA 1988, s.6E;
- where there has not been an accident causing injury to another person, a police constable who follows an errant motorist on to his private property must rely on a general implied licence to be there rather than on any power conferred by statute;
- where an accident has actually occurred and injury has been caused, a police constable may enter premises with or without force in order to require a preliminary breath test or to arrest a driver;
- any use of force to enter the premises must be an action of 'last resort';
- the police constable must reasonably believe that the motorist was either driving, attempting to drive or in charge of the vehicle at the time the accident occurred and that injury has been caused to another person;
- a police constable has an implied licence in these circumstances to enter property to require a motorist to provide him with a preliminary breath test;
- once that licence has been revoked, the police constable is a trespasser and any evidence subsequently obtained is subject to discretionary exclusion under PACE 1984, s.78;
- where the officer acts in a *bona fide* manner it is unlikely that the discretion will be exercised; where he acts *mala fides* then the discretion is engaged;
- whether or not an implied licence to enter has been revoked is a question of fact, which depends on the words used and the manner in which they are expressed.

3.5 DETENTION OF PERSONS AFFECTED BY ALCOHOL OR A DRUG

Section 10 of the RTA 1988 provides for the detention of those who provide positive specimens either at a police station or elsewhere:

(1) Subject to subsections (2) and (3) below, a person required under section 7 or 7A to provide a specimen of breath, blood or urine may afterwards be detained at a police station (or, if the specimen was provided otherwise than at a police station, arrested and taken to and detained at a police station) if a constable has reasonable grounds for believing that, were that person then driving or attempting to drive a mechanically propelled vehicle on a road, he would commit an offence under section 4 or 5 of this Act.

(2) Subsection (1) above does not apply to the person if it ought reasonably to appear to the constable that there is no likelihood of his driving or attempting to drive a mechanically propelled vehicle whilst his ability to drive properly is impaired or whilst the proportion of alcohol in his breath, blood or urine exceeds the prescribed limit.

(2A) A person who is at a hospital as a patient shall not be arrested and taken from there to a police station in pursuance of this section if it would be prejudicial to his proper care and treatment as a patient.

(3) A constable must consult a medical practitioner on any question arising under this section whether a person's ability to drive properly is or might be impaired through drugs and must act on the medical practitioner's advice.

Section 10 was amended by the Railways and Transport Safety Act 2003, but the amendments had not been implemented at the time of writing. The section was further amended by the Serious Organised Crime and Police Act 2005 which provisions were implemented from 1 July 2005.

The purpose of these amendments is that although the police may complete the evidential breath testing procedure satisfactorily at the roadside they may need in some circumstances to arrest the person and detain him at a police station until he is fit to drive. The amended RTA 1988, s.10 provides that a person may be detained at a police station if a constable has reasonable grounds for believing that, were that person then driving or attempting to drive a mechanically propelled vehicle on a road, he would commit an offence under s.4 or s.5 of that Act.

3.6 HOSPITAL PATIENTS

Finally, in dealing with the arrest provisions of the RTA 1988 it should be noted that there is an express exclusion contained in s.6D(3) that precludes an arrest where the motorist is at a hospital as a patient. The effect of this particular provision is dealt with in **Chapter 4**.

CHECKLIST The arrest

---

1. Was there an actual arrest?
2. What was the reason for the arrest?
3. What was the basis of the police constable's reasonable suspicion?
4. Was there a refusal or failure to provide a screening sample of breath?

5. If there was a refusal or failure to provide, does this constitute a possible defence to a charge of failing to provide a specimen under RTA 1988, s.6(6)?
6. If the arrest was invalid, what is the effect of this on any other evidence relating to other offences that may have come to light as a result of subsequent procedures?
7. Was more than one request made for a screening sample of breath? If so, are the prosecution able to show that because of the lapse of time, the motorist was still driving or attempting to drive?
8. Did the police constable exercise his right to enter property under the provisions of s.6E?
9. If so, had an accident occurred involving injury to another person or had there been a refusal or failure to co-operate with a preliminary test following an accident?
10. If the pre-conditions applicable to s.6E do not apply did the police constable have an implied right to enter the premises?
11. If there was such an implied licence to enter, was it ever revoked?
12. If so, how? What words were used? Are the words used likely to be held to be mere vulgar abuse or an actual revocation of the implied licence?
13. If the arrest was unlawful, can the evidence and any subsequent evidence obtained be held to be inadmissible by the court by virtue of PACE 1984, s.78?
14. What were the actions of the arresting police officers? Were they in themselves oppressive in such a way as to have an adverse effect on the nature of the proceedings?
15. Was the motorist, at the time of the arrest, at a hospital as a patient?

CHAPTER 4

Protection for hospital patients and testing of incapacitated drivers

4.1 THE LEGISLATION

Section 7A of the Road Traffic Act 1988 was inserted by the Police Reform Act 2002, s.56(1) with effect from 1 October 2002 and provides:

(1) A constable may make a request to a medical practitioner for him to take a specimen of blood from a person ('the person concerned') irrespective of whether that person consents if –

   (a) that person is a person from whom the constable would (in the absence of any incapacity of that person and of any objection under section 9) be entitled under section 7 to require the provision of a specimen of blood for a laboratory test;

   (b) it appears to that constable that that person has been involved in an accident that constitutes or is comprised in the matter that is under investigation or the circumstances of that matter;

   (c) it appears to that constable that that person is or may be incapable (whether or not he has purported to do so) of giving a valid consent to the taking of a specimen of blood; and

   (d) it appears to that constable that that person's incapacity is attributable to medical reasons.

(2) A request under this section –

   (a) shall not be made to a medical practitioner who for the time being has any responsibility (apart from the request) for the clinical care of the person concerned; and

   (b) shall not be made to a medical practitioner other than a police medical practitioner unless –

      (i) it is not reasonably practicable for the request to be made to a police medical practitioner; or

      (ii) it is not reasonably practicable for such a medical practitioner (assuming him to be willing to do so) to take the specimen.

(3) It shall be lawful for a medical practitioner to whom a request is made under this section, if he thinks fit –

   (a) to take a specimen of blood from the person concerned irrespective of whether that person consents; and

   (b) to provide the sample to a constable.

(4) If a specimen is taken in pursuance of a request under this section, the specimen shall not be subjected to a laboratory test unless the person from whom it was taken –

    (a) has been informed that it was taken; and
    (b) has been required by a constable to give his permission for a laboratory test of the specimen; and
    (c) has given his permission.

(5) A constable must, on requiring a person to give his permission for the purposes of this section for a laboratory test of a specimen, warn that person that a failure to give the permission may render him liable to prosecution.

(6) A person who, without reasonable excuse, fails to give his permission for a laboratory test of a specimen of blood taken from him under this section is guilty of an offence.

(7) In this section 'police medical practitioner' means a medical practitioner who is engaged under any agreement to provide medical services for purposes connected with the activities of a police force.

Section 9 of RTA 1988 provides:

(1) While a person is at a hospital as a patient he shall not be required to co-operate with a preliminary test or to provide a specimen for a laboratory test unless the medical practitioner in immediate charge of his case has been notified of the proposal to make the requirement; and –

    (a) if the requirement is then made it shall be for co-operation with a test administered, or for the provision of a specimen, at the hospital, but
    (b) if the medical practitioner objects on the ground specified in subsection (2) below, the requirement shall not be made.

(1A) While a person is at a hospital as a patient, no specimen of blood shall be taken from him under section 7A of this Act and he shall not be required to give his permission for a laboratory test of a specimen taken under that section unless the medical practitioner in immediate charge of his case –

    (a) has been notified of the proposal to take the specimen or to make the requirement; and
    (b) has not objected on the ground specified in subsection (2).

(2) The ground on which the medical practitioner may object is –

    (a) in a case falling within subsection (1), that the requirement or the provision of the specimen or (if one is required) the warning required by section 7(7) of this Act would be prejudicial to the proper care and treatment of the patient; and
    (b) in a case falling within subsection (1A), that the taking of the specimen, the requirement or the warning required by section 7A(5) of this Act would be so prejudicial.

Section 7(7) of RTA 1988 provides:

(7) A constable must, on requiring any person to provide a specimen in pursuance of this section, warn him that a failure to provide it may render him liable to prosecution.

Note that RTA 1988, s.10 (2A) provides:

> (2A) A person who is at a hospital as a patient shall not be arrested and taken from there to a police station in pursuance of this section if it would be prejudicial to his proper care and treatment as a patient.

Section 10 provides for the detention of a motorist who has provided positive evidential specimens and who would, otherwise if released, commit a further offence by driving over the prescribed limit if released.

Prior to 30 March 2004, what was then s.6(2) provided that a police officer could only require a motorist to provide a specimen of breath for a breath test at a police station. This is no longer the case. Section 9 has been amended by the Railways and Transport Safety Act 2003, s.107 and Sched.7 so that a constable can now require a driver to co-operate with a preliminary test or provide an evidential specimen anywhere, including at a hospital, provided he has notified the medical practitioner in immediate charge of the case of such a proposal. The only other limitation in the legislation which relates to the preliminary testing stage is s.6D(3) which provides that a motorist shall not be arrested by virtue of his having provided a positive preliminary breath test, or for refusing or failing to provide such a specimen if he is at a hospital as a patient.

The amended provision no longer prevents a police officer from making a request to a patient at a hospital to provide a specimen of breath using a roadside screening device. In *Jones (Vivian)* v. *DPP* [2005] RTR 184 the defendant was at a hospital following a road traffic accident and was required by a constable to provide a specimen of breath with a roadside screening device. She refused and the constable, after checking with the doctor treating her, asked her to supply a specimen of blood. On analysis this was found to be in excess of the prescribed limit. She subsequently appealed against conviction on the grounds that she should have been offered the opportunity to provide a specimen of breath and that she had not been aware, because of her drowsy state following the accident, that part of the specimen had been placed in her handbag after its provision by the officer.

The appeal was dismissed. As the procedure for taking specimens for analysis had been carried out, from first to last, in accordance with RTA 1988, s.7(2) while the defendant was in hospital there was no power to take a specimen of breath for analysis. The defendant had been supplied with a sample of her blood pursuant to RTOA 1988, s.15(5) when it had been placed in her handbag.

4.2 DEFINITIONS

The term 'hospital' is defined in RTA 1988, s.11 as 'an institution which provides medical or surgical treatment for in-patients or out-patients'.

Whilst not specifically stated to be the case, it would appear that the reasons for this protection are twofold: first, to ensure that patients at a hospital are not disturbed during their treatment by requests to provide various samples and, second, to ensure that whilst patients are receiving that treatment there is no room for possible conflict between doctors seeking to treat their patients and police officers seeking evidence for a prosecution.

The requirement that the hospital provide medical or surgical treatment, on either an in- or an out-patient basis, would appear to be sufficiently wide to cover both public and private sector establishments. It is submitted that the use of the words 'as a patient' in the section requires that the person involved must have been through some form of admission procedure in order to qualify as a patient. Therefore, if for some reason he was taken to a hospital that did not cater for emergency or casualty admissions, then he would not be at the hospital 'as a patient' and would not be subject to the protection of RTA 1988.

In *Hollingsworth* v. *Howard* [1974] RTR 58 it was held that a patient was not at a hospital when in an ambulance on his way to a hospital. This point was given further clarification, however, in *Attorney General's Reference (No. 1 of 1976)* [1977] 1 WLR 646 where it was held that the words in themselves meant anywhere within the precincts of a hospital; so that, for example, the patient in the ambulance referred to above would have been able to claim the protection of s.9 once the ambulance had turned into the drive of the hospital grounds.

It should be noted that the legislation merely states that 'the requirement' to provide a specimen of blood be made either at a police station or a hospital. Thus, in *Russell* v. *Devine* [2001] NIECA 28, a case heard in the Court of Appeal of Northern Ireland, but in relation to legislation worded in similar terms to RTA 1988, s.7, it was held that, provided the requirement to provide the specimen was made at a police station (or at a hospital), the actual taking of the specimen might sensibly be done anywhere and there was no compelling reason for it to be done at the police station or at a hospital.

Whether a patient has ceased to be such is a fact for the court to decide in individual cases. In *Askew* v. *DPP* [1988] RTR 303 the defendant had been involved in a collision and had been taken to hospital for examination. A police constable spoke to a doctor who was examining X-rays of the defendant's injuries and ascertained from him that the defendant was free to go home. On being told of this by a nurse, the defendant complained of pains in the arm and it was suggested to him that he take analgesic tablets to relieve the pain.

He was then seen by the police officers in the foyer of the hospital and asked to step outside the building, which he did. He then provided a positive screening breath test. Subsequently, at the police station, he provided specimens of breath above the prescribed limit. The next day he was informed by the hospital that he had in fact suffered broken ribs and a collapsed lung in the accident.

His appeal to the Divisional Court was dismissed. The justices could only have concluded that the defendant was no longer a patient at the hospital within the meaning of s.9 when the breath test specimen was required of him outside the building.

4.3 TREATMENT

For some time it was thought to be the case that where a person attended hospital for treatment, he continued to be a patient until such time as that treatment had been completed. This view extended to the requirement that the patient wait after the treatment had finished for a short period in order to ascertain whether there were going to be any after-effects of either the accident or the treatment.

However, in the Scottish case of *Watt* v. *MacNeill* 1980 SLT 178 (and noted at [1988] RTR 310)) the High Court of Justiciary refused to follow the decision in *Attorney-General's Reference (No. 1 of 1976)* (see above). In this case the defendant had been injured in a motor vehicle accident and was taken to a hospital where he was treated by the casualty officer on duty. Following the treatment he was lying on a hospital trolley, naked from the waist up and with no shoes on, when he was approached by a police officer who ascertained from him that he had been the driver of the vehicle. The police officer then approached the casualty doctor, who gave permission to the police officer to obtain a specimen of breath and, if that were positive, specimens of blood or urine. These were taken and proved positive. After they had been taken, the defendant put on his shoes and clothes and left the hospital without being seen by any other members of the hospital staff.

It was held that at the relevant time the defendant continued to be a patient at a hospital and that, therefore, it was permissible for the casualty doctor to give permission for the relevant specimens to be taken. It would appear that it is a question of fact for the tribunal in each case to decide whether or not the defendant continues to be a patient at a hospital, the question of cessation of treatment being only one of the factors to be taken into account when making the necessary decision. Indeed, the common sense approach to what is essentially a factual problem will involve ascertaining whether or not a person has had treatment at a hospital, whether or not that treatment has come to an end, whether the doctor in charge of the case has informed the police that the treatment has come to an end, whether that fact has been ascertained and whether the patient himself has begun to prepare himself to leave the hospital (*Askew* v. *DPP* [1988] RTR 303).

Even where the driver is discharged from hospital, after treatment, any previous request for a sample can be used to re-initiate the procedure. In

Webber v. *DPP* [1998] RTR 111 the driver of a car was involved in an accident and taken to hospital without providing a screening test. At the hospital she was asked to take that test, but refused. She was then required to provide specimens of blood, but before she could do so she was discharged from the hospital. She was then arrested in reliance on RTA 1988, s.6(5)(b) by reference to her earlier refusal to provide the roadside test.

Her subsequent appeal against conviction was dismissed. The requirement made by the officer under s.7 was lawful and set in train a procedure which, if not acquiesced to, led to further sanctions. The procedure was not to be seen as varied or discharged just because the defendant had been allowed to leave hospital. Nothing in the statute drove the court to the view that the locus at which the specimen was provided was so vital that, if it was not provided at a hospital its analysis ceased to be admissible.

4.4   PRELIMINARY BREATH TEST

There is no reason why a police officer cannot request a patient in a hospital to co-operate with a preliminary test as defined in ss.6A–6C provided that the medical practitioner in immediate charge of the case has been notified of the proposal and there is no objection on the ground that the requirement would be prejudicial to the proper care and treatment of the patient.

This protection extends not only to deciding whether or not the patient is sufficiently well to be able to supply the screening sample, but also to whether or not he is able to have the requirement put to him.

4.5   PROVIDING THE SPECIMEN

Following the provision of a positive screening sample of breath, a requirement can then be made under RTA 1988, s.7 for the provision of a specimen for a laboratory test.

Again, the medical practitioner in immediate charge of the case has to be notified of the proposal to make the requirement and, again, he can object either to the requirement or to the provision of a specimen on the grounds that to consent would be prejudicial to the proper care and treatment of his patient.

Because RTA 1988, s.7 allows a police officer to make a requirement for an evidential specimen '[i]n the course of an investigation into whether a person has committed an offence under section 3A, 4 or 5 of [the] Act' it is not necessary for there to be the prior supply of a positive preliminary sample of breath before the police constable moves on to this part of the procedure. It may well be the case, therefore, that a proposal made to a medical practitioner to supply a screening sample of breath, which is turned down, could almost immediately be renewed as a proposal to supply evidential specimens of breath, blood or urine. If the prejudice to the proper care and treatment of the patient was that which would have been caused by the requirement to supply breath, then there may be circumstances where it would be possible to argue that the same prejudice would not apply if the requirement was to supply blood or urine.

The procedure to be followed by a police officer requiring the provision of an evidential specimen from a patient in hospital was laid down in *Ogburn* v. *DPP* [1994] 1 WLR 1107. In essence, thereafter, the details of the procedure as laid down in *DPP* v. *Warren* [1993] RTR 58, and subsequently amended in *DPP* v. *Jackson*; *Stanley* v. *DPP* [1998] RTR 397, have to be strictly followed by the constable (see **Chapter 7**).

The above case was not specifically referred to in *R* v. *Burton on Trent Justices, ex parte Woolley* [1995] RTR 139 in which the Divisional Court said that there was no requirement to inform a driver at a hospital why a specimen of breath could not be taken provided that the motorist was given ample opportunity to raise any objection he might have to giving blood 'either on medical grounds or for any other reason which might afford a reasonable excuse under section 7(6)'. This latter comment needs to be read in the light of the House of Lords' decision in *Stanley* v. *DPP* and *DPP* v. *Jackson* where the gloss of 'any other reason' would have to be struck out.

In *Butler* v. *DPP* [2001] RTR 28 the defendant failed a roadside breath test and was taken to a police station. There he told a police officer that he suffered from 'immune system breakdown', but was found to be fit enough to provide a specimen of breath by the police doctor. However, during the subsequent procedure he collapsed and was taken to hospital. No one told the doctor at the hospital of the defendant's assertions regarding his health and the doctor consented to the taking of blood samples.

His appeal against conviction was allowed. The safeguards in RTA 1988, s.7 applied equally to the procedure under s.9 at a hospital. Under s.7 the constable was required to inform a medical practitioner of any potential medical reasons put forward for not providing a blood sample and similar considerations applied in s.9 cases. The information had not been passed to the doctor in the hospital and the specimen subsequently obtained was not admissible.

Refusal or failure to provide the required specimens is an offence unless the defendant has a reasonable excuse for the failure (see **Chapter 10**).

4.6 SPECIMENS OF BLOOD TAKEN FROM PERSONS INCAPABLE OF CONSENTING

The protection afforded to hospital patients has been diminished by implementation of RTA 1988, s.7A. The changes, which were designed to ensure that samples can be taken from drivers suspected of drink driving even if they have been injured in an accident, were implemented from 1 October 2002.

The section provides that a constable may request a medical practitioner to take a specimen of blood from a driver who is not capable of giving consent to the taking of that sample where it appears to the constable that the driver has been involved in an accident that the constable is investigating and where the constable would normally be entitled to require an evidential specimen from the individual concerned. The constable must be of the opinion that the person is incapable of giving valid consent to the taking of the blood sample and that the incapacity is attributable to medical reasons. The wording of the legislation leaves it open for the constable to make such a request where the medical reasons are either physical or relate to mental capacity.

Such a request cannot be made to a medical practitioner who, at the time, has the responsibility for the clinical care of the person concerned. The request must be made to a medical practitioner who is engaged under an agreement to provide medical services for purposes connected with the activities of a police force unless it is not reasonably practicable for the request to be made to such a police medical practitioner or it is not reasonably practicable for such a medical practitioner to take the specimen.

The British Medical Association (BMA) has issued guidelines to help doctors to apply the new law. The guidelines state that a blood sample may be taken for the purposes of alcohol or drug testing where:

(a) a police constable has assessed the person and found they are incapacitated due to medical reasons;
(b) the police medical practitioner taking the sample should be satisfied that the person is not able to give valid consent and ensure the person does not object to, or resist, the sample being taken;
(c) in the view of the doctor in immediate charge of the patient's care, taking the sample would not be prejudicial to the proper care and treatment of the patient.

Section 7A(4) requires that if a blood specimen is taken in this way, there can be no forensic analysis of the specimen by way of laboratory test unless the person from whom it was taken has been informed that it has been taken and gives his permission for a laboratory test of the specimen to be carried out. Provided that the driver has also been warned by the constable that a failure to give this permission will result in a prosecution for an offence under s.7A(6) any failure to give permission will still lead to a prosecution which, if successful, will see the driver subject to the same penalties as if the specimen had tested positive.

In *R* v. *Grimwood* (2005) 169 JP 373, a case of causing death by dangerous driving, the Court of Appeal said that it was more prejudicial than probative to place before a jury evidence of the existence of a sample of blood taken in hospital pre-transfusion for purposes other than ascertaining the level of alcohol in the driver's blood and which had been exposed to the air prior to any analysis being carried out. A doctor was entitled to refuse a police attempt to obtain a sample of blood under RTA 1988 where the taking of the sample would be prejudicial to the proper care and treatment of the patient.

CHECKLIST   Hospital patients

1. Was the defendant at a 'hospital' as defined by RTA 1988?
2. Had he been admitted there as a patient?
3. Where was the requirement to co-operate with a preliminary test made?
4. At the time the request was made, had the patient's treatment concluded?
5. Had the medical practitioner in charge of the case informed the police that treatment was at an end? If not, how were the police aware that this was the case?
6. Were the circumstances such that the patient had begun to make his preparations to leave the hospital?
7. In making the requirement, did the constable reasonably believe there to have been an accident, injury caused and some involvement on the part of the patient?
8. Did the police officer notify the medical practitioner in charge of the case of his intention to make a requirement to supply a specimen of breath?
9. What was his response?
10. Was any medical information given by the driver that should have been passed on to the medical practitioner to enable an informed decision to be made?
11. Was the patient informed of the police officer's request and of the response of his medical practitioner?
12. Did the police officer make a request for a screening sample to be given or did the officer proceed straight to a request for provision of an evidential specimen?
13. Was the medical practitioner aware that a request for an evidential specimen was to be made as well as the initial request for a screening sample of breath?
14. Was there a failure or refusal to supply what was required?
15. Was there a reasonable excuse for the failure or refusal to supply?
16. Was the request for a specimen of blood made under RTA 1988, s.7A?
17. If so, if the driver were not at a hospital and unable to give consent to the taking of a blood specimen, would the circumstances normally allow the constable to make the request?
18. Was the request to take blood made to a police medical practitioner?

CHAPTER 5

Driving or in charge whilst unfit

5.1 THE LEGISLATION

Section 4 of RTA 1988 provides:

(1)   A person who, when driving or attempting to drive a mechanically propelled vehicle on a road or other public place, is unfit to drive through drink or drugs is guilty of an offence.

(2)   Without prejudice to subsection (1) above, a person who, when in charge of a mechanically propelled vehicle which is on a road or other public place, is unfit to drive through drink or drugs is guilty of an offence.

(3)   For the purposes of subsection (2) above, a person shall be deemed not to have been in charge of a mechanically propelled vehicle if he proves that at the material time the circumstances were such that there was no likelihood of his driving it so long as he remained unfit to drive through drink or drugs.

(4)   The court may, in determining whether there was such a likelihood as is mentioned in subsection (3) above, disregard any injury to him and any damage to the vehicle.

(5)   For the purposes of this section, a person shall be taken as unfit to drive if his ability to drive properly is for the time being impaired.

(6)–(8)   [*Repealed, with effect from 1 January 2006, by the Serious Organised Crime and Police Act 2005, s.111 and Sched.7, para. 27(2) and Sched.17, Pt 2.*]

5.2 DEFINITIONS

Introduction

Section 11(2) of RTA 1988 defines 'drug' as including any intoxicant other than alcohol. There is no need for the drug to be classified as a medicine. Whilst the word 'intoxicant' is not similarly defined, normal usage would suggest a meaning whereby loss of self-control to a greater or lesser degree is occasioned by taking the substance concerned. This could, in certain circumstances, include insulin injected for the purpose of controlling diabetes. In *R* v. *Ealing Magistrates' Court ex parte Woodman* (1994) 158 JP 997 the Divisional Court held that s.4 could be used to prosecute a diabetic who had administered insulin if it could clearly be shown that the unfitness to drive as a result of a hypoglycaemic attack was the direct result of an injection of insulin. However, in this case, the court also found that where the injection had been properly administered, the court had to be sure that the unfitness to drive had been caused by the insulin and not, for example, the consequence of blood sugar imbalance or an attack brought on despite the insulin injection.

The offences under s.4 have, until recently, tended to take second place to the more commonly prosecuted offences under s.5 of driving or being in charge with an alcohol level above the prescribed limit. Their retention within the statutory scheme is important, affording as they do a viable alternative to the offences under s.5 by merely requiring some evidence of impairment of driving and covering the situation where that impairment is occasioned by the consumption of drugs and not alcohol. Additionally, with the recent changes to s.6 and especially the extension of the ability to test and screen for drugs, it is now likely that s.4 will be increasingly used as an alternative to the s.5 offence.

In *Bradford* v. *Wilson* [1984] RTR 116 the defendant was found slumped over the steering wheel in a stationary car and holding a plastic bag over his face. He admitted that he had been glue-sniffing. A plastic bag and a tin of Evo-stik were found on the floor of the car and were subsequently ascertained to contain toluene. Evidence was called to show that toluene contained a narcotic which, when inhaled, had the effect of alcohol, namely giddiness, light-headedness, slurred speech and loss of control. The defendant was convicted of being unfit to drive, the justices having found that he had deliberately inhaled toluene to achieve the effect of a narcotic and that it had been used as a drug.

His appeal against conviction was dismissed on the basis that as a general rule, a drug was a substance, not being drink or food, taken in the human body by any means, which affected the control of the body. The defendant had taken the drug and it had affected him so that he did not have proper control over the vehicle and was therefore unfit to drive.

'Driving or attempting to drive'

Sections 4 and 5 are not dissimilar. Both require that there has been some driving or an attempt to drive or that the person to be prosecuted was in charge of the vehicle.

'Driving' requires that there is a person who, by use of the steering controls of the vehicle, together with clutch, brakes and possibly accelerator, is able to produce movement by the vehicle, which movement is subject to some control by the person said to be driving.

There is, in effect, a two-stage test to be applied in determining whether or not someone was driving for the purposes of the legislation. This approach was adopted by the Divisional Court in *DPP* v. *Alderton* [2004] RTR 367 where the defendant was seen by police officers in the driving seat of a stationary vehicle on a grass verge forming part of the road outside the defendant's house. He admitted that, prior to the arrival of the police, he had been sitting in the driving seat of the vehicle 'wheel spinning' which involved the engine running and the use of the accelerator, clutch and steering wheel with the vehicle in gear and the handbrake on.

The Divisional Court said that, applying, first, a test of degree of control over the movement and direction of the vehicle, there was a suffcient degree of control being exercised by the defendant by ensuring that the handbrake prevented the movement of the vehicle despite the fact that the wheels were turning, to say that the defendant was driving the vehicle. Secondly, applying a test of whether what was being done fell within the ordinary meaning of 'driving', a person 'wheel spinning' could properly be said to be driving a vehicle within the ordinary meaning of that word.

Whether or not someone is driving in the ordinary sense of the word is a question of fact or degree. Where a passenger interfered with the driving of a car by momentarily seizing the steering wheel, it was held in *DPP* v. *Hastings* [1993] RTR 205 that his actions did not amount to driving, but were merely an interference with the driving.

Where a motor vehicle has broken down and is being pushed, anyone sitting in the vehicle who is controlling its movements can be said to be driving the vehicle, provided that there is some common purpose with any persons who may be pushing the vehicle. However, where the vehicle is being pushed and control is exercised by means of leaning through the open window of the vehicle in order to gain access to the steering wheel, it is unlikely that this would be held to be driving for the purposes of RTA 1988.

In *McKoen* v. *Ellis* (1987) 151 JP 60 the appellant was found by a police officer on a public road sitting astride his motorbike. He was subsequently convicted of consuming alcohol whilst above the prescribed limit. He appealed against his conviction on the grounds that he could not have been found to be driving at the time. The justices had found as facts that he had pushed the bike in such a way as to cause the engine to engage, following which he had been able to turn on the lights and had used the brakes to stop the machine. They concluded that he had substantial control of the movement and direction of the motorbike. He controlled it at his will. He was driving in the ordinary sense of the word.

The Divisional Court approved the approach taken by the justices whereby they had taken into account the whole circumstances of the incident, including the circumstances surrounding the defendant's conduct. Provided that the court had properly directed itself in this way, the question was one of fact and degree and could only be overturned if the court could be shown to have been acting unreasonably.

Whether or not a person has been driving is again a question of fact and degree to be determined by reference to the time, place and circumstances in which the driver is found. In *Whelehan* v. *DPP* [1995] RTR 177, these factors together with a pre-caution admission from the driver that he had driven to the location (but consumed alcohol thereafter) were found to be sufficient to reach a conclusion on driving.

Of more difficulty to the courts has been determining the question of whether a person is attempting to drive a vehicle. In *Kelly* v. *Hogan* [1982] RTR 352 the defendant, who was unfit to drive because of drink and was sitting in the driving seat of a car stationary on a public road, tried to insert keys into the ignition. None of the keys were, in fact, the right keys for that particular car, although it was accepted that had he had the right keys he would have started the engine.

It was held by the Divisional Court that the act of putting the keys into the ignition, whether the wrong keys or not, was sufficiently proximate to the commission of the full offence as to constitute an offence of attempting to drive. The fact that commission of the full offence was impossible, either through ineptitude or inefficiency, was irrelevant since he had intended to drive. He had therefore been rightly convicted.

It should be noted that the offence of attempting to drive is one created by RTA 1988 itself and does not rely on the Criminal Attempts Act 1981 for its provenance. Indeed, in that drink-driving offences are purely summary, the Criminal Attempts Act could not create such offences by virtue of the provision within it limiting the Act to offences only capable of being tried on indictment (s.1(4)).

A person, whilst not being the driver of a motor vehicle, may be guilty of aiding and abetting the principal offence. In *DPP* v. *Anderson* (1991) 155 JP 157 the defendant rode as a pillion passenger on a motorbike ridden by a learner driver, who had consumed a substantial amount of drink. It was held that in order to prove aiding and abetting the principal offence, the prosecution must show:

(a) that the principal offender had committed the offence of driving with excess alcohol;
(b) that the aider and abettor knew that the principal offender had consumed an excessive amount of alcohol, or was reckless as to whether he had or not; and
(c) that the defendant had aided, abetted, counselled or procured the commission of the offence.

Similarly, in *DPP* v *Janman* [2004] RTR 522 the defendant was alleged to have been in charge of a motor vehicle whilst over the prescribed limit in circumstances where his partner, a learner driver, was the actual driver of the vehicle. The Divisional Court held that whether a person was qualified to supervise a learner was irrelevant to the question of whether they were, in fact, supervising a learner, and, accordingly, the prosecution did not have to establish that the person supervising was statutorily qualified to do so. In addition, where a driver with a provisional driving licence was driving a motor vehicle on a road, the person supervising him would, at least in normal circumstances, be 'in charge' of the motor vehicle. The court also rejected the defendant's argument that the statutory defence applied to him because there was no likelihood of his driving on the basis that his partner, albeit a learner driver, was so competent a driver that there would be no need in any circumstances for the defendant to take over the control of the vehicle.

'In charge'

The question of whether a person is in charge of a motor vehicle is one that can only be decided on the particular facts of individual cases.

Guidance was given by the Divisional Court in *DPP* v. *Watkins* [1989] QB 821. The appellant was found in a drunken state, seated in the driver's seat of a car. He did not own the car and there was no evidence he was there with the owner's permission. He had an ignition key in his hand, but it was the wrong key for that particular type of car. The lights were not on and the engine was not running. It was held that there had to be a causal connection between the appellant and control of the vehicle before the appellant could be found to be in charge and it was for the court to consider all the relevant factors and reach its decision as to fact and degree.

In addition, if the person was the owner of the car, or had recently driven it, he would have been in charge of it. The question for the court would be whether he was still in charge or whether he had relinquished control of it. If, for example, there was no realistic possibility of his realising actual control whilst unfit because he had gone to bed, or if it had been taken by another, then obviously he could no longer be said to be in charge. If the person was not the owner, other lawful possessor, or recent driver, but was merely sitting in the vehicle, the question for the court was whether he had assumed charge of it. Such a person would be in charge if, whilst unfit, he was voluntarily in de facto control of the vehicle. Usually, this would mean a gaining of access to the vehicle with an intention to drive it away.

The following facts were held to be relevant in deciding such cases:

(a) whether and where the person was in the vehicle or how far he was from it;
(b) what he was doing at the relevant time;
(c) whether he was in possession of a key that fitted the ignition;
(d) whether there was evidence of an intention to take or assert control of the car by driving or otherwise; and
(e) whether any other person was in, at or near the vehicle and, if so, the like particulars in respect of that person.

'Road or other public place'

In RTA 1988, s.192 – the general interpretation section – 'road' is defined as meaning any highway and any other road to which the public has access, including any bridge over which a road passes. The term should be distinguished from its counterpart in the Vehicle and Registration Excise Act 1994 which utilises the term 'public road' to mean a road repairable at the public expense.

It should be noted that the definition in s.192 is sufficiently wide to encompass not only those routes that the ordinary man in the street would class as a road, but also any other way that is classified as a highway or to which the public have access. Usually, it is a matter of fact and degree for the court to decide whether or not a public way is a road for the purposes of RTA 1988 or not. The Divisional Court will hesitate to interfere with a decision provided that it has been arrived at reasonably and the court has been properly directed.

In *Cutter* v. *Eagle Star Insurance Company* [1998] 1 WLR 1647 the House of Lords, in determining an appeal in civil proceedings, was required to consider whether a car park was a 'road' for the purposes of RTA 1988. The court determined that the question to be asked, if the place was not a highway, was whether it was a road to which the general public had actual and legal access. A road could be said to have the physical character of a defined or definable route or way, with ascertained or ascertainable edges, leading from one point to another with the function of serving as a means of access enabling travellers to move conveniently from one point to another along a definable route. Accordingly, the question of whether a place was a road was always a question of fact. In the ordinary use of language, a car park was not a road since it had a separate and distinct character and function. However, for the purposes of s.4 and s.5, a car park may be an 'other public place' which, with unrestricted public access, could be sufficient for a conviction.

In *DPP* v. *Vivier* (1991) 155 JP 970 the respondent was involved in a traffic accident shortly after midnight on a road within a privately owned caravan park. The caravan park was surrounded by a ditch and there were field gates designed to be kept locked. At the site entrance there was a reception area to which casual visitors wishing to stay had to report and at which they were issued with a car pass. The justices found that the owners of the site had taken special precautions to ensure that unwanted visitors did not enter the site. At the material time the site had been open to the public, but not to the general public – only to a special class of persons who had legitimate access to the site. However, although there were large numbers of such persons, this did not of itself make the site a public site.

It was held by the Divisional Court that those attending the caravan site were attending for their own purposes and not the purposes of the site owner and that there was no sufficient segregation or selection to cause them to cease to be members of the general public. The case was therefore remitted to the justices with a direction to convict the defendant of the s.5 offence.

A car park attached to a public house has been held to be sufficient to satisfy the section (*Elkins* v. *Cartlidge* [1947] 1 All ER 829) although where the car park was closed because it was outside licensing hours and the owner did not permit parking there at that time, the car park did not fall within the definition (*Sandy* v. *Martin* (1974) 139 JP 241).

This line of reasoning was followed in *Howell* v. *DPP* (1994) 158 JP 680 where the appellant's car was parked in the car park of a community centre, which was readily accessible from the public road without any physical obstruction to prevent access by members of the public. The community centre was a members' club, membership rules requiring nomination by an existing member. The Divisional Court held that the car park was the car park of a private members' club and was not a public place.

In *Bowman* v. *DPP* (1990) 154 JP 524 the appellant was convicted of driving a motor car in a public place (a car park) with excess alcohol in his breath. There was evidence to show that the appellant had been seen driving his car around the car park late at night, that there were other cars parked there and that the car park barrier was raised. There was further evidence to show that the barrier was only functional during normal shopping hours. The car park was well known to two of the justices, who took into account their local knowledge that the barrier was up at night and that such was a clear indication to the public to use the car park at that time. They therefore held that the appellant had been driving in a public place and convicted him of the offence.

In dismissing the appeal, the Divisional Court held that the justices were entitled to use their local knowledge and to draw the inferences that they did. In this case there had been ample evidence to show that the car park at the material time had been a public place and the defendant had been rightly convicted.

However, in *R* v. *Spence* [1999] RTR 353 the appellant was alleged to have driven dangerously in a small car park that consisted of a yard outside a small office building flanked on three sides by a wall, a hedge and a fence. Access from the road was prevented by bollards. A swing gate, open during the day but closed at night, permitted entrance. The car park was used by employees, customers and other business visitors. As those who used it were a special class as distinct from members of the general public and there was no evidence of a general public 'user', it was held that the car park was not a road or other public place for the purposes of RTA 1988.

Similarly, in *Brewer* v. *DPP* [2005] RTR 5 a railway station car park bordered partly by a fence and with a gate at the entrance was held by justices to be a road for the purposes of a prosecution under s.5. Vehicular access to the car park was gained by pressing a button to produce a ticket and the removal of the ticket in turn caused the barrier to lift. Employees at the station gained access to their own private car park by driving through the larger car park.

The decision was overturned on appeal. The only feature which was capable of rendering the car park a road was that staff drove through it on their way to their own staff car park, but that was insufficient public usage to render the car park capable of being a road.

In *Planton* v. *DPP* [2002] RTR 9 it was held that a causeway linking the mainland to a small island, which was sometimes passable and sometimes submerged by tidal water, was not a public place for the purposes of a prosecution under s.5. The use of the causeway was compatible with access to residences on the island, but there was no evidence of any general public access to the island for any purpose.

It is for the prosecution to prove that a place is a public place at the time of the offence (*Pugh* v. *Knipe* [1972] RTR 286). Even if an area is only open to a section of the public, and entry is subject to conditions, that area is a public place for the purposes of the legislation provided that entry is permitted not because of some special characteristic or reason personal to particular individuals, but on a criterion possessed by the public at large (*DPP* v. *Neville* (1996) 160 JP 758).

'Mechanically propelled vehicle'

Section 185 of RTA 1988 defines 'motor vehicle' as a mechanically propelled vehicle intended or adapted for use on roads. The Vehicles Excise and Registration Act 1994 refers to mechanically propelled vehicles used or kept on any public road. Section 189 of RTA 1988 specifically exempts from the definition of 'motor vehicle' a mechanically propelled vehicle which is a grass-cutting implement controlled by a pedestrian and not adapted for any other use, and also any other mechanically propelled vehicle controlled by a pedestrian which may be specified by the Secretary of State as so exempt.

Whilst a vehicle that is broken down and has no hope of repair does not fall within the definition, temporary removal of a vehicle's engine does not render it incapable of being a mechanically propelled vehicle, as it is capable of replacement, after which time it would presumably once more be capable of fitting the definition.

In *Chief Constable of Avon and Somerset* v. *Fleming* [1987] 1 All ER 318 it was held that a vehicle is intended or adapted for use on roads when a reasonable person sees the vehicle and reasonably forms the view that its general user would be such as would normally be used on a road. Where this issue is in doubt it is for the prosecution to prove that the vehicle was so intended or adapted.

The test in the above case was further defined in *DPP* v. *Saddington* [2001] RTR 15 where the defendant was charged with driving an unregistered motor scooter – a motorised 'Go-Ped' – on a road whilst disqualified and without insurance. The Divisional Court said that the test of whether a vehicle was mechanically propelled or not was not whether a reasonable person would use a Go-Ped on a road, which in ordinary circumstances would be unlikely, given the attendant dangers. The test to be applied was whether a reasonable person would say that one use of the Go-Ped would be use on a road. A reasonable person must consider whether some general use on the roads must be contemplated – and not merely some isolated use or use by a man losing his senses.

'Unfit to drive'

For the purposes of s.4, the test of whether a person is unfit to drive depends upon whether his ability to drive properly at the material time is impaired. Thus, where the driving at the time falls below the standard that would be expected of a normal, competent driver, the test of impairment can be satisfied and unless the statutory defence in s.4(3) can be made out, a conviction is likely.

Prior to the introduction of the breathalyser procedure, the offence had always been one of driving whilst unfit through drink or drugs. The Road Traffic Act 1962 (RTA 1962) temporarily changed the definition of the offence to one of driving whilst impaired, but it was always accepted that there was no discernible difference between the two phrases. The RTA 1962 had also introduced provisions whereby the courts could take account of blood–alcohol levels in order to find evidence of impairment, but in practice convictions at the time depended almost entirely on the manner in which the accused had driven, or on the evidence of his personal appearance or behaviour.

It was the need to prove impairment that led to the introduction of prescribed limits above which drivers could be prosecuted for an offence of driving whilst blood, urine (and now breath) levels exceeded that prescribed level. The statutory level of 80 mg of alcohol per 100 ml of blood was set after the BMA produced figures to show that this was the lowest figure at which it could be stated beyond doubt that almost every driver was impaired by alcohol in the sense that he was more likely to be involved in an accident because he had taken alcohol. However, it was pointed out at that time that lower levels produced an impairment in a driver's ability to drive safely, and that the critical level for most drivers would be at around 50 mg of alcohol per 100 ml of blood.

Police forces in England and Wales are developing a series of field impairment tests at the roadside to determine the question of impairment. In December 2004 the Department for Transport issued a Code of Practice for Preliminary Impairment Tests under the power contained in RTA 1988, s.6B(2). The Code deals with:

- the kind of task that may be specified for the purpose of a preliminary impairment test;
- the kind of observation of physical state that may be made in the course of a preliminary impairment test;
- the manner in which a preliminary impairment test should be administered; and
- the inferences that may be drawn from the observations made in the course of a preliminary impairment test.

The tests are to be carried out in two stages commencing with a pupillary examination of the eyes of the suspect and followed up by a series of tests of 'divided attention'. The pupillary examination is conducted using a gauge held adjacent to the appropriate side of the subject's face to enable the constable to compare the size of the subject's pupils with those of someone not affected by drink or drugs. The constable is also required to look out for and record whether the subject's eyes are 'watery' and/or 'reddened'.

The second stage requires a constable to carry out tests designed to measure the subject's ability to concentrate:

- the Romberg test measures changes in an individual's internal body clock and measures the ability to balance. The subject is required to stand perfectly still and assess the passage of between 25 and 30 seconds of time – any body sway or tremors being indicative of possible ingestion of drink or drugs and failure to estimate the time within defined limits being indicative of use of some form of drugs;
- the 'one-leg' stand where the officer requires the subject to raise the right foot 15–20 centimetres off the ground, to keep the arms down by the side and to count progressively upwards from 'one thousand and one', etc. until told to stop. Whilst carrying out this exercise, the officer looks for swaying, putting the foot down to regain balance or arm raising;
- the 'walk and turn' test which requires the suspect to walk along a defined line putting the heel of each foot against the toes of the preceding foot and where the officer is looking for signs of imbalance, incorrect turns or stepping off the line; and
- the 'finger to nose' test where the officer tests for perception of depth and balance looking for appropriate co-ordination and body sway.

The results of any preliminary impairment test are to be recorded by the police officer on Form MG DD/F.

5.3 BLOOD/URINE OPTION WHERE EVIDENCE OF DRUG IMPAIRMENT

Section 7 of RTA 1988 provides for the situation in which a police constable has arrested a motorist whose driving has been obviously impaired, but where the breath test device at the police station does not subsequently show the motorist to have been consuming alcohol.

In these circumstances:

(3)   A requirement under this section to provide a specimen of blood or urine can only be made at a police station or at a hospital; and it cannot be made at a police station unless –

     (a)   the constable making the requirement has reasonable cause to believe that for medical reasons a specimen of breath cannot be provided or should not be required, or

     (b)   specimens of breath have not been provided elsewhere and at the time the requirement is made a device or a reliable device of the type mentioned in subsection (1)(a) above is not available at the police station or it is then for any other reason not practicable to use such a device there, or

    (bb) a device of the type mentioned in subsection (1)(a) above has been used (at the police station or elsewhere) but the constable who required the specimens of breath has reasonable cause to believe that the device has not produced a reliable indication of the proportion of alcohol in the breath of the person concerned, or

    (bc) as a result of the administration of a preliminary drug test, the constable making the requirement has reasonable cause to believe that the person required to provide a specimen of blood or urine has a drug in his body, or

     (c)   the suspected offence is one under section 3A or 4 of this Act and the constable making the requirement has been advised by a medical practitioner that the condition of the person required to provide the specimen might be due to some drug;

but may then be made notwithstanding that the person required to provide the specimen has already provided or has been required to provide two specimens of breath.

Section 7(3)(bc) was inserted with effect from 30 March 2004 by the Railways and Transport Safety Act 2003 specifically to enable a constable to require a specimen of blood or urine where, as the result of the administration of a preliminary drug test, he has reasonable cause to believe that the person required to provide the specimen has a drug in his body. At the time of writing, however, the Secretary of State has not approved any analytical device capable of detecting the presence of a drug. Once such a device is available, there will then be two means whereby a sample of blood or urine can be required from a person suspected of committing a s.4 offence. Where the result of the preliminary drug test gives a constable reasonable cause to believe that the person concerned has a drug in his body, s.7(3)(bc) will apply and a specimen can be required. Alternatively, where the constable making the requirement has been advised by a medical practitioner that the person's condition might be due to some drug then s.7(3)(c) will apply and a requirement can be made.

In *Cole* v. *DPP* [1988] RTR 224 the defendant failed to provide a screening breath test and was arrested and taken to a police station where he supplied specimens of breath which gave a reading of zero. The officer suspected that his erratic driving was due to consumption of drugs and requested a doctor to examine him prior to a request for blood samples to be given. The doctor was of the opinion that the defendant's condition might be due to drugs or epilepsy, but did not advise that it might be due to some drug. The constable then required a blood sample, which was refused.

The motorist's appeal against conviction was allowed on the grounds that s.7(3)(c) intends a doctor to give a clear indication orally of the view found by him as to the possible cause of the motorist's condition. In the absence of such an opinion, the constable's request for blood was invalid, and there could be no conviction for failing to provide the specimens.

Whilst *Bell* v. *DPP* (1998) WRTLB 92 confirmed the view that there must be a clear indication by a doctor that the cause of the motorist's condition is due to some drug, it should be noted that in *Leetham* v. *DPP* [1999] RTR 29 on the facts of the particular case, the observations of the police officer at the scene were held to be sufficient to justify a conclusion that drugs had impaired the defendant's ability properly to drive. In this case, police officers stopped a car being driven at speed and erratically. It was observed that the driver's eyes were red and glazed, that his speech was slurred and that his answers to questions were given slowly. He admitted having smoked a cannabis cigarette earlier in the evening. It was held that despite the fact that no doctor was called to confirm the matter, there was evidence in relation to the driving of the vehicle, the admitted consumption of cannabis, the effects of the drug and the police officer's evidence to justify the conclusion that drugs had impaired the defendant's ability to drive.

It is, of course, possible to argue that where there is a charge under the provisions of RTA 1988, s.4 the fact that there is proof that the specimen provided is above the prescribed limit for a successful prosecution under s.5 is not of itself sufficient proof that the person providing the specimen was unfit to drive – evidence of impairment being dependent on other factors such as an inability to control the vehicle properly or the fact of the motorist's condition or demeanour. However, it is submitted that in the present climate of road safety awareness, there is a sufficient body of evidence that can be called upon to show that even where the level of alcohol in the body is below the prescribed limit, the effect of alcohol on a normal person is such that any intake of alcohol that is more than merely minor consumption will have the effect of impairing a driver's ability to drive and as such render him liable to prosecution under s.4 for driving whilst unfit.

In many cases in the past it was usual for the police to charge alternative offences under s.4 and s.5 on the basis that the evidence of the specimen would decide whether the charge was to be one of driving whilst unfit or above the prescribed limit. However, the introduction of the procedure for requiring instantly analysed breath specimens at the police station has to a large extent made the need for alternative charges unnecessary. Where there is a need to rely on the evidence of blood or urine alternatives, however, police authorities would do well to consider making the charging of alternatives standard procedure.

A comparison between the offences under s.4 and s.5 was undertaken in *DPP* v. *Frost* [1989] RTR 11 in which the Divisional Court took the opportunity to compare the effect of the statutory defence on both sections. In this case, the defendant, who had been driven to a party, felt unwell and went to sit in the driver's seat of his car. He subsequently fell asleep there and was awoken with some difficulty by two police officers at about 3 a.m. They described him as being in a befuddled condition and unsteady on his feet when walking, as a result of which he was arrested for being in charge of a motor vehicle whilst under the influence of drink or drugs. At the police station he provided specimens of breath that were substantially over the prescribed limit and was then charged with offences contrary to s.4 and s.5.

The appeal to the Divisional Court turned to a large extent upon whether or not justices needed to have expert evidence on the breakdown rates of alcohol in the body in order to justify dismissals where the statutory defence had been made out (see **Chapter 6**). What becomes obvious from the appeal, though, is that evidence of impairment under s.4, where the prosecution do not rely on scientific evidence, becomes a matter of opinion as to the state of the defendant at the material time. A situation could therefore arise where a limited consumption of alcohol that is below the prescribed limit but causes impairment could lead to a conviction under s.4.

5.4   ARREST PROVISIONS

Sub-sections 4(6)–(8) of RTA 1988 were omitted from 1 January 2006 following implementation of Serious and Organised Crime and Police Act 2005, s.111 and Sched.7, para. 27(2) and Sched.17, Pt 2. Any arrest of a driver in respect of an offence under RTA 1988, s.4 must now take place under s.6(D).

CHECKLIST   Unfit to drive through drink or drugs

---

1. Does the charge refer to impairment through 'drink' or 'drugs'?
2. If the charge does not so specify, what consumption does the prosecution intend to rely on?
3. If the prosecution are relying on 'drug', is the substance a 'drug' covered by the definition in RTA 1988, s.11(2)?
4. Was the motorist aware that he had taken such a drug and that it would have this effect on him?

5. Is there an allegation that the motorist was 'driving' or 'attempting to drive'? Do the facts as alleged by the prosecution fall within the definition of one or the other?

6. Is the motorist alleged to have been 'in charge' of the vehicle? Again, do the facts support this allegation?

7. Does the vehicle fall within the definition of 'mechanically propelled vehicle' or one of the exemptions to that definition?

8. Was the vehicle being used on a road at the material time?

9. Or is it alleged that the vehicle was being used in some other public place? What are the facts?

10. What evidence does the prosecution intend to rely on to show impairment of driving?

11. How was that evidence obtained?

12. If the evidence of impairment is solely the result of the analysis of a specimen provided by the motorist, is it possible to argue that that alone was not, on this occasion, evidence of impairment as to show unfitness to drive?

13. Has an alternative charge been preferred under RTA 1988, s.5 and what effect will this have on the proceedings?

14. Did the constable have reasonable cause to suspect that an offence under RTA 1988, s.4 had been committed? Was an arrest necessary?

15. If force was used to enter premises, why was it necessary for the police officer to use force and was its use reasonable?

CHAPTER 6

The 'in charge' statutory defence

6.1 THE LEGISLATION

Both s.4 and s.5 of RTA 1988 provide a statutory defence to the offences of being in charge of a mechanically propelled vehicle whilst unfit to drive through drink or drugs and of being in charge of a motor vehicle after consuming so much alcohol that the proportion of it in breath, blood or urine exceeds the prescribed limit.

Section 4 of RTA 1988 provides that:

> (3) For the purposes of subsection (2) above, a person shall be deemed not to have been in charge of a mechanically propelled vehicle if he proves that at the material time the circumstances were such that there was no likelihood of his driving it so long as he remained unfit to drive through drink or drugs.
>
> (4) The court may, in determining whether there was such a likelihood as is mentioned in subsection (3) above, disregard any injury to him and any damage to the vehicle.

Section 5 of RTA 1988 provides:

> (2) It is a defence for a person charged with an offence under subsection (1)(b) above to prove that at the time he is alleged to have committed the offence the circumstances were such that there was no likelihood of his driving the vehicle whilst the proportion of alcohol in his breath, blood or urine remained likely to exceed the prescribed limit.
>
> (3) The court may, in determining whether there was such a likelihood as is mentioned in subsection (2) above, disregard any injury to him and any damage to the vehicle.

6.2 APPLYING THE DEFENCE

Whilst there are minor differences between the two sections, these are differences more of form than of substance. The defendant is required under s.4 to show that he would not have driven so long as he remained unfit to do so, in which case he is deemed not to be in charge, whilst the defence under s.5

requires the defendant to prove that he had no intention of driving whilst the level of alcohol in his breath, blood or urine remained above the prescribed limit. In both cases, the normal rules of evidence apply, so that the burden of proving the matter lies with the defendant, to the civil standard of 'balance of probabilities'.

In keeping with other similar defences that seek to reverse the burden of proof and impose a burden on the defendant, the statutory defence in s.5 (and by analogy, s.4) has been the subject of judicial consideration post-implementation of the Human Rights Act 1998. In *Sheldrake* v. *DPP* [2005] RTR 2 the defendant was found asleep slumped over the steering wheel of his car in a public place. The proportion of alcohol in his breath was four times the prescribed limit. The magistrates rejected the defendant's contention that the statutory defence in s.5(2) contained a reverse burden of proof which interfered with the presumption of innocence guaranteed by Article 6(2) of the Convention for the Protection of Human Rights and Fundamental Freedoms and that it should be interpreted as placing only an evidential burden as opposed to a persuasive legal burden on him. The magistrates concluded that RTA 1988, s.5(2) did not interfere with the presumption of innocence, but that, if it did, it pursued a legitimate aim and was proportionate.

The case eventually reached the House of Lords following the driver's successful appeal to the High Court. In reinstating the decision of the justices to convict, the House held that the burden of proof provision in s.5(2) imposed a legal burden on an accused charged with an offence under s.5(1). Section 5(2) of RTA 1988 was directed to a legitimate objective and the burden placed on the defendant was not beyond reasonable limits or in any way arbitrary.

In practice, the major difference between the two provisions lies in the relative difficulty that a defendant seeking to rely on either provision will have if he is to be ultimately successful. Under s.4, the question of whether he would have been unfit to drive at the relevant time is one that can be decided without recourse to scientific evidence. Under s.5, however, unless the case is obvious, to show that the level of alcohol in the body would have been below the prescribed limit at the relevant time requires expert assistance as to how alcohol affects the defendant. Courts have been extremely slow to find the statutory exception to apply unless there is such expert evidence before them.

In *DPP* v. *Frost* [1989] RTR 11 the distinction between the two sets of provisions was considered by the Divisional Court. The defendant was charged with offences under s.4 and s.5 following an incident whereby he had left a party because he felt ill, although it had been his intention at the outset to sleep at the premises. The police later found him in the driver's seat of his parked car where he was fast asleep, but with the car keys in the ignition.

He gave evidence to the justices that it had been his intention to stay the night and that, had he done so, he would not have driven until 9 a.m. the following morning. The justices, without hearing expert evidence concerning rates of alcohol dissipation, were of the opinion that the statutory defence applied, and dismissed the two charges.

The Divisional Court dismissed the prosecutor's appeal against acquittal on the charge under s.4. The question for the court was whether the defendant had proved by evidence that at the time of the offence there was no likelihood of his driving whilst unfit. The relevant inquiry should therefore centre around the effect on the defendant's unfitness to drive during the interval of time between the offence and the time of driving. On that question, it was held, laymen could be expected to hold views and to be able to express opinions without always having the evidence of experts.

On the other hand, the appeal against dismissal of the charge under s.5 was allowed. Here, the defendant had to prove that at the time of the offence the circumstances were such that there was no likelihood of his driving while the proportion of alcohol in his breath remained above the prescribed limit, the relevant inquiry being centred around the effect of the time lapse on the defendant's breath–alcohol proportion. However, the rate of decline of the breath–alcohol level over a given period was not within the ordinary experience of a layman and (in this case) was not plain to a layman. Accordingly, there was no material on which the justices could properly have concluded without expert medical or scientific evidence that the defendant's breath–alcohol level would have been below the prescribed limit at 9 a.m. the following morning.

As a side issue in this case the Divisional Court also pointed out that it was not permissible for the justices to have taken judicial notice of Annex A of Home Office Circular 32/1984 (issued 11 April 1984) containing a table of changes in body fluid–alcohol concentrations over time.

In determining whether the defendant has proved whether there was any likelihood of his driving whilst unfit or over the prescribed limit, the court has a discretion to disregard the fact that the vehicle has been involved in an accident and is thus incapable of being driven, or that the defendant has received injuries as a result of an accident that prevent him from driving further, but which do not hide the fact that he was driving or in charge of the vehicle at some time. A driver should not be able to rely on the statutory defence, therefore, where his driving would have continued had it not been for the intervention of an accident. However, where there has been some intervening event that significantly reduces the likelihood of a driver being able to drive his car whilst over the limit, this is a matter that the court should take into account. Thus, in *Drake* v. *DPP* [1994] Crim LR 855 the defendant's car had been wheel-clamped, he had refused to pay the fee to remove the clamp and had unsuccessfully attempted to remove the clamp with a hammer. As there was no likelihood of his driving the vehicle, his conviction for being in charge whilst over the prescribed limit was quashed.

CHECKLIST   The statutory defence

1. Has the motorist been charged under s.4 or s.5?
2. If so, is it possible to rely on the statutory defence to prove that continued impairment or continued exceeding of the prescribed limit would not have occurred when driving was next likely to take place?
3. Is there sufficient evidence for the driver to show that on the balance of probabilities the statutory defence applies?
4. Was there any injury to the motorist or damage to the vehicle?
5. What likelihood is there of the court disregarding such evidence? What are the circumstances surrounding the incident?
6. Will expert evidence be required to show that at the material time an alcohol level over the prescribed limit would not have been the case?
7. If such evidence is not available, is this a case that can be decided by a layman taking a view of the whole matter, i.e. that it is 'obvious'?
8. What was the lapse of time between the final consumption of alcohol and the provision of the specimen for analysis?
9. If there was a lengthy period involved, is the prosecutor likely to seek 'back-tracking' evidence to show the highest level of alcohol in the body reached by the motorist?

CHAPTER 7

Driving whilst over the prescribed limit

7.1 THE LEGISLATION

Section 5 of RTA 1988 provides:

(1) If a person –

(a) drives or attempts to drive a motor vehicle on a road or other public place, or

(b) is in charge of a motor vehicle on a road or other public place,

after consuming so much alcohol that the proportion of it in his breath, blood or urine exceeds the prescribed limit he is guilty of an offence.

(2) It is a defence for a person charged with an offence under subsection (1)(b) above to prove that at the time he is alleged to have committed the offence the circumstances were such that there was no likelihood of his driving the vehicle whilst the proportion of alcohol in his breath, blood or urine remained likely to exceed the prescribed limit.

(3) The court may, in determining whether there was such a likelihood as is mentioned in subsection (2) above, disregard any injury to him and any damage to the vehicle.

It was held in *DPP* v. *Short* (2002) 166 JP 474 that an offence under s.5 was still disclosed where an information alleged a motor vehicle had been 'used' rather than driven. The defect in the information did not fall into the category of errors that are so fundamental that they are incapable of cure by amendment. The magistrates in the case should have exercised their discretion to permit an amendment.

7.2 PRESCRIBED LIMIT

Section 11(2) of RTA 1988 defines the 'prescribed limit' as:

(a) 35 microgrammes of alcohol in 100 millilitres of breath,

(b) 80 milligrammes of alcohol in 100 millilitres of blood, or

(c) 107 milligrammes of alcohol in 100 millilitres of urine, or such other proportion as may be prescribed by regulations made by the Secretary of State.

Section 5(1) provides that a motorist is only guilty of an offence if the proportion of alcohol in the specimen provided exceeds the prescribed limit. Where the analysis shows the proportion to be the same as the prescribed limit, then no offence under s.5 can be made out, although it is always open to the prosecutor to prefer a charge under s.4 of driving whilst unfit.

Home Office Circular 46/1983 advised Chief Constables not to proceed against an offender where the breathalyser analysis was less than 40 µg. This was to ensure that any offender prosecuted would be significantly in excess of the prescribed limit and is comparable with the allowance subtracted from any specimen of blood or urine analysed in a laboratory.

In *McGarry* v. *Chief Constable of Bedfordshire* [1983] RTR 172 the defendant sought to compare mathematically the different prescribed levels. His urine sample had shown a level of 108 mg of alcohol in 100 ml of urine. The defendant argued that in order to convert the analysis to a blood analysis, the calculation (108 × 80) divided by 107 should be used, which would then give a figure of 80.74 for blood. As it was usual practice to ignore fractions, the 0.74 should not be taken into account. Therefore he was not in excess of the prescribed limit.

Rejecting this argument and dismissing his subsequent appeal against conviction, the Divisional Court said that s.5(1) and s.11(2) did not authorise or require the making of any calculation beyond treating 107 mg of alcohol in 100 ml of urine as equivalent to the prescribed limit of 80 mg in blood. This being so, the defendant had been driving above the prescribed limit as regards the sample provided. There was no room for application of the principle of *de minimis*, and the conviction would be upheld.

In *Oswald* v. *DPP* [1989] RTR 360, DC the practice by analysts of deducting 6 mg from the blood analysis in order to give some room for possible error was considered. It was held that there was no need for a further rounding down of the figure provided to take account of any fractions that may have occurred during analysis.

7.3   PROVISION OF SPECIMENS FOR ANALYSIS

The legal background

Section 7 of the Act provides:

(1)   In the course of an investigation into whether a person has committed an offence under section 3A, 4 or 5 of this Act a constable may, subject to the following provisions of this section and section 9 of this Act, require him –

    (a)   to provide two specimens of breath for analysis by means of a device of a type approved by the Secretary of State, or

    (b)   to provide a specimen of blood or urine for a laboratory test.

(2)   A requirement under this section to provide specimens of breath can only be made –

    (a)   at a police station,

    (b)   at a hospital, or

    (c)   at or near a place where a relevant breath test has been administered to the person concerned or would have been so administered, but for his failure to co-operate with it.

(2A) For the purposes of this section, 'a relevant breath test' is a procedure involving the provision by the person concerned of a specimen of breath to be used for the purpose of obtaining an indication whether the proportion of alcohol in his breath or blood is likely to exceed the prescribed limit.

(2B) A requirement under this section to provide specimens of breath may not be made at or near a place mentioned in subs (2)(c) above unless the constable making it –

    (a)   is in uniform, or

    (b)   has imposed a requirement on the person concerned to co-operate with a relevant breath test in circumstances in which section 6(5) of this Act applies.

(2C) Where a constable has imposed a requirement on the person concerned to co-operate with a relevant breath test at any place, he is entitled to remain at or near that place in order to impose on him there a requirement under this section.

(2D) If a requirement under section (1)(a) above has been made at a place other than at a police station, such a requirement may subsequently be made at a police station if (but only if) –

    (a)   a device or a reliable device of the type mentioned in subs 1(a) above was not available at that place or it was for any other reason not practicable to use such a device there, or

    (b)   the constable who made the previous requirement has reasonable cause to believe that the device used there has not produced a reliable indication of the proportion of alcohol in the breath of the person concerned.

(3)   A requirement under this section to provide a specimen of blood or urine can only be made at a police station or at a hospital; and it cannot be made at a police station unless –

    (a)   the constable making the requirement has reasonable cause to believe that for medical reasons a specimen of breath cannot be provided or should not be required, or

    (b)   specimens of breath have not been provided elsewhere and at the time the requirement is made a device or a reliable device of the type mentioned in subsection (1)(a) above is not available at the police station or it is then for any other reason not practicable to use such a device there, or

  (bb) a device of the type mentioned in subsection (1)(a) above has been used (at the police station or elsewhere) but the constable who required the specimens of breath has reasonable cause to believe that the device has not produced a reliable indication of the proportion of alcohol in the breath of the person concerned,

(bc) as the result of the administration of a preliminary drug test, the constable making the requirement has reasonable cause to believe that the person required to provide a specimen of blood or urine has a drug in his body, or

(c) the suspected offence is one under section 3A or 4 of this Act and the constable making the requirement has been advised by a medical practitioner that the condition of the person required to provide the specimen might be due to some drug;

but may then be made notwithstanding that the person required to provide the specimen has already provided or been required to provide two specimens of breath.

(4) If the provision of a specimen other than a specimen of breath may be required in pursuance of this section the question whether it is to be a specimen of blood or a specimen of urine and, in the case of a specimen of blood, the question who is to be asked to take it shall be decided (subject to subsection (4A)) by the constable making the requirement.

(4A) Where a constable decides for the purposes of subsection (4) to require the provision of a specimen of blood, there shall be no requirement to provide such a specimen if –

(a) the medical practitioner who is asked to take the specimen is of the opinion that, for medical reasons, it cannot or should not be taken; or

(b) the registered health care professional who is asked to take it is of that opinion and there is no contrary opinion from a medical practitioner,

and, where by virtue of this subsection there can be no requirement to provide a specimen of blood, the constable may require a specimen of urine instead.

(5) A specimen of urine shall be provided within one hour of the requirement for its provision being made and after the provision of a previous specimen of urine.

(6) A person who, without reasonable excuse, fails to provide a specimen when required to do so in pursuance of this section is guilty of an offence.

(7) A constable must, on requiring any person to provide a specimen in pursuance of this section, warn him that a failure to provide it may render him liable to prosecution.

Section 7 was substantially amended from 1 July 2005 following implementation of Serious Organised Crime and Police Act 2005, s.154(4)–(6).

The requirement that the specimens are provided during the course of an investigation into offences under RTA 1988, s.3A, s.4 or s.5 merely requires that the ordinary plain meaning of the words is used, namely 'inquiring into'. In *Graham* v. *Albert* [1985] RTR 352 a police constable arrested a motorist for failing to provide a screening sample of breath. At the police station, the duty sergeant informed her of the reason for her arrest, established that she had not consumed alcohol during the previous 20 minutes and required her to provide specimens of breath for analysis.

The justices dismissed the information on the grounds that the arresting officer's purpose had been to investigate a road traffic accident and not an offence under the drinking and driving provisions. The prosecutor's appeal was allowed as the station officer had been inquiring into the possibility that the defendant had committed an offence and as such he was lawfully able to make the necessary requests of her.

Where a police constable reasonably believes that one of a number of persons was driving a vehicle and had consumed alcohol then he may, in the course of his investigation, lawfully require each of those persons to provide specimens of breath (*Pearson* v. *Metropolitan Police Commissioner* [1988] RTR 276). It does not matter that the charge for which the defendant was arrested in the first place has been subsequently withdrawn, provided that the investigating police officer was acting *bona fide* at the time of the offence. Thus, in *Hawes* v. *DPP* [1993] RTR 116 the defendant was driving a car in a public house car park that was being used as a car park for officials at another function nearby. A police officer formed the opinion that the defendant was drunk and arrested him. He was charged with driving in a public place whilst unfit through drink or drugs and with failing to provide specimens of breath.

At the hearing, the prosecutor took the view that the car park was not a public place at the material time and withdrew the first allegation. The defendant then submitted that there was no case to answer on the second charge as no offence had been committed under s.4 and thus the officer had no power to require the provision of breath specimens. He was convicted by the justices.

The Divisional Court dismissed the defendant's appeal. Where a question arose as to whether a police officer had lawfully required a person to provide a specimen under s.7, the court trying the matter was simply concerned to know whether there was or was not a *bona fide* investigation of the question of whether the defendant had committed an offence under RTA 1988, s.4 or s.5. The officer in this case had been concerned only to discover whether the defendant had been guilty of an offence, and with nothing else, and the requirement for a breath test had been lawfully administered.

The requirement to provide specimens of breath could previously only be made at a police station, whereas a requirement to supply blood or urine could either be made at a hospital or, in five specific cases, at a police station. However, since implementation of the Serious Organised Crime and Police Act 2005, s.154 from 1 July 2005, the requirement to provide an evidential breath specimen can now be made at a police station, hospital or elsewhere – thus allowing police forces to introduce devices capable of analysing breath specimens at the roadside which will be admissible as evidence in subsequent court proceedings. Blood or urine specimens can only be required at a police station:

(a)   where the constable making the requirement has reasonable cause to believe that for medical reasons a specimen of breath cannot be provided; or

(b)   where there is no reliable device available; or

(c)   where it is believed the device has produced an unreliable reading; or

(d)   where, following a preliminary drug test there is reasonable cause to believe that the person concerned has ingested a drug; or

(e)   where the condition of the person required to provide the specimen may be due to some drug.

No more than two specimens of breath may be requested and only the lower reading is admissible in evidence. In *Howard* v. *Hallett* [1984] RTR 353 the police officer operating the device erroneously completed the procedure without asking the defendant to provide the second of the two specimens. On realising his mistake, he then recommenced the procedure and obtained a second and a third specimen. The defendant's appeal against conviction was allowed in that as there was no evidence of the first test before the court – and therefore no evidence that it could have been the lower of the specimens provided – the conviction could not stand.

A constable may require the provision of breath specimens for analysis in a situation where a request has already been made and refused (*Owen* v. *Morgan* [1986] RTR 151). Indeed, subject to the tolerance of the officer involved, there would appear to be no limit to the number of such requests that he is allowed to make.

In *Denny* v. *DPP* (1990) 154 JP 461 the defendant was arrested following an accident and taken to a police station, where he was required to provide specimens of breath for analysis. After he had provided the first specimen, the machine indicated that it was no longer functioning normally. As a result, the defendant was taken to another police station where he was able to provide two positive specimens of breath. His appeal against conviction was dismissed, the Divisional Court applying *Sparrow* v. *Bradley* [1985] RTR 122, which had held that if a police officer considered that the first device was not working properly then it could not be said to be a departure from the statutory procedure to give the motorist a further opportunity to provide a specimen with another device.

As previously stated, s.7(2) limits any request to provide a breath specimen to a request at a police station. A police officer must require a breath specimen rather than blood or urine unless one of the five situations listed above occurs. These are discussed in more detail below.

(a)   Reasonable cause to believe that for medical reasons a specimen of breath cannot be provided

Once at a police station, a motorist will be required to provide specimens for analysis under the provisions of RTA 1988, s.7. It does not matter, however, that the requirement for the specimens of breath is made at a police station where there is no approved device, nor indeed that the specimens are to be provided at another police station.

In *Chief Constable of Kent* v. *Berry* [1985] RTR 321 the defendant was required to provide two specimens of breath at a police station. When he had provided the first of these, the machine malfunctioned. As a result, the police officer who made the requirement transferred the defendant to another police station in order to make a further request to supply blood or urine. The defendant provided a specimen of blood at the second police station even though there was a breathalyser device available and working. The justices found that the police constable had not complied with the relevant procedures as he had been in a position to require the defendant to supply breath on a reliable device at the second police station and had not done so. Therefore, the evidence of the blood analysis could not be admitted and the case was dismissed.

In allowing the prosecutor's appeal, the Divisional Court held that the effective and operative requirement for a specimen of blood was that made in accordance with the statutory procedure at the first police station and that the requirement had led directly to the provision of the specimen relied on. That specimen could properly be taken at another police station and the presence of an approved device at that police station in no way affected the validity of the original requirement, which the prosecution were entitled to rely upon as a means of proving their case.

It is a necessary pre-condition to an alternative requirement for the provision of blood or urine that the police constable making the request has reasonable cause to believe that there are medical reasons why a specimen of breath cannot be provided or should not be required. In *Horrocks* v. *Binns* [1986] RTR 202 the defendant attempted to blow into the breathalyser device, but no sample was recorded. He explained that he had suffered injuries in the road accident that had led to his arrest, which were the cause of his failure to supply the breath specimens. The police officer, whilst not believing that the injuries were capable of having such an effect and not thinking that the defendant was suffering from concussion, gave him the benefit of the doubt as he felt that the defendant was the best judge of his own injuries. The Divisional Court said that as the police officer had no reasonable cause to believe that the injuries prevented a sample of breath from being required or provided, there was no medical reason for failing to supply breath. The defendant's acquittal for failing to supply specimens of blood or urine was upheld.

However, in *White* v. *Proudlock* [1988] RTR 163 the defendant was required to provide two specimens of breath for analysis at a police station and failed to do so. The police officer in the case, without forming any view as to whether there were any medical reasons for so doing, required the defendant to supply a specimen of blood, which again was refused. The justices held that the police officer had been mistaken in requiring a blood specimen because he had not formed a view that the failure to provide the breath specimens was for medical reasons. The charges against the defendant were dismissed.

The Divisional Court allowed the prosecutor's appeal and said that the finding by the justices was an erroneous one. What had to be established was that the police officer making the requirement had reasonable cause to believe that for medical reasons a specimen of breath could not be provided. He did not have to form any view as to the nature of the medical condition. What constituted a medical reason for the purposes of RTA 1988 was a decision for the police officer in the case. It would seem that it is not a decision susceptible to challenge in the Divisional Court.

The burden on the police officer in such cases was explained in *Davis* v. *DPP* [1988] RTR 156 where the defendant attempted on three occasions to blow into the Lion Intoximeter 3000 and was unable to do so on each occasion. He explained to the officer that he had a heavy cold, was an asthma sufferer and could not blow properly into the machine. The sergeant formed the view that he had reasonable cause to believe that for medical reasons a specimen of breath should not or could not be required, even though he was personally of the opinion that a specimen of breath could have been provided. It was held that what was or was not a reasonable cause was a question of fact to be objectively determined by the justices. It was immaterial that the police officer actually believed, was dubious, sceptical or unbelieving as to the medical reason, so long as there was a reasonable cause for his belief on which the justices could make a finding.

Further explanation of the requirement on the officer was provided in *Dempsey* v. *Catton* [1986] RTR 194 where the defendant stated that he was unable to provide specimens of breath because he had a phobia of machines. The police officer accepted this as a possible medical reason why breath could not be provided, and required the defendant to supply a specimen of blood, which he refused to do. The justices convicted the defendant of failing to supply, on the basis that the statement by the defendant was sufficient to enable the police officer to have reasonable cause to believe that breath could not be provided for medical reasons.

The Divisional Court, in dismissing the defendant's appeal, said that the officer was not required to determine whether the phobia asserted by the defendant was or was not a phobia recognised by medical science. All he could do, as a layman, was to determine whether it was capable of being such a condition and then to consider whether he had reasonable cause to believe that breath should not be provided or required for medical reasons. Provided there was sufficient material to justify such a decision, the decision was entirely that of the police officer and he was not required to summon a doctor to give a medical opinion.

It would appear that a reasonable belief can be formed even in circumstances where the defendant refuses to give details of the medical condition that he alleges is preventing him from supplying the specimens of breath. In

DPP v. *Boden* [1988] RTR 188 it was held that the test is an objective one and that, provided the police officer has formed a reasonable belief, lack of information from the defendant as to the medical reason did not necessarily make the officer's belief unreasonable.

In *Steadman* v. *DPP* [2003] RTR 2 the Divisional Court said that there was nothing in s.7(3)(a) which suggested that a police officer, who was having to decide whether medical reasons existed for believing that a specimen of breath could not be provided or should not be required, should be required to take medical advice; the section only required him to have reasonable cause to believe. The decision was one for the police officer himself and was a decision to be based on the facts known to the officer at the time bearing in mind that he was to be treated as a layman in such matters.

Where a police officer is informed by a driver of reasons which may be capable of being medical reasons for not providing a specimen of blood, it is not within the reasonable power of the officer to conclude that the reasons are incapable of amounting to medical reasons. The opinion of a medical practitioner should be sought as to whether the specimen cannot or should not be taken for medical reasons. Thus, in *Townson* v. *DPP* (13 June 2006, unreported), the police officer should have sought medical advice on being told by the driver of recent repeated blood tests, difficulty in finding a vein, pain, diabetes and high blood pressure.

Whether there is a distinction between a medical excuse under s.7(3)(a) and a reasonable excuse for failing to provide a specimen under RTA 1988, s.7(6) was considered in *Davies* v. *DPP* [1989] RTR 391 where the defendant refused to supply specimens of breath because he was taking a drug that a psychiatrist had told him would influence the alcohol content of his bloodstream. He was then required to supply blood and said he was unable to do so because he suffered from haemophilia as evidenced by a small cut received earlier which was still bleeding.

This explanation was accepted and the defendant was requested to supply specimens of urine within the hour. The defendant said that whilst there was no medical reason for not doing so, he was taking large doses of various vitamins that would influence the analysis and so he would not supply urine either. He was charged and convicted of failing to supply specimens of urine.

In dismissing the defendant's appeal, the Divisional Court held:

(a) the question of whether the police officer had reasonable cause to believe that a specimen of breath could not be provided was a question of fact to be objectively determined by the justices;

(b) as the test was an objective one, it was immaterial that the police officer was sceptical about the reason given to him or might even be left in a state of disbelief;

(c) the officer was to be treated as a layman in medical matters;

(d)   there was a clear distinction between the medical evidence relevant to the question of reasonable excuse under s.7(6) and the evidence relevant to s.7(3)(a). A reasonable excuse only arose if there was some evidence of incapacity or of some risk to health and the concern was with the knowledge and belief of the driver as well as with his actual state of health. Under s.7(3)(a) the concern was with the state of knowledge of the police officer and with the reasonable belief of someone with that knowledge;

(e)   even if the words 'cannot be provided' related exclusively to physical or mental capacity to provide a specimen, no similar restriction could be placed on the words 'should not be required'; and

(f)   although the officer in the present case had directed his attention to the 'could not provide' test, the court was not concerned with the actual belief of the officer, but with whether a constable with that state of knowledge had reasonable cause to hold the belief that the breath specimens should not be required when he asked whether there was any medical reason why urine could not be provided.

In *Grix* v. *Chief Constable of Kent* [1987] RTR 193 the defendant was required to provide specimens of breath, but was unable to do so for medical reasons, which the police constable reasonably believed. The police constable then required him to provide blood, to which the defendant replied: 'No, specimen of urine – no blood.' He was convicted of failing to supply a specimen of blood.

In dismissing the defendant's subsequent appeal, the Divisional Court held that a police constable was under no duty, when requiring a specimen of blood to be provided, which was then refused, to ascertain the reason for the refusal or indeed whether there was a medical reason why blood could not be provided.

In that it is usually over-consumption of alcohol that leads to a motorist being brought to a police station and the breathalyser procedure being invoked, is it open to a prosecutor to argue that, because of intoxication, there is a medical reason for not providing specimens of breath? This argument was considered in *Young* v. *DPP* [1992] Crim LR 893 in which a police officer conducting the procedure had required the defendant to supply a specimen of blood after concluding that she was unable to supply breath, owing to her intoxication. The defendant argued that intoxication was not normally regarded as a medical condition and that, in any case, intoxication could not give rise to a defence of reasonable excuse for a motorist accused of failing to provide a specimen. Therefore, it would be inconsistent to regard intoxication as a medical reason for the purposes of s.7(3). As the purpose of RTA 1988 was to give the police powers to test possibly intoxicated motorists, but to restrict their powers to requesting breath in other than exceptional cases, the mere fact of intoxication could not constitute such an exceptional case.

In rejecting all three arguments the Divisional Court emphasised that there is no necessary connection between a medical reason that leads to a request for blood and a medical condition that provides a possible defence of reasonable excuse for not providing the specimen. In determining the existence of a possible defence to a charge such as this, the court must have regard to the fact that the excuse has been 'manufactured' by the defendant, as the intoxication was self-induced. On the other hand, where the existence of a medical reason leads the prosecutor to pursue a different means of securing the evidence, there is little or no disadvantage to the defendant and the intoxication need not be held against her in this way.

The court held that intoxication was a condition recognised by the medical profession as a medical condition and that, therefore, the police officer had properly formed a reasonable belief that there was a medical condition that allowed him to make a requirement that blood be provided.

In *Webb* v. *DPP* [1992] RTR 299 the defendant made three attempts to blow into the Lion Intoximeter, all of which were unsuccessful. She indicated to the officer that she was trying as hard as she could and that she did not suffer from any medical condition. The officer observed that she was of slight build, that her breath smelt of alcohol and that she was shaken and upset and appeared to be in a distressed condition. He concluded that she was in a state of shock, and that he had reasonable cause to believe that for medical reasons a specimen of breath could not be provided.

In dismissing her subsequent appeal against conviction, the Divisional Court said that whether the constable had a reasonable cause to believe was a question of fact for the justices who should take into account the fact that he was a layman and that his personal belief was immaterial. Since the defendant was apparently doing her best, there could be no reason other than a medical one why she should not comply with the requirement to provide specimens of breath. Her distressed condition, her being shaken and upset, consumption of alcohol and being of slight build were factors capable of amounting to a medical reason, and it had been open to the officer to form a reasonable belief that such existed.

(b)   Reliable device not available for use

The second limb of s.7(3), allowing for a blood or urine substitute to be requested, applies where there is no reliable device available at the police station at the time or where it is not practicable to use such a device there.

The exact meaning of the phrase 'practicable to use' was considered in *Chief Constable of Avon* v. *Kelliher* [1987] RTR 305, in which justices dismissed information alleging an offence of failing to provide specimens of breath on the grounds that it would have been practicable to bring an officer trained in the use of the device from a neighbouring police station in a situation where there was no such trained officer available at the time the request for a breath specimen to be provided was made.

The Divisional Court, in allowing the prosecutor's appeal, held that the phrase 'practicable to use' demanded an answer to the question whether it was practicable to use the breath device at the time when the requirement was made. In this case it was not possible to use the device at the relevant time and, therefore, the constable had been correct to require a specimen of blood from the defendant. It was not practicable to expect a police constable to break off in the middle of such a procedure in order to telephone neighbouring police stations in the hope of finding a trained operator.

Whether or not the device to be used is reliable is a question in each case for the police officer who is operating it. Provided the police officer reasonably believes that the device is not reliable or is not available, then he is entitled to require specimens of blood or urine in order to obtain the evidence upon which the prosecution is to be based. In *Haghigat-Khou* v. *Chambers* [1988] RTR 95 a specimen of blood was required in circumstances where the police sergeant operating the intoximeter believed it to be unreliable because the printer mechanism was not functioning properly. It was accepted, however, that oral evidence of the reading could have been given by the police sergeant who would have been able to read from the screen the evidence of the analysis of breath.

It was held that as the police officer had formed a reasonable belief that the device was unreliable, he was entitled to make the request of the defendant that he provide a specimen of blood, which could then be lawfully admitted in evidence in order to prove the case.

This decision was applied in *Stokes* v. *Sayers* [1988] RTR 89 where, before any request was made to the defendant, the police officer in the case noticed that the screen on the Lion Intoximeter 3000 was displaying the words '34 low abort'. He concluded that the device was not reliable and required the defendant to provide a specimen of blood. At the subsequent trial, the officer did not explain how the reading had been produced, or whether the defendant had ever been required to supply specimens of breath. The justices concluded that the prosecutor had failed to establish that the device had not been a reliable device and dismissed the information.

The appeal by the prosecutor was dismissed. The prosecutor had to establish by evidence in such cases first, that the police officer did believe that the device to be used was unreliable and second, that there was some material or evidence on which, at the time, he could reasonably have formed that view.

It is for the prosecution to prove that the device was properly calibrated and therefore reliable (*Mayon* v. *DPP* [1988] RTR 281). Failures of printer devices attached to the machine do not provide evidence of unreliability especially where the police officer administering the procedure is able to give oral evidence of the readings displayed on the VDU screen. Thus, in *Thom* v. *DPP* [1994] RTR 11 the fact that the printout paper became tangled in the machine was held not to be evidence of unreliability. Neither was it evidence of the machine not working properly or being unreliable where the first two characters on each line of the printout were missing (*DPP* v. *Barber* (1999) 163 JP 457).

The inaccuracy of the intoximeter clock or the failure to distinguish between GMT and BST are similarly not matters that will render the device unreliable. The question is not concerned with the accuracy or otherwise of the data supplied to the computer, but with any inaccuracy in the content of the information produced by the computer (*DPP* v. *McKeown*; *DPP* v. *Jones* [1997] 1 WLR 295).

In *Ashton* v. *DPP* [1998] RTR 45, which was followed in *Louis* v. *DPP* (1998) 162 JP 287, it was decided that a Lion Intoximeter 3000 was a 'reliable device', even though there was evidence to show that the machine had been designed to compensate for the presence of acetone in breath by giving a slightly lower reading. (It is now accepted scientifically that alcohol and acetone cannot co-exist in breath.) Despite the fact that the machine could not produce a wholly accurate analysis of the proportion of alcohol in breath, it was still held to be a reliable device.

More recent cases challenging the reliability of the device used in a police station have centred around the instruction given by the manufacturers of the Intoximeter EC/IR device that 'as a precaution, all radio sets and mobile telephones in the room where the evidential breath testing instrument is in use should be turned off'. In *Scheiner* v *DPP* [2006] All ER(D) 110 the appellant argued that as no evidence had been adduced by the prosecutor about how often mobile telephones would interfere with a breathalyser, there must clearly have been the possibility of such interference given the scope of the manufacturer's instructions and that it was for the prosecutor to show that it could never interfere with the result. In the instant case, all the prosecutor had done was to show that on this particular occasion there was no evidence of the results being inaccurate.

The Court of Appeal found no difficulty in rejecting this submission and sought to bring to an end unmeritorous appeals on similar grounds:

> This appeal should, in my view, mark the end of arguments before magistrates' courts and crown courts that, merely because a mobile telephone or police radio was – still less, may have been – present and switched on, so the result of the analysis of the samples of breath produced by the Intoximeter EC/IR device should not be admitted and/or should be found unreliable. Evidence is required at least to raise the realistic possibility that the device on the occasion with which the court is concerned may have malfunctioned and produced a false reading. Assertions based merely on an alleged failure to comply with the manufacturer's recommendations do not amount to such evidence. They do not amount to such evidence not least because there is no common understanding, of which a court could take notice, of the impact upon the operation of such a device of a radio wave transmitted by a mobile telephone or short wave police radio. For those reasons, in my view, this appeal discloses no ground of appeal.

79

(c) Device has not produced a reliable indication of the proportion of alcohol in breath

The Lion Intoxilyzer 6000 UK was granted Home Office approval on 22 February 1998 and came into use on 1 January 2000. The following devices received Home Office approval in July 2005:

- Camic Datamaster
- Intoximeter EC/IR
- Lion Intoxilyzer 6000 UK – software version 2.33 or 2.34.

These and similar devices are able to indicate that the breath specimen provided is unreliable because:

- of the presence of an interfering substance;
- of the presence of mouth alcohol – although such a message will only be displayed where the reading is greater than 30 µg of alcohol in 100 ml of breath;
- the reading is 'out of range' to the extent that the driver's breath–alcohol concentration is in excess of 220 µg per 100 ml of breath. (It was held in *DPP* v. *Brown*; *DPP* v. *Teixeira* (2002) 166 JP 1 that where there was evidence that a particular machine was unable to detect unacceptable specimens of mouth alcohol, such was not a ground to find that the original type approval authorisation by the Secretary of State was incorrect.);
- there are significant differences between the two breath samples to the extent that the difference between the two readings is greater than 15 per cent based on the lower figure, but only if the actual difference is greater than 5 µg of alcohol per 100 ml of breath.

The devices will indicate one of the above messages if either or both specimens of breath are found to be unsuitable for analysis.

In *Zafar* v. *DPP* [2005] RTR 18 the appellant contended that the prosecution was obliged to show that the reading from the intoximeter related solely to 'deep lung alcohol' and not in any respect to 'mouth alcohol'. The defendant gave evidence that he had only consumed one pint of lager and that he suffered from heartburn which caused an occasional reflux of the stomach contents to the mouth for which he took medicine. He said he remembered feeling discomfort just before he took the breath test at the police station. Expert evidence was given that the intoximeter was designed to detect alcohol in deep lung air as opposed to alcohol in the mouth or upper respiratory tract and that the particular machine used in this case was very poor at detecting mouth alcohol and providing a warning to the operator.

The Divisional Court adopted the definition of 'breath' in the New Shorter Oxford English Dictionary as 'air exhaled from anything' stating that neither the normal use of the word 'breath' nor the dictionary definition limit the meaning to 'deep lung breath'. There was nothing in RTA 1988 to suggest that the word should be given some special meaning or that the dictionary definition should not apply.

Zafar v. *DPP* was followed in *Woolfe* v. *DPP* [2006] All ER(D) 261. The justices found as a fact that the appellant suffered from a medical condition of regurgitation of stomach content into the oesophagus. However, they felt bound by the decision in *Zafar* v. *DPP* and convicted him of driving with excess alcohol.

The Court of Appeal said that, although at first sight *Zafar* may appear harsh, this had to be seen in context. Breath specimens do not provide a precise calculation of how much alcohol a person has consumed. Nor would several people, each having consumed the same amount of alcohol, all produce the same analytical result. There are numerous variables, including age, size, gender and metabolic rate. Parliament had nevertheless prescribed a universal pragmatic test, falling well short of a total prohibition on driving with alcohol in the body. It had done so in the knowledge that different people will be able to consume the same quantities of alcohol with different physical and legal effects. There could be no principled objection to that. Moreover, a defendant who produced a positive specimen as analysed by the intoximeter had chosen to drive after consuming alcohol and would already have provided a positive roadside specimen of breath. At least 20 minutes would have elapsed between the last consumption of alcohol and the provision of the roadside test. A prosecution would only follow if the intoximeter yields two readings above the 35 µg limit (in practice, above 39 µg for a decision to prosecute) and, where the readings do not exceed 50 µg, there is a statutory right to require an alternative specimen of blood or urine. For regurgitation or reflux to prejudice a defendant, it must have occurred twice (once before each specimen) and with substantially similar results. In addition, the present prescribed procedure required the suspect to be asked twice (once before and once after the evidential breath test procedure) whether he had brought up anything from his stomach. The scope for real injustice was extremely slight and, where it arose, there remained the further possibility of mitigating the penalty through a finding of special reasons.

The difference between the current generation of approved devices and their predecessor, the Lion Intoximeter 3000, was that the latter would complete a cycle even if there was what was now known as an interfering substance within the specimen taken, whereas the current generation were designed to cease the existing cycle without recalibrating when meeting such a substance. In *Mercer* v. *DPP* [2004] RTR 8 it was held that the test to be applied was whether there had been ascertainment by means of an approved device of the proportion of alcohol in a specimen which had been performed in conformity with the operating procedures of the device in question. In this case, the Divisional Court dismissed an appeal by a convicted driver in circumstances where the evidence before the court consisted of the first specimen taken during the first cycle and the first specimen taken during a second, subsequent cycle.

Even where an approved device gives an unreliable reading following the provision of breath specimens, there is no requirement on the officer to immediately require alternative specimens of blood or urine. In *Stewart* v. *DPP* (2004) 168 JP 82 the officer gave the appellant the choice of either providing two more breath specimens, or specimens of blood or urine. A further two breath specimens were provided and the appellant convicted on the evidence of the lower reading. The Divisional Court held that there was nothing in the statute which obliged the officer to require blood or urine nor was there an indication that the option of a further breath test might not be offered. On any sensible interpretation of s.11(3)(b) each of the first two specimens did not permit an analysis to be 'satisfactorily achieved' and once it was accepted that effectively no specimen of breath was provided, there was nothing to prevent the officer requiring further specimens of breath.

Similarly, in *Jubb* v. *DPP* (2003) 167 JP 50, the Divisional Court, in a case turning on other aspects of ss.7(1)(b) and 7(3)(bb), tacitly approved the practice of a police officer offering the option of further breath tests in a situation where the first set of specimens had been rejected by the approved device because an unreliable indication of breath-alcohol had been recorded.

Further, in *Edmond* v. *DPP* [2006] RTR 18, the Divisional Court said that where an officer sought a second set of breath specimens from the driver where the first set had been deemed to be unreliable, there was no need for the officer to give the driver the statutory warning as required by RTA 1988, s.7(7) provided it had been given at the time the first request for breath specimens had been made. The section obliged a police officer to give a warning on 'requiring' a person to provide a specimen and there was no requirement on the officer to repeat the warning where he made a second request for the same type of sample.

(d) Following a preliminary drug test the constable believes the person to have a drug in his body

Section 6C was inserted into RTA 1988 by the Railways and Transport Safety Act 2003 from 30 March 2004 and gives statutory form to the concept of the preliminary drug screening test. In time, it is intended that approval be given to a device capable of analysing samples of saliva or sweat for drug ingestion. However, as no such device has at the time of writing been approved, s.7(3)(bc) remains unused.

(e) Condition of driver might be due to some drug

See **para. 5.2**.

7.4   APPROVAL OF DEVICES

Section 7(3)(bb) was inserted into RTA 1988 by the Criminal Procedure and Investigations Act 1996, s.63 with effect from 1 April 1997. The intention of the amendment was to pave the way for installation in police stations of a new generation of evidential breath test devices capable of indicating to the operator that either or both specimens of breath are unsuitable for analysis because of:

- an interfering substance other than alcohol;
- the presence of mouth alcohol;
- a reading in excess of 220 µg per 100 ml of breath;
- a difference between the two readings of more than 15 per cent based on the lower figure.

Since 1997 a number of 'second generation' machines have been approved (see **para. 7.3(c)**).

The Lion Intoxilyzer 6000 UK machines consist of different specifications, the first two incorporating gas delivery systems A, B or C and software version 2.33, whilst the latter machine incorporates software version 2.34. It is submitted that the software forms part of the Approval Order and cannot be amended without recourse to a further order.

All 'first generation' machines in police stations – mainly the Lion Intoximeter 3000 and Camic Breath Analyser – were replaced by second generation machines by 31 December 1999, owing to the fear that the original equipment would not be Year 2K compliant.

In *Hayward* v. *Eames* [1985] RTR 12 it was stated that the purpose of an Approval Order was to afford an easy means of providing evidence to courts that a device had been approved by the Secretary of State. Section 11(2) expressly requires that the Secretary of State exercise a positive duty to approve a device and to do so by issuing an Approval Order. However, the section requires that the Secretary of State do no more than approve a type of device. Thus, where an Order was in error (by naming as the manufacturer of a device a company that did not exist), this did not invalidate the Order (*Chief Constable of Northumbria* v. *Browne* [1986] RTR 113).

At the same time as approval was being given to the new generation of machines a standard drink-driving pro forma was developed for use by police forces in England and Wales. The pro forma is a layman's guide to a practical and simplified understanding of the various procedures contained in RTA 1988 and provides guidance on exercising discretion where a choice exists for the police officer and on how a choice of different steps will lead on to different stages in the procedure. The proforma is divided into six parts:

- Part A – Drink/Drugs Station Procedure – general;
- Part B – Drink/Drugs Station Procedure – specimens/impairment;

- Part C – Drink/Drugs Hospital Procedure;
- Part D – Alcohol Technical Defence Form;
- Part E – Drug Sample Information Form;
- Part F – Preliminary Impairment Test

Parts A and B of the pro forma were considered and received judicial approval in *DPP* v. *Smith* [2000] RTR 341.

7.5 CHALLENGES TO APPROVED DEVICES

Challenges mounted in the courtroom to devices approved by the Secretary of State have tended to follow three distinct lines:

- challenges based on general unreliability where it is argued that the device should never have received approval;
- challenges to the reliability of individual devices on the evidence available in a particular case;
- challenges to the reliability of individual devices having regard to post-approval tests on reliability.

Challenges on general unreliability

Challenges of this nature have invariably foundered because of the reluctance of the courts to countenance 'fishing expeditions' in which attempts have been made to seek discovery of documents ancillary to the use of breath-analysis devices.

In *R* v. *Coventry Magistrates' Court, ex parte Perks* [1985] RTR 74 an application was made for the issue of a witness summons directed to a police officer and requiring him to produce the Lion Intoximeter 3000 logbook relating to the month during which the motorist's breath had been tested, the purpose being to ascertain whether the printout from the machine contained an error as to his date of birth.

In granting an order of certiorari to quash the witness summons, the Divisional Court held that the logbook would be of no probative value at the trial as its only potential use would be for cross-examination of the appropriate prosecution witness about the reliability of the machine on that particular date. In that the application had been in the nature of a fishing expedition, the application had been misconceived.

Similar attempts were made in *R* v. *Skegness Magistrates' Court, ex parte Cardy*; *R* v. *Manchester Crown Court, ex parte Williams* [1985] RTR 49. In these cases motorists applied for production of documents relating to the Lion Intoximeter 3000 and, again, the Divisional Court refused to allow the applications to stand. It was said, *per incuriam*, that a printout from an approved device was no more than evidence and on the principle *omnia prae-*

sumuntir rite esse acta there was a presumption that the device was in order when used. However, it was open to a motorist to rebut the presumption by calling evidence challenging the reliability of the device at the relevant time. Whilst a defendant may think it appropriate to challenge the reliability of the particular device used for analysing his breath specimens, he had no right of discovery of documents with a view to searching for material that might support a submission that the device was defective at the relevant time.

However, a different view was taken by the Divisional Court in *Young* v. *Flint* [1987] RTR 300 where evidence was called by the prosecutor in the form of an expert witness who gave evidence that there had been minor modifications made to the device before use in this particular case. The justices refused to allow the defence to cross-examine the witness about the modifications in order to ascertain whether the device still came within the scope of the Breath Analysis Devices (Approval) Order 1983.

In allowing the defendant's appeal, the Divisional Court held that there was an undeniable right to cross-examine a prosecution witness on any relevant admissible matter. As the prosecutor had called evidence to show that the device had been modified, the defendant had the right to discover whether the device now fell outside the scope of the Order. That right had been denied by the justices and the motorist's conviction would be quashed.

Advice as to the correct time to make an application for a witness summons in order to examine documents relating to the use of an approved device was given in *R* v. *Tower Bridge Magistrates' Court, ex parte DPP* [1989] RTR 118. Here, the defendant wished to show that, at the time he had provided breath, the machine was not operating properly and thus he required production of relevant documents. A written request was refused by the Crown Prosecution Service on the grounds that the device had shown itself to have been properly calibrated at the time of the test. A further application for a witness summons was then made at the outset of the trial and was granted.

In allowing the prosecutor's appeal and quashing the witness summons, the Divisional Court held that the application for the witness summons had been in the nature of a fishing expedition which, it was hoped, would lead to the disclosure of some information which would be of assistance to the defence. The application had been made at a time when there was nothing to show that the device had been malfunctioning and the Divisional Court was not prepared to countenance such applications. It was for the defence at the conclusion of the prosecution case to call evidence, which of itself tended to suggest that the evidence provided by the printout was unreliable because the machine was not working correctly. Whether or not the evidence proved to be worthy of credit was a matter to be discovered at the appropriate time during the course of the trial.

In *DPP* v. *Wood; DPP* v *McGillicuddy* (2006) 170 JP 177 the two defendant drivers had been charged with driving in excess of the prescribed limit. Breath specimens had been measured in each case by a device manufactured by a private company, Intoximeters (UK) Limited which supplied intoximeter devices to police forces.

The defence applied under the Criminal Procedure and Investigations Act 1996 (CPIA 1996), s.8 for disclosure of a range of material relating to device printouts, engineers' reports, service and calibration sheets and engineers' logs. Their case challenged technical aspects of the devices, contending that wrongful calibrations had taken place.

Disclosure of the materials sought was ordered on the grounds that the case could not be properly tried without the information. When disclosure did not take place, the defence successfully applied for a stay of the prosecution on the grounds that non-disclosure constituted an abuse of process.

The prosecutor successfully appealed. Section 8(3)(a) of CPIA 1996 required that the material of which disclosure was to be ordered had to be in the possession of the prosecutor and had to have come into his hands in connection with the case for the prosecution against the accused.

The material in question had never been in the possession of the prosecution. The only basis upon which it could have been said that the material in question satisfied the requirement that it had been in the possession of the prosecutor would have been if it could be said that Intoximeters (UK) Limited was a part of the prosecution. Such a contention was plainly impossible. The fact that, upon request, Intoximeters (UK) Limited had voluntarily provided certain material to the defence had not altered the relationship it had with the prosecution.

In addition, the material in the hands of Intoximeters (UK) Limited was not material which the prosecutor was entitled to inspect or copy under CPIA 1996, s.8(4). As such, there should have been no order for disclosure in the first place.

The court said that there should have been some consideration of the need by the prosecutor to obtain and use witness summonses under the Magistrates' Court Act 1980, s.97. The significance of the material withheld by the company should have been set against a proper appreciation of the defence, other evidence as to the reliability of the device and the legal position about arguments over type approval.

It is unlikely, however, that an application for a witness summons seeking production in evidence of documentation relating to type approval, the proper functioning of the approved device and calibration records/service sheets will be successful *unless* it can be shown that such evidence will be material to the issues to be contested by the defence. In *R (on the application of Cunliffe)* v. *West London Magistrates' Court* [2006] EWHC 2081 (Admin), the Divisional Court said that such applications were 'no more than fishing expeditions' and that unless there was a proper basis for admission of the material in evidence, then no witness summons should be granted under s.97.

It would seem, therefore, that the Divisional Court is only prepared to allow a challenge to a machine in this way where, at the time of the trial, there is some evidence that the device was either not working correctly at the material time, or there had been some change to the machine during the course of its operational lifetime that was known and that may have turned the device into one not sanctioned by the Approval Order.

Reliability of the evidence in individual cases – expert and non-expert witnesses

Section 15(2) of RTOA 1988 provides:

(2) Evidence of the proportion of alcohol or any drug in a specimen of breath, blood or urine provided by or taken from the accused shall, in all cases (including cases where the specimen was not provided or taken in connection with the alleged offence) be taken into account and, subject to subsection (3) below, it shall be assumed that the proportion of alcohol in the accused's breath, blood or urine at the time of the alleged offence was not less than in the specimen.

The assumption is not that the device is working correctly, but an assumption that the proportion of alcohol in the relevant specimen was not less than the proportion of alcohol at the time of the offence. In the case of a breath specimen there is a presumption that the machine is reliable, but if that presumption is challenged by relevant evidence, the court has to be satisfied that the machine has provided a reading upon which it can rely before making the assumption.

In *Slender* v. *Boothby* [1986] RTR 385 the defendant was arrested on 28 February; he provided the first sample of breath at 11.59 p.m. on that date and the second two minutes later. Unfortunately, the printout from the machine dated the second sample as having been provided on 1 March, even though the year was a leap year, which the machine had not been programmed to distinguish. The police sergeant dealing with the case took the view that the machine was not working properly and therefore requested the defendant to supply a specimen of blood for analysis. The defendant refused and was subsequently convicted of failing to provide the necessary specimen.

In dismissing the defendant's appeal, the Divisional Court made it clear that the word 'reliable' (in what is now RTA 1988, s.7(3)(b)) means reliable for the purposes of the Act of Parliament. At the relevant time, the machine was not capable of producing an accurate date on the printout and could not therefore be held to be an accurate device. The officer had been right to make a request for blood to be provided and the justices had been correct to convict.

Similarly, in *Parker* v. *DPP* (1993) 157 JP 218 where the printout showed the time in GMT when it was, in fact, BST, it was held that the justices were well aware of the Summer Time Act 1972 and were fully entitled to advance the time on the printout by one hour.

Slender v. *Boothby* was considered in *Fawcett* v. *Gasparics* [1986] RTR 375. In this case the error on the printout was that the material date, which was Sunday 14 October, was shown on the printout as Saturday 14 October. The constable operating the device gave evidence that it had correctly calibrated itself at the end of the sequence. However, the case was dismissed, the court determining that the device was not reliable in that the date had not been shown correctly.

The prosecutor's appeal was allowed. The device's failure to state the correct combination of the day and date might go to the weight or value to be placed on what appeared on the printout, but such an error could not undermine the admissibility in evidence of the printout purporting to be a statement relating to a specimen provided by the defendant in accordance with the Act. Provided the device functioned and produced what purported to be a statement and a certificate, it was to be admitted in evidence subject to any criticism it received about the weight to be attached to it as evidence.

The question of the information on the printout and its effect on the subsequent admissibility of it in evidence was considered in *Badkin* v. *Chief Constable of South Yorkshire* [1988] RTR 401. In this case the defendant was arrested and subsequently provided two samples of breath at a police station. The device failed to produce a printout and one of the constables operating the device concluded that it was not reliable and requested the defendant to provide a specimen of blood. At the hearing, the defendant was charged with driving whilst the proportion of alcohol in his breath was over the prescribed limit. The two police constables who had operated the machine gave oral evidence as to the readings they had seen.

In allowing the defendant's appeal against conviction, the Divisional Court held that, as the device was obviously unreliable, evidence based on the officer's view of what appeared on the screen during the test could not be relied upon. The officer was unable to say whether the machine was working correctly or not and there was no other evidence to confirm that the machine was reliable at the time.

It is not an easy thing to rebut the presumption that the specimen contains the same proportion of alcohol in breath as was the case at the time of the offence.

In *DPP* v. *Hill* [1991] RTR 351 the defendant provided a positive screening test at the roadside after an accident and was taken to a police station where it was noticed that his breath smelt strongly of intoxicants and that his eyes were glazed. He then provided a breath specimen that was above the prescribed limit. He gave evidence at his trial that he had consumed just one half-pint of lager and that the smell of alcohol arose because of his job as a barman. The justices believed him and dismissed the information.

The prosecutor's appeal was allowed. Whilst it was possible as a matter of law to rebut the presumption that the proportion of alcohol in the accused's breath at the time of the alleged offence was not less than in the specimen, it did not follow that that was a comparatively easy thing to do. In this case, the roadside test, the test at the police station and the evidence of the defendant's condition all pointed to the reliability of the device and thus to the guilt of the defendant.

It would seem that if a defendant is to be successful in mounting an attack against the calibrated evidence of the device used to obtain an analysis of his breath, then he must rely upon the type of error that occurred in *Mayon* v. *DPP* [1988] RTR 281. Here, the case stated by the justices failed to disclose that there had been a proper calibration by the machine. Accordingly, there was no evidence to corroborate the two readings that had been produced to show that the defendant had been driving whilst over the limit or evidence that the readings were accurate.

In *Leeson* v. *DPP* [2000] RTR 385 a driver provided a positive reading at a police station and was subsequently charged with driving whilst over the prescribed limit. At the magistrates' court the prosecution and defence both gave evidence, but the prosecution produced no evidence as to the calibration of the machine. The defence invited a dismissal of the case on the basis that the prosecution had not adduced any proof of the reliability of the intoximeter. The justices declined to dismiss the case and allowed the printout to be handed in, showing the machine was properly calibrated.

The Divisional Court said that the case against the defendant could not be proved without the printout showing the results of the self-calibration of the machine to establish its reliability. However, it would not be consonant with the proper and due administration of justice for the defendant to be acquitted where the prosecution's failure to adduce such evidence was simply an oversight. The justices had a discretion to admit the printout and it could not be said they had exercised it incorrectly.

A situation that arises regularly in court is where the defendant claims that he could not possibly have been over the limit, owing to the limited amount of drink that he had consumed prior to being stopped by the police. In *Hughes* v. *McConnell* [1986] 1 All ER 268, which was followed in *Price* v. *Nicholls* [1986] RTR 155 it was held that a device could not be shown to be unreliable by means of an inference drawn from facts such as evidence of limited drink taken, the apparent condition of a defendant as seen by others, or evidence falling short of expert testimony as to the amount of alcohol that would need to be drunk in a theoretical amount of time in order to produce such a reading.

The decisions in *Hughes* v. *McConnell* and *Price* v. *Nicholls* were expressly overruled by the decision in *Cracknell* v. *Willis* [1988] AC 450. The defendant was convicted of driving with excess alcohol in his breath and of failing to provide a specimen of breath. He had provided one reading of 78 µg at the police station, but thereafter had not blown into the machine properly so as to provide the second reading. His appeal to the House of Lords was on the ground, *inter alia*, that he should have been allowed to adduce evidence of the amount of alcohol he had consumed in order to show that the Lion Intoximeter 3000 was defective.

In overruling *Hughes* v. *McConnell* and *Price* v. *Nicholls* and allowing the defendant's appeal, the House of Lords concluded that the evidence of the breath specimen reading was not conclusive evidence of the quantity of alcohol in the appellant's breath at the time of driving. The wording of (what is now) RTOA 1988, s.15(2), and the presumption that the proportion of alcohol in the accused's breath, blood or urine at the time of the alleged offence was not less than in the specimen provided, were not such as to limit any challenge to the reliability of the device to any particular type of evidence. The appellant was entitled to challenge the breath specimen reading and to adduce evidence of the amount of alcohol he had consumed. Evidence was admissible which, if believed, provided material from which the inference could reasonably be drawn that the machine was unreliable. Lord Griffiths commented as follows:

> We all know that no machine is infallible, and if, despite this knowledge, Parliament had intended that breath-testing devices should be treated as virtually infallible I would have expected such an intention to be expressed in clear and direct language. I say virtually infallible because that is the effect of limiting a challenge to 'direct evidence of malfunction' which the motorist cannot, in practice, obtain from a blood or urine test which the police are entitled to refuse unless the reading is below 50 microgrammes. Nowhere in the legislation can I find any indication that Parliament intended such a result.
>
> Suppose that a teetotaller after dining with people of the highest repute, two Bishops if you will, forgets to turn on his lights and is stopped by the police. He is asked to provide a roadside breath test and indignantly, but inadvisedly refuses. He is arrested and taken to the police station. There he thinks better of his refusal. He agrees to supply two specimens of breath and the machine to his astonishment shows very high readings. He asks to be allowed to prove the machine wrong by supplying a blood or urine specimen. The police agree and he gives a blood specimen. An analysis shows no alcohol in the specimen. It is virtually certain that the police would accept the analysis and he would not be prosecuted. But if he were prosecuted it is virtually certain that the magistrates would prefer the analysis and he would be acquitted. But now suppose that the police refuse his request to supply a blood or urine specimen because the reading on the machine was over 50 microgrammes. Is he to be convicted without the opportunity of calling the two bishops as witnesses to the fact that he had drunk nothing that evening and inviting the magistrates to draw the inference that the machine must have been unreliable? If he can invite the magistrates to draw such an inference from the word of the analyst, why should he not invite them to draw the inference from the word of the bishops?

In assessing the type of challenge to be mounted in cases where there is evidence that the machine may have been defective or unreliable, the normal course would be by way of case stated, so that there is either a remittal to the justices in the case of a successful appeal by the prosecution or a dismissal of the case in the instance of a successful appeal by the defence. However, where there has been a gross irregularity in the proceedings stemming from an unjustifiable and indefensible conviction on no evidence, the supervisory role of the High Court can be invoked in order to quash the conviction (*R* v. *Kingston upon Thames Justices, ex parte Khanna* [1986] RTR 364).

The decision in *Cracknell* v. *Willis* was distinguished in *DPP* v. *Hill* [1991] RTR 351 where justices found in favour of a nightclub employee who argued that his breathalyser reading of 46 µg could not have been correct in that he was not allowed to drink on duty and, in any event, had drunk only a half-pint of lager. The Divisional Court remitted the case to justices with a direction to convict and pointed out that whilst the statutory presumption could be challenged, it was impossible on the facts of the case in point to come to the conclusion that the machine was unreliable.

However, the principles in *Cracknell* v. *Willis* were applied subsequently by the Divisional Court which gave valuable guidance on the approach to be adopted by a fact-finding tribunal to the evidence in a case where the reliability of the device is challenged and the evidence is not that of an expert witness. In *DPP* v. *Spurrier* [2000] RTR 60, the defendant was stopped by police at 11.45 a.m. There was no evidence of erratic driving on her part, she was not unsteady on her feet, her eyes were not glazed, but her breath did smell of intoxicants. She provided a positive roadside screening test and, at the police station, a specimen which, when analysed, was four times the prescribed limit.

The justices found she had consumed a quarter bottle of whisky and two cans of lager, but had ceased drinking at 11.30 p.m. the night previous to being stopped.

The court concluded that the intoximeter reading was unreliable because:

- the reading was incompatible with alcohol consumption the night before;
- there was an absence of any observable signs of intoxication; and
- her behaviour was rational and co-operative and she was of previous good character.

The court also concluded that there was no need for expert/technical evidence to rebut the statutory presumption.

The Divisional Court, in upholding the prosecutor's appeal, said that where lower consumption was alleged than that indicated by the intoximeter, it was not necessary for the defendant to adduce expert evidence of the reading that would have been produced had consumption been as alleged by the defendant. There was no justification in law for such an evidential regime. In some cases, expert evidence as to the effect of consumption, coupled with the absorption rate of a particular person, it being possible for such rates to vary enormously depending upon the size, make-up and physical processes of a particular person, may be essential to reach a proper conclusion on the facts.

It was a matter for the court to look critically at the facts in each case and to decide whether such evidence was necessary. Justices should bear in mind:

1. A discrepancy between claimed consumption and a reading could point to unreliability of the device, or the unreliability of the defendant's evidence as to how much he consumed. It is essential to consider the reliability of the defendant's evidence while having in mind the presumption of reliability of the device.
2. Where there is a minimal claimed consumption, a high reading and little other evidence, the discrepancy is solely derived from the defendant's claimed consumption; rebutting the presumption of reliability in such circumstances would be likely to be difficult.
3. Where there were no observable signs of alcohol save on the breath, justices should have in mind the fact that certain people can develop a high tolerance to alcohol and have high levels of alcohol without there being observable signs. Many cases depend on the facts and it might be necessary to adjourn a hearing to obtain expert evidence.
4. In cases where claims of lower consumption are raised, signs of surprise by the defendant at the reading, or the very fact of a positive test, are to be expected. The absence of surprise would be a factor for justices to consider in the light of the defendant's caution that he was not obliged to say anything, and it is for the justices to decide what weight to give that absence.
5. Where the prosecution is given no notice that the defendant intended to claim the device was defective, it is for the prosecution to consider whether to apply for an adjournment. Justices are likely to respond favourably to such an application. It would be within the justices' discretion to order the defendant to pay the cost of the adjournment.
6. As a general rule, there is no reason why a defendant should not be taken to be required to give notice in advance of trial that he intends to rely on the fact that the device was defective. Having regard to the presumption of reliability, the efficient administration of justice requires the prosecution to know that the defendant intends to rebut the presumption.

Challenging approval following post-approval testing

The third avenue of potential challenge to the reliability of a device encompasses the situation where a driver alleges that the device should never have received the approval of the Secretary of State or that approval in respect of the device should be withdrawn. In *DPP* v. *Brown*; *DPP* v. *Teixeira* (2002) 166 JP 1 the two appellants sought to challenge the reliability of the Intoximeter EC/IR device on the basis that post-approval and independent testing of the devices had shown the machine to be defective.

In *Brown*, the respondent was acquitted of driving whilst over the prescribed limit, the magistrates having heard technical evidence as to experiments carried out by experts that demonstrated that the device was unable to detect unacceptable specimens of mouth alcohol. They found that the device was defective in its material function and unreliable.

In *Teixeira* an acquittal followed after magistrates heard medical evidence and concluded that the device was not functioning to the same standard as the device approved by the Secretary of State and could not be relied upon to provide accurate evidence from witnesses as to the level of alcohol consumed by the respondent.

In allowing the prosecutor's appeals, the Divisional Court said that the assumption in RTOA 1988, s.15(2) is an assumption that the proportion of alcohol in the relevant specimen was not less than the proportion of alcohol at the time of the offence. When the reliability of a device used to analyse breath is challenged, justices are solely concerned with the reliability of the particular device used in the individual case; it is not part of their function to consider generally whether the device ought to have received the Secretary of State's approval. Courts should approach the issue of the reliability of breath-testing devices in the following way:

1. It is no function of the court to consider whether approval should have been given.
2. Justices were aware of the strength of the evidence provided by a printout of a specimen of breath. The assumption in RTOA 1988, s.15(2) was an assumption that the proportion of alcohol in the relevant specimen was not less than the proportion of alcohol at the time of the offence. In the case of a specimen of breath there was a presumption of law that the device was reliable. If that assumption were challenged by relevant evidence, the justices would have to be satisfied that the device had provided a reading on which they could rely before making the assumption.
3. Justices should look with a critical eye to see whether any tests conducted by expert witnesses correspond to the realities of the particular case.
4. Justices should examine carefully whether the presumption that the device was reliable was challenged by relevant evidence. For example, the challenge to the reliability of the particular device would not be relevant to a case where:

    (a) it was common ground that in one of the instant cases there would not have been mouth alcohol or alcohol vapour in the dead space of the upper respiratory tract;
    (b) the reliability of the particular device was challenged by expert evidence confined to the effect on the device of mouth alcohol or alcohol vapour;
    (c) the justices were satisfied that the device was otherwise reliable.

5. Justices should remember that expert evidence related only to part of the case and that, whilst it might be of assistance in reaching a decision, they must reach a decision having considered all the evidence. If, after considering all the evidence (the burden of proof being on the prosecution), the justices are sure the defendant is guilty, they must find the defendant guilty.

DPP v. *Brown* and *DPP* v. *Teixeira* were cited with approval by the Divisional Court in *DPP* v. *Memery* [2003] RTR 18. The court accepted that whilst the Intoximeter EC/IR manufactured by Alcotek Inc. sometimes could not accurately detect mouth alcohol, it was not open to the Crown Court to find that, in approving the device, the Secretary of State was acting unlawfully and/or *Wednesbury* unreasonable (*Associated Picture Houses Ltd* v. *Wednesbury Corporation* [1948] 1 KB 223). The reliability of a particular device was always open to challenge by admissible evidence and, in the event of such a challenge, the prosecution had to prove reliability. Moreover, looking at the scheme as a whole, including the procedural safeguards relating to the possibility of inaccurate reading because of mouth alcohol, the approval could not be described as irrational.

However, *DPP* v. *Memery* was specifically disapproved in the Scottish case *(Gary) Brown* v. *Procurator Fiscal, Falkirk* [2003] RTR 17. In this case the High Court of Justiciary in Scotland held that the Secretary of State had been satisfied that the examples of the Intoximeter EC/IR tested for the purposes of type approval, in accordance with the procedures set out in the type approval document, met the requirements in the document and thus were capable of measuring accurately the concentration of alcohol in end-expiratory air; that the evidence was that the Intoximeter EC/IR in question met those requirements for its function as an evidential breath testing instrument approved by the Secretary of State when it was installed and the fact that it might have been demonstrated that it reacted inconsistently to mouth alcohol when tested biologically did not deprive it of type approval nor did it demonstrate that when the defendant's breath was analysed by the device it did not function as a device in relation to which the statutory requirement could be made of the defendant under s.7(1)(a).

A similar approach was taken in *DPP* v. *Fearnley* (2005) 169 JP 450 in which the Divisional Court stated that there was a legal presumption that a breath analysis machine was reliable and approved. If this was to be challenged, it was for the defendant driver to adduce some evidence to call that into question. Such evidence was not adduced where the defendant sought to call evidence that related to other machines of a similar nature and approval – it was the machine used in the instant case that was important to determination of the case.

A similar result ensued in *Skinner* v. *DPP* [2005] RTR 17 where it was held that the Intoximeter EC/IR was, in all observable respects, compliant with its type approval and, when supplied, should have had the approved version of the operating software installed. There had been no evidence called of any changes that involved the software and, in the absence of any evidence to suggest otherwise, the court had been correct to assume that the machine was functioning correctly.

7.6 DRIVER'S OBLIGATION AND OPTION TO PROVIDE BLOOD OR URINE

The legal background

Section 7 of RTA 1988 provides:

(1) In the course of an investigation into whether a person has committed an offence under section 3A, 4 or 5 of this Act a constable may, subject to the following provisions of this section and section 9 of this Act, require him –

    (a) to provide two specimens of breath for analysis by means of a device of a type approved by the Secretary of State, or

    (b) to provide a specimen of blood or urine for a laboratory test.

(2) A requirement under this section to provide specimens of breath can only be made –

    (a) at a police station,

    (b) at a hospital, or

    (c) at or near a place where a relevant breath test has been administered to the person concerned or would have been so administered, but for his failure to co-operate with it.

(2A) For the purposes of this section, 'a relevant breath test' is a procedure involving the provision by the person concerned of a specimen of breath to be used for the purpose of obtaining an indication whether the proportion of alcohol in his breath or blood is likely to exceed the prescribed limit.

(2B) A requirement under this section to provide specimens of breath may not be made at or near a place mentioned in subsection (2)(c) above unless the constable making it –

    (a) is in uniform, or

    (b) has imposed a requirement on the person concerned to co-operate with a relevant breath test in circumstances in which section 6(5) of this Act applies.

(2C) Where a constable has imposed a requirement on the person concerned to co-operate with a relevant breath test at any place, he is entitled to remain at or near that place in order to impose on him there a requirement under this section.

(2D) If a requirement under section (1)(a) above has been made at a place other than at a police station, such a requirement may subsequently be made at a police station if (but only if) –

    (a) a device or a reliable device of the type mentioned in subs 1(a) above was not available at that place or it was for any other reason not practicable to use such a device there, or

    (b) the constable who made the previous requirement has reasonable cause to believe that the device used there has not produced a reliable indication of the proportion of alcohol in the breath of the person concerned.

(3) A requirement under this section to provide a specimen of blood or urine can only be made at a police station or at a hospital; and it cannot be made at a police station unless –

(a) the constable making the requirement has reasonable cause to believe that for medical reasons a specimen of breath cannot be provided or should not be required, or

(b) specimens of breath have not been provided elsewhere and at the time the requirement is made a device or a reliable device of the type mentioned in subsection (1)(a) above is not available at the police station or it is then for any other reason not practicable to use such a device there, or

(bb) a device of the type mentioned in subsection (1)(a) above has been used (at the police station or elsewhere) but the constable who required the specimens of breath has reasonable cause to believe that the device has not produced a reliable indication of the proportion of alcohol in the breath of the person concerned, or

(bc) as the result of the administration of a preliminary drug test, the constable making the requirement has reasonable cause to believe that the person required to provide a specimen of blood or urine has a drug in his body; or

(c) the suspected offence is one under section 3A or 4 of this Act and the constable making the requirement has been advised by a medical practitioner that the condition of the person required to provide the specimen might be due to some drug;

but may then be made notwithstanding that the person required to provide the specimen has already provided or been required to provide two specimens of breath.

(4) If the provision of a specimen other than a specimen of breath may be required in pursuance of this section the question whether it is to be a specimen of blood or a specimen of urine and, in the case of a specimen of blood, the question who is to be asked to take it shall be decided (subject to subsection (4A)) by the constable making the requirement.

(4A) Where a constable decides for the purposes of subsection (4) to require the provision of a specimen of blood, there shall be no requirement to provide such a specimen if –

(a) the medical practitioner who is asked to take the specimen is of the opinion that, for medical reasons, it cannot or should not be taken; or

(b) the registered health care professional who is asked to take it is of that opinion and there is no contrary opinion from a medical practitioner.

(5) A specimen of urine shall be provided within one hour of the requirement for its provision being made and after the provision of a previous specimen of urine.

(6) A person who, without reasonable excuse, fails to provide a specimen when required to do so in pursuance of this section is guilty of an offence.

(7) A constable must, on requiring any person to provide a specimen in pursuance of this section, warn him that a failure to provide it may render him liable to prosecution.

Section 8 of RTA 1988 provides:

(1) Subject to subsection (2) below, of any two specimens of breath provided by any person in pursuance of section 7 of this Act that with the lower proportion of alcohol in the breath shall be used and the other shall be disregarded.

(2) If the specimen with the lower proportion of alcohol contains no more than 50 microgrammes of alcohol in 100 millilitres of breath, the person who provided it may claim that it should be replaced by such specimen as may be required under section 7(4) of this Act and, if he then provides such a specimen, neither specimen of breath shall be used.

(2A) If the person who makes a claim under subsection (2) above was required to provide specimens of breath under section 7 of this Act at or near a place mentioned in subsection (2)(c) of that section, a constable may arrest him without warrant.

(3) The Secretary of State may by regulations substitute another proportion of alcohol in the breath for that specified in subsection (2) above.

Meaning of 'constable'

The requirement under RTA 1988, s.7 and the implied requirement in s.8 is that only a constable may request a motorist to provide a specimen of breath. It has been usual for police forces to designate and train selected officers to operate the breathalyser procedure in the police station and to use whichever of the approved devices is in operation in that particular police force area. However, the wording of the section is such that provided the person operating the device is a constable in the generally acknowledged sense of that word, then the statutory requirement is fulfilled. It would appear, therefore, that a Ministry of Defence police officer, a British Transport police officer and even a special police constable are covered by the legislation and, therefore, able to operate the device and carry out the necessary procedure.

Supplying specimens

Section 11(3)–(4) of RTA 1988 provides that:

(3) A person does not co-operate with a preliminary test or provide a specimen of breath for analysis unless his co-operation or the specimen –

    (a) is sufficient to enable the test or the analysis to be carried out, and

    (b) is provided in such a way as to enable the objective of the test or analysis to be satisfactorily achieved.

(4) A person provides a specimen of blood if and only if –

    (a) he consents to the taking of such a specimen from him; and

    (b) the specimen is taken from him by a medical practitioner, or, if it is taken in a police station, either by a medical practitioner or by a registered health care professional.

'Registered health care professional' is defined in RTA 1988, s.11(2) as meaning a person (other than a medical practitioner) who is a registered nurse or a registered member of a health care profession as is mentioned in Health Act 1999, s.60(2) other than the profession of practising medicine and the profession of nursing.

97

The necessity for ensuring that the correct procedures have been carried out was emphasised in *Murray* v. *DPP* [1993] RTR 209 where justices found as a fact that the necessary warning to a motorist that failure to provide the appropriate specimens would lead to prosecution had not been given, but nevertheless convicted him of driving with excess alcohol in his breath, on the basis that no prejudice had been caused to him. On appeal, Watkins LJ said that the effect of the decision in *Howard* v. *Hallett* [1984] RTR 353 was that the result of a breath, blood or urine test was only admissible under the relevant provisions of RTA 1988 if the procedural requirements of s.7 and s.8 had been fully complied with.

The essence of that conclusion led to the court's construction of RTOA 1988, s.15(2) that it should be read as if implicit in the provisions, after the words, 'specimen of breath, blood or urine provided by the accused' were the words 'pursuant to the provisions of the Act'.

It is, therefore, of the utmost importance that a police officer follows the correct procedures when seeking to obtain evidence that will lead to a prosecution. In *DPP* v. *Rous* [1992] RTR 246 the challenge to the procedure used came from an attempt to equate the use of the pro forma booklets as being the product of a formal interview for the purposes of Code C of the Codes of Practice made under PACE 1984 and therefore to attempt to exclude the evidence contained in the pro forma by virtue of the provisions of PACE 1984, s.78. It was held, however, that this was not a situation in which the justices could exercise their discretion under s.78 and the case was remitted to them with a direction that the evidence of the breath analysis be admitted.

Over and above the provisions in RTA 1988, s.7(3) which allow a police officer to decide that the evidence to be obtained will be that of an analysis of blood or urine rather than an analysis of breath, RTA 1988, s.8(2) states that a motorist who provides a specimen of breath, the lower proportion of which contains no more than 50 µg of alcohol in 100 ml of breath, may claim that it should be replaced by such specimen as may be required under s.7(4). Moreover, if such a specimen is provided, neither of the two specimens of breath that have previously been provided may be relied on in evidence.

The claim to have the specimens of breath replaced by those of blood or urine only becomes possible where the lower of the two readings contains no more than 50 µg of alcohol in 100 ml of breath.

In *Anderton* v. *Lythgoe* [1985] 1 WLR 222 a motorist supplied two specimens of breath, both containing 50 µg of alcohol in 100 ml of breath. He was not told of his right to have the specimens replaced and the prosecution sought to rely on the evidence of his breath analysis at his trial. The justices held that, although the statutory provisions did not require that he be told of the statutory option, natural justice did so require. Therefore they dismissed the allegation against him.

In dismissing the prosecutor's appeal, the Divisional Court stated that the statute contemplated two possible ways in which a defendant's guilt or innocence was to be established, namely by a breath specimen or, at the defendant's election, by a specimen of blood or urine. Both alternatives had to be made available to the defendant where appropriate. To obtain a breath specimen of no more than 50 µg and to rely on it alone as conclusive of the defendant's guilt was an inadequate performance of the statutory duty imposed by the section.

It is axiomatic that where the breath analysis is such that the defendant has the right to have it replaced, the defendant is fully informed of the extent of the option.

In *Johnson* v. *West Yorkshire Metropolitan Police* [1986] RTR 167 the defendant was entitled to have the specimens of breath replaced by blood or urine specimens. Following a policy decision of the West Yorkshire police, the police constable offered the defendant the option of providing blood, but did not refer to the possibility of replacing the specimen with urine.

The defendant would not supply blood, claiming an aversion to needles having fainted whilst having a blood test some years before. The police constable did not believe that this constituted a medical reason for the purposes of RTA 1988, did not seek the advice of a medical practitioner and charged the defendant with driving with excess alcohol in his breath. He was convicted by the justices of this offence, but successfully appealed to the Crown Court on the basis that the defendant's expression of repugnance for the needle could have constituted a medical reason, and it was for a medical practitioner, not the police constable, to judge the validity of that reason.

The prosecutor's appeal to the Divisional Court was dismissed. The defendant's aversion to a blood test was capable of being a medical reason. In addition, where a motorist was offered the option to exercise his right to have his breath specimens replaced, it was first for the motorist to choose whether to exercise the right, and second for the police officer to choose whether the motorist was to provide a specimen of blood or of urine. However, if the motorist raised an objection amounting to a medical reason for refusing to accede to the police constable's choice, the issue as to the validity of that reason fell to be determined by a medical practitioner and not by the police officer.

In this case the police constable's improper choice of a blood specimen denied the defendant the full benefit of the statutory option. The procedural requirements of the section had not been fully met and, as compliance with the section was a condition precedent to the admission of the evidence of the analysis of the breath specimens, the Crown Court had been correct to exclude the evidence of the breath analysis.

A police officer has a broad discretion under RTA 1988, s.7(4) to determine what sort of specimen should be required. It is only in very rare circumstances that the courts will seek to interfere with the exercise of the police officer's discretion, since there is nothing in the statute to require the officer to question the motorist as to whether he would prefer a specimen of blood or urine to be the one selected. However, in *Joseph* v. *DPP* [2004] RTR 341 it was held that where there was no reason for not choosing urine in preference to blood and a valid reason was put forward why urine should be the choice instead of blood, the officer must at least consider whether blood or urine should be the choice. If the officer then concluded that the required specimen should be the one to which the driver objected, without any basis for doing so, the decision was capable of being categorised as perverse or, alternatively, it could be said that the officer had misunderstood the legal position and, accordingly, the statutory procedure had not been validly gone through.

Once given the opportunity to exercise the option to have the breath specimen analysis replaced, the defendant must make the decision reasonably quickly in order to ensure that this advantage is not lost, especially where the time taken to make the decision is seen by the police officer as an attempt to dissemble and thus allow alcohol to dissipate from the body.

In *Smith* v. *DPP* (1990) 154 JP 205 the defendant was offered the opportunity to have his breath analysis replaced by an analysis of a specimen of blood. He refused, but one hour later and after consulting a solicitor, he changed his mind, agreed to supply blood and was allowed to do so. However, he was then charged with driving with excess alcohol in his breath and was convicted.

The Divisional Court held that the question of whether the defendant's rejection of the opportunity to claim replacement of the breath specimen had ended the statutory procedure was one for the justices to decide. Notwithstanding that the police officer had given the defendant a later opportunity to supply blood, the justices were entitled to decide that the statutory procedure had ended when the defendant firmly rejected the option in the first place.

Admitting evidence

Whilst the court must be vigilant to ensure that the correct procedures have been carried out, subsequent tainting of the alternative analysis does not necessarily render the evidence of the other part of it totally unreliable. There is still evidence upon which the court can proceed and, in any case, the prosecution are precluded from reverting to the evidence obtained as a result of the analysis of breath.

In *Yhnell* v. *DPP* [1989] Crim LR 384 the defendant had provided two specimens of breath, the lower of which had shown a reading of 42 µg. He had been offered the statutory option and had then supplied a sample of blood. This had been divided in the usual way and the part retained by the police had then been analysed to contain 97 mg of alcohol in 100 ml of blood. The defendant's part of the sample had been analysed and revealed 74 mg of alcohol. The justices found that the defendant had injected alcohol-free blood into this sample before analysis and convicted the defendant after allowing the prosecution the opportunity to tender evidence of the original breath analysis.

The defendant appealed, saying that the justices should not have admitted the breath-analysis evidence as such was precluded once the statutory option had been invoked. However, it was held that the justices had been correct to admit the evidence of the breath analysis, provided it was for the purpose of showing that there had been a reason for invoking the statutory option in the first place. In this case there had been evidence before the justices to show that the reason for the difference in analysis of the blood specimens had been due to contamination of the defendant's sample, and that they had not, therefore, relied on the breath-analysis evidence to convict the defendant. Had they done so the conviction could not have been upheld because they would have been relying on inadmissible evidence in that s.8 had been brought into play, and evidence of blood or urine analysis would have been necessary.

Replacement specimen – driver's preference

In *Surinder Singh Dhillon* v. *DPP* (1993) 157 JP 420 it was held that, where the statutory option existed, any response to the police officer's explanation of the option had to be unequivocal. Thus, where the defendant responded 'No, I can't stand the sight of blood', the court interpreted this as merely an indication that the defendant did not wish to supply blood and held that the police officer should have made further inquiry of the defendant in order to ascertain a clear answer to the statutory question.

A line of cases during the 1980s and early 1990s beginning with *Hobbs* v. *Clark* [1988] RTR 36 and extending through to *DPP* v. *Byrne* (1991) 155 JP 601 created a doctrine of 'driver preference' related to the extent to which a driver could express a preference as to whether he should be allowed to supply a specimen of blood or urine.

These decisions, and especially the decision in *Byrne*, were challenged in the House of Lords in *DPP* v. *Warren* [1993] AC 319 where the prosecutor argued that the interpretation given to s.8 in *Byrne* was an unwarranted judicial gloss on the statutory language. In giving the opinion of the House of Lords, Lord Bridge compared the wording of s.7(4) with that of s.8(2) and concluded that, whilst the two provisions could not be interpreted differently according to whether the option arose for consideration out of s.7(3) or s.8(2), it did not necessarily follow that the procedures that ensued had to be identical without regard to which provision gave rise to them. By reference to the language of the statute, there was no reason why, when a constable explained a motorist's right under s.8(2), he should not tell him that if he exercised the right to have a replacement specimen taken under s.7(4), it will be for the constable to decide whether that specimen is to be of blood or urine. If the police officer intends to require a specimen of blood to be taken by a medical practitioner, the driver should be told that his only right to

101

object to giving blood, and to give urine instead, will be for medical reasons, to be determined by the medical practitioner.

However, when the option arose under s.7(3) the constable need do no more than tell the motorist the reason under that provision why specimens of breath could not be taken or used; tell him that in these circumstances he is required to give a specimen of blood or urine, but that it is for the police officer to decide which, warn him that a failure to provide a specimen may render him liable to prosecution and then, if the police officer decides to require blood, ask the driver if there are any reasons why a specimen could not or should not be taken. The driver is thereby afforded an opportunity to raise any objection he may have to giving blood, either on medical grounds or for any other reason that may provide him with a reasonable excuse under RTA 1988, s.7(6).

Nothing in the language itself, in either s.7(3) or s.8(2), required any invitation to be extended to the defendant to express any preference for blood or urine.

In allowing the prosecutor's appeal against the decision of the Divisional Court to follow *DPP* v. *Byrne*, Lord Bridge concluded that much of the reasoning in the judgments following *Hobbs* v. *Clark* and in particular the summary of the law given in *Byrne* had to be considered unsound.

The decision in *DPP* v. *Warren* makes it clear that when making a decision under s.7(4) or s.8(2) as to whether the alternative specimen to be provided should be of blood or urine, the police officer does not have to invite the driver to express his own preference before making that decision. However, subsequent cases were decided on the basis that the words of Lord Bridge in *Warren* had created a regime that, if departed from, would render inadmissible any evidence of analysis of a specimen of blood or urine. In *Fraser* v. *DPP* [1997] RTR 373 a strong Divisional Court held that where the right of election arose under s.8(2) the statutory provisions required a motorist to be informed of a number of matters, but they did not require him to be informed of all of them at the outset. The provisions only required him to be told that if he exercised his right under s.8(2) it would be for the officer to decide, pursuant to s.7(4), whether the replacement specimen should be of blood or urine and, if the former, that his only right to object would be for medical reasons to be determined by a doctor. The officer was not required to tell the defendant at the outset in terms that a specimen of blood, if selected, would be taken by a doctor; accordingly there had been sufficient compliance with the statutory provisions and the defendant had been properly convicted.

Fraser v. *DPP* also reviewed a number of unreported decisions after *DPP* v. *Warren* and noted the five criteria that were relevant to the s.8(2) procedure:

(a)   the lower of the specimens of breath provided by the driver exceeds the statutory limit but does not exceed 50 µg of alcohol per 100 ml breath;

(b) in these circumstances the driver may claim to have the specimen replaced by one of blood or urine if he wishes;

(c) if he does so it will be for the constable to decide whether the replacement specimen is to be of blood or urine;

(d) if the constable requires a specimen of blood, it will be taken by a doctor unless the doctor considers that there are medical reasons for not taking blood, when urine may be given instead;

(e) if the constable intends to require a specimen of blood to be taken by a medical practitioner, the driver should be told that his only right to object to giving blood and to giving urine instead will be for medical reasons to be determined by the medical practitioner.

Having reviewed the numerous cases on the subject since the decision in *DPP v. Warren*, Rose LJ then set out the various principles to be distilled from those authorities:

1. The statutory requirements must be strictly complied with because an accused is being asked to provide evidence against himself (*Murray* v. *DPP* [1993] RTR 209).

2. The requirements enunciated by Lord Bridge in *Warren* concerning the procedure to be followed by police when offering a s.8(2) option are not the words of a statute to be analysed as such (*Hayes* v. *DPP* [1993] Crim LR 966). They are to be complied with to the extent that Lord Bridge's guidance represents 'a reproduction of the statutory requirements. To the extent that they exceed the strict requirement of the statute, they fall into the category of guidance only' (*DPP* v. *Ormsby* [1997] RTR 394 (Note)).

3. Although the statutory provisions, as interpreted in *Warren*, must be complied with:

   it is also important to have regard to the overall intention of Parliament when the statute was enacted. The relevant provisions were intended to enable a driver to provide a replacement specimen in a situation in which he faces conviction on the basis of a specimen already provided. The provisions were not intended to provide a series of hazards for police officers which if not skilfully negotiated with complete precision would enable drivers to escape conviction entirely (*DPP* v. *Charles* [1996] RTR 247 (Note)).

4. Failure precisely to follow the particularly long procedure does not necessarily mean that non-compliance with the statutory procedure renders inadmissible a specimen obtained in consequence of it (*DPP* v. *Ormsby* [1997] RTR 394 (Note)).

5. The fundamental question to be determined is whether failure to give the full formula deprived the driver of the opportunity to exercise the option or caused him to exercise it in a way that he would not have done had everything been said (*DPP* v. *Charles* [1996] RTR 247 (Note)). What is required is that 'the driver is fairly and effectively exposed to all of the

information and choices identified in Lord Bridge's speech' (*R* v. *Burton on Trent JJ, ex parte Woolley* [1995] RTR 139), 'so long as the option given by the statute is explained fairly and properly so that the driver can make an informed decision, the requirements of justice and the efficacy of the driver's option given by the statute under s.8(2) are ensured' (*Baldwin* v. *DPP* [1996] RTR 238).

6. In addition to the observation in *Ormsby* already referred to, the general tenor of the more recent decisions is best exemplified by Simon Brown LJ in *Baldwin*:

> I cannot accept that the decided authorities now so encrust and gloss the statute so as to require not merely adherence to the procedure laid down in Lord Bridge's speech in *Warren*, but the slavish adoption of a form of words which, in terms, involves stating to the defendant at the earlier stage that he has 'a right to object'.

7. To comply with the statutory requirements, a driver must be asked whether there are reasons why a specimen of blood should not be taken (*Ogburn* v. *DPP* [1994] 1 WLR 1107). A driver must consent to the taking of blood by a doctor and therefore, it seemed to the court, a driver must be specifically told that, if he consents, a doctor will take blood and he must then be asked whether there are reasons why blood should not be taken.

8. Failure to comply with the fifth criterion (as set out by the court in *Fraser*) is not in itself fatal to the admissibility of a previously obtained breath sample (*Robinson (Dena)* v. *DPP* [1997] RTR 403 (Note)).

9. It is not necessary for an officer to refer to medical reasons when inquiring whether there are reasons why a blood sample should not be taken by a doctor (*Baldwin* v. *DPP* [1996] RTR 238).

Medical reasons

Despite the above, problems continued to be caused where there was reference by police officers to 'any reasons' for not providing blood, qualified in some way by a further reference to these reasons being 'medical' ones. The differing and often conflicting lines of authority eventually returned to the House of Lords in *DPP* v. *Jackson; Stanley* v. *DPP* [1998] RTR 397.

The facts of *Jackson* are that police officers saw the defendant driving a motorcar in an erratic manner. They stopped him and one of the officers saw that his eyes were red and glazed and noticed that his speech was slurred. The officer arrested the defendant on suspicion of having driven whilst unfit to do so through drink or drugs and brought him to the police station, where the facts of his arrest were outlined to the police sergeant in the station. In the police station the defendant was examined by a doctor who then informed the sergeant that the defendant's symptoms could be consistent with him having taken drugs.

The officer then asked the defendant to provide a sample of blood or urine, warned him of the consequences of failure to provide and asked if he had any representations whether the sample should be blood or urine. The defendant said he would not give a sample and, upon being pressed as to whether there was any medical reason for not giving blood, the defendant replied, 'I don't like needles, but I'm not giving anything anyway.' He was charged and subsequently convicted of failing to provide a specimen.

The defendant appealed to the Divisional Court, submitting that the words 'I don't like needles' raised a potential medical reason for not providing blood, which should have been referred to a doctor. In addition he argued that the use of the phrase 'medical reasons' had limited the extent to which he could respond, in direct contravention of the formula approved by Lord Bridge in *DPP* v. *Warren*. The Divisional Court accepted this latter argument with reluctance, feeling itself bound by the authority in *DPP* v. *Warren*. It certified the following point of law for the House of Lords:

> To what extent if at all should the guidance given by the House in *DPP* v. *Warren* as to the procedure to be followed when a request is made for a sample of blood under the provisions of section 7(4) of the Road Traffic Act 1988 be applied beyond the issue arising in that case of whether the driver should be invited to express a preference for giving blood or urine? If that guidance does not apply other than in respect of that issue what, on the true construction of the Road Traffic Act 1988, is the procedure to be followed when a request is made under sections 7(3), 7(4) and 8(2) of that Act?

In *Stanley* v. *DPP* the defendant was stopped when driving and taken to a police station. His specimen of breath with the lower reading contained 47 µg of alcohol. The constable read from a pro forma telling him he could opt to replace the specimen with blood or urine, that the police would decide the type of specimen and that normally this would be of blood unless there were medical reasons, to be determined by a medical practitioner.

The defendant replied, 'No, I don't want no needle.' He was subsequently convicted on the basis of his earlier breath specimen and appealed to the Divisional Court. That court rejected his argument that his reply to the police officer indicated that there may have been a medical reason that required further examination by the police officer. Whilst accepting that the words could, in different circumstances, against a different background and depending on intonation, be construed as putting forward a medical reason, the Divisional Court was satisfied on the evidence that the words had not amounted to a medical reason in this case. However, the issue of the words used to limit the defendant's choice caused the Divisional Court to certify the following point for the House of Lords:

> When a motorist who is entitled to make a claim under section 8(2) of the Road Traffic Act 1988 declines to do so, is it incumbent on a police officer to ensure that

the motorist has understood his rights by asking whether there are any medical reasons for his refusal to supply an alternative specimen?

The House of Lords took the view that unmeritorious acquittals would take place if the *Warren* requirements were to be regarded as mandatory to the extent that any breach of them would result in the dismissal of the charge even if the breach had caused no unfairness or prejudice to the driver.

In giving the leading judgment in the case, Lord Hutton said:

> I am of the opinion that the guidance given in *Warren*'s case should be regarded as having the following effect. The requirements stated by Lord Bridge, with three exceptions, are not to be treated as mandatory but as indicating matters of which a driver should be aware so that, whether in a section 7(3) case or a section 8(2) case, he may know the role of a doctor in the taking of a specimen of blood and in determining any medical objections which he may raise to the giving of such a specimen. The requirements, constituting the three exceptions, which should be regarded as mandatory so that non-compliance should lead to an acquittal, are:
>
> (1) in a section 7(3) case the warning as to the risk of prosecution required by section 7(7);
> (2) in a section 7(3) case the statement of the reason under that subsection why breath specimens cannot be taken or used; and
> (3) in a section 8(2) case the statement that the specimen of breath which the driver has given containing the lower proportion of alcohol does not exceed 50 microgrammes of alcohol in 100 millilitres of breath.
>
> As well as complying with these three mandatory requirements police officers, in order to seek to ensure that the driver will be aware of the role of the doctor, should continue to use the formula in a section 7(3) case and the formula in a section 8(2) case set out by Lord Bridge [1993] AC 319, 327–328 or words to the same effect (subject to two points to which I refer later). But what is necessary is that the driver should be aware (whether or not he is told by the police officer) of the role of the doctor so that he does not suffer prejudice. Therefore, if the driver appreciates that a specimen of blood will be taken by a doctor and not by a police officer, the charge should be dismissed by the justices because the police officer failed to tell the driver that the specimen would be taken by a doctor.
>
> Accordingly, in relation to the *Warren* requirements there will be two issues for the justices to decide. The first issue is whether the matters set out in the *Warren* formula appropriate to a section 7(3) case or a section 8(2) case (with the respective changes to which I refer later) have been brought to the attention of the driver by the police officer. The second issue, if the answer to the first issue is 'No', is whether in relation to the non-mandatory requirements, the police officer's failure to give the full formula deprived the driver of the opportunity to exercise the option, or caused him to exercise it in a way which he should not have done had everything been said. If the answer to the second issue is 'Yes' then the driver should be acquitted, but if the answer is 'No' the failure by the police officer to use the full formula should not be a reason for an acquittal.
>
> As the second issue is directed to the question whether the driver has suffered prejudice, I consider that it would only be in exceptional cases that the justices would acquit on that ground without having heard evidence from the driver himself raising the issue that he had suffered prejudice. Both issues are issues of

fact, and therefore if the justices, having heard the evidence of the driver to raise the second issue, are left with a reasonable doubt as to whether or not he was prejudiced, they should acquit.

As I have indicated, there are two respects in which I would word the requirements stated by Lord Bridge in a different way.

(1) I consider that there is nothing in the wording of the relevant subsections and there are no considerations of fairness which require a police officer to ask the driver if there are any non-medical reasons why a specimen of blood cannot or should not be taken. If there is some non-medical reason which would support a reasonable excuse under section 7(6) this is a matter for the justices to decide. Therefore, I am of the opinion that in Lord Bridge's speech in relation to a section 7(3) case the words 'ask the driver if there are any reasons why a specimen cannot or should not be taken from him by a doctor' should read 'ask the driver if there are any medical reasons why a specimen cannot or should not be taken from him by a doctor'. Therefore, my opinion on this point accords with the sixth observation made by the Divisional Court in *Jackson*'s case:

> 'While it may well be prudent for the police officer to inquire whether there are reasons other than medical ones for a sample not being given, in order to avoid the (outside) possibility of prosecutions for refusal in which the court holds that a reasonable excuse was present under section 7(6), there is in our view nothing in the 1988 Act that justifies a requirement that the officer should make such enquiry, and every reason in common-sense to assume that if a driver has a reason for not giving a specimen that is sufficiently compelling to qualify under section 7(6) he will volunteer that reason of his own motion.'

(2) I also consider that in a section 8(2) case, in addition to telling the driver that a specimen of blood 'will be taken by a doctor unless the doctor considers that there are medical reasons for not taking blood', the police officer should ask the driver if there are any medical reasons why a specimen cannot or should not be taken from him by a doctor. I observe that the pro-forma instructions of some police forces do set out this question in a section 8(2) case.

The judgments of the Divisional Court in both *Jackson* and *Stanley* referred to the decisions in *Fraser* v. *DPP* [1997] RTR 373 and *DPP* v. *Donnelly* [1998] RTR 188. In those two cases the Divisional Court considered that the argument on behalf of the respective defendants that the full *Warren* formula had not been followed by the police was unmeritorious and held that the failure should not lead to an acquittal. The Divisional Court came to these decisions by ruling that the matters set out in the *Warren* formula relating to the role of the doctor need not be stated to the driver at the outset but can be stated at a later stage in the procedure. I consider, with respect, that this approach is erroneous and that the driver should be told of the role of the doctor at the outset before he has to make the decision to give blood. If the driver is not told at the outset of the role of the doctor it will be for the justices to decide whether that omission prejudiced the driver and deprived him of the opportunity to make an informed decision.

This decision cast much-needed light on a difficult area of law upon which courts have regularly been required to adjudicate. As a result of the decision, cases on points such as those raised under s.7(4) and s.8(2) are to be decided upon the facts of the individual case, rather on whether or not there has been strict compliance with the words used by Lord Bridge in *DPP* v. *Warren*.

CHECKLIST   **Driving whilst over the prescribed limit**

---

1. What is the proportion of alcohol on which the prosecutor intends to rely?
2. Is it above the prescribed limit for the type of specimen?
3. If the constable's requirement to the motorist was to supply blood or urine at a police station, which of the five pre-conditions to this request in RTA 1988, s.7(3) applied?
4. Was the device used at the police station, or elsewhere, an 'approved device'?
5. Is there any real information available to show that the device was not functioning correctly? Are there grounds for applying for a witness summons to obtain the evidence?
6. Are there any errors on the face of the printout that suggest the machine was not reliable at the relevant time?
7. Was the motorist entitled to have the analysis of the specimen of breath replaced by a specimen of blood or urine (because it was under 50 µg)?
8. Was this option put to him?
9. If an alternative specimen was supplied, is there a large discrepancy between the two readings? Can it be argued that the breathalyser was therefore unreliable?
10. Is there evidence of any kind that will suffice to mount a challenge to the reliability of the device?
11. Can expert evidence be called to challenge the reliability of the device?
12. Has the prosecution called evidence to prove the machine properly calibrated itself?
13. Was the defendant warned of the consequences of failing or refusing to supply the specimen?
14. Has there been some other omission in the procedure that will invalidate the evidence obtained?
15. Was a pro forma used to document the procedure? Should there be a request for disclosure of the document to check for omissions?
16. If blood or urine specimens were required, what was the reason given by the officer for this? Does the reason fall within the exceptions in RTA 1988, s.7(3)?
17. Was there a reason for requiring blood or urine? Did the officer reasonably believe there to be such a reason?
18. Has the officer properly exercised his discretion in light of all the information available to him at the time?
19. What led the officer to conclude that a reliable device was unavailable or not practicable for use?
20. Where the officer requires an alternative specimen from the motorist, was the option fully explained to him in terms of its extent and the discretion vested in the officer?
21. Was the opportunity given to the motorist to explain why a blood specimen should not be given?

22. If the lower of the two breath specimens produced a reading of no more than 50 µg, was the option of providing blood or urine given to the defendant?
23. Was the extent of the option fully explained to the defendant?
24. If a reason was put forward for not supplying a specimen of blood, did the police officer seek medical advice as to the nature of the reason?
25. Was the role of the doctor or health care professional properly explained to the defendant before a decision was made on blood or urine?

CHAPTER 8

Evidence of analysis

8.1 THE LEGISLATION

Section 16 of RTOA 1988 states:

(1) Evidence of the proportion of alcohol or a drug in a specimen of breath, blood or urine may, subject to subsections (3) and (4) below and to section 15(5) and (5A) of this Act, be given by the production of a document or documents purporting to be whichever of the following is appropriate, that is to say –

    (a) a statement automatically produced by the device by which the proportion of alcohol in a specimen of breath was measured and a certificate signed by a constable (which may but need not be contained in the same document as the statement) that the statement relates to a specimen provided by the accused at the date and time shown in the statement, and

    (b) a certificate signed by an authorised analyst as to the proportion of alcohol or any drug found in a specimen of blood or urine identified in the certificate.

(2) Subject to subsections (3) and (4) below, evidence that a specimen of blood was taken from the accused with his consent by a medical practitioner or a registered health care professional may be given by the production of a document purporting to certify that fact and to be signed by a medical practitioner or a registered health care professional.

(3) Subject to subsection (4) below –

    (a) a document purporting to be such a statement or such a certificate (or both such a statement and such a certificate) as is mentioned in subsection (1)(a) above is admissible in evidence on behalf of the prosecution in pursuance of this section only if a copy of it either has been handed to the accused when the document was produced or has been served on him not later than seven days before the hearing, and

    (b) any other document is so admissible only if a copy of it has been served on the accused not later than seven days before the hearing.

(4) A document purporting to be a certificate (or so much of a document as purports to be a certificate) is not so admissible if the accused, not later than three days before the hearing or within such further time as the court may in special circumstances allow, has served notice on the prosecutor requiring the

attendance at the hearing of the person by whom the document purports to be signed.

(5) [*Relates to Scotland.*]

(6) A copy of a certificate required by this section to be served on the accused or a notice required by this section to be served on the prosecutor may be served personally or by registered post or recorded delivery service.

(6A) Where the proceedings mentioned in section 15(1) of this Act are proceedings before a magistrates' court inquiring into an offence as examining justices, this section shall have effect with the omission of subsection (4).

(7) In this section 'authorised analyst' means –

   (a) any person possessing the qualifications prescribed by regulations made under section 27 of the Food Safety Act 1990 as qualifying persons for appointment as public analysts under those Acts, and

   (b) any other person authorised by the Secretary of State to make analyses for the purposes of this section.

By virtue of RTOA 1988, s.15(1) expressions used in s.16 of that Act have the same meaning as in RTA 1988, ss.3A–10.

8.2 STATUS OF THE STATEMENT

One of the first challenges to the use of an approved device to analyse a breath specimen was whether the test record printout was a statement of the measurement of alcohol within the meaning of RTOA 1988, s.16(1)(a).

In *Gaimster* v. *Marlow* [1984] QB 218 the defendant objected to the production in evidence of the test record printout on the basis that it was not a statement within the meaning of the section and was inadmissible as evidence of the proportion of alcohol in the defendant's breath. The justices acceded to this argument as they felt that mere production by an automatic device could not presuppose the existence of a valid statement. In their view, a statement had to be comprehensible and understandable to the ordinary man in the street and the document produced by the machine was palpably not so understandable. There was no clear indication that the figures on the test record referred to the proportion of alcohol in the accused's breath or that the machine had been working properly at the time.

In allowing the prosecutor's appeal, the Divisional Court was of the opinion that in deciding cases such as this it was necessary to have regard to 'reality' and 'to deal with the real, not some fanciful world'. The test record printout was clearly capable of fulfilling the requirements of the section and clearly provided a statement of the amount of alcohol in the defendant's breath. Even though it might not have been immediately clear to all who saw it that this was what it purported to do, further explanation was possible from the police officer in court who had been trained in the use of the device and who could explain the various parts of the statement where appropriate.

The statement is no more than a printout of the information that the operator observes on the screen during the course of the breathalyser procedure. Thus, there is nothing to prevent a police officer from obtaining a second set of printouts from the device in a situation where the first set has disappeared. In *DPP* v. *Hutchings* [1991] RTR 380 the prosecution sought to adduce a second set of printouts in just such circumstances, prompting the Divisional Court to reach the conclusion that the second set was not a copy of the first set, but was the result of a second operation of the device in relation to the same material and as much an original document as the first printout.

8.3 REQUIREMENT TO SERVE THE STATEMENT

The requirement on the prosecution to tender in evidence the original printout from the device does not apply where there has been a guilty plea, where it had become the practice of the court to require the original document to check the readings (*R* v. *Tower Bridge Magistrates' Court, ex parte DPP* [1988] RTR 118).

Without s.16, prosecutors would have to call to give evidence the police officer who conducted the procedure at the police station or the analyst who determined the amount of alcohol in the specimen of blood or urine provided by the defendant. Section 16 is therefore, in the main, an enabling one, allowing a more convenient method of presenting such evidence to the court.

In *Steward* v. *DPP* (2004) 168 JP 146 evidence was laid before justices by a police constable who had witnessed the procedure that a medical practitioner had taken a blood sample from the driver with consent. No certificate was produced from the surgeon in conformity with s.16(2). The evidence of an authorised analyst that the alcohol level in the blood had been in excess of the limit was given by way of a witness statement producing the analyst's certificate as to the proportion of alcohol in the specimen. The defendant unsuccessfully argued that, in the absence of oral evidence or a certificate from the police surgeon who had taken the blood sample, there could be no compliance with s.16(2).

The Divisional Court held that s.16(2) was permissive, enabling the prosecutor to present, with minimal cost and inconvenience, evidence that a blood sample had been taken with consent by a medical practitioner, but it was not the only evidence that was admissible as to such matters. It was plain from the case that the justices had been provided with evidence that the police surgeon was a medical practitioner and that he had taken the sample by consent. The justices were entitled to rely on other evidence to show that the sample had been taken by a medical practitioner.

There are, however, occasions where the evidence of the amount of alcohol in the defendant's breath, which would normally be shown on the printout produced is not available in that form because the machine has malfunctioned or because the printer has failed to produce the document. As the section confers a discretion to allow for evidence of the reading to be given in documentary form, the lack of such evidence is not fatal to the case because oral evidence can be called as an alternative. However, the oral evidence must cover not only the analysis of the specimen, but also evidence that the machine had properly self-calibrated and was functioning properly.

In *Owen* v. *Chesters* [1985] RTR 191 the defendant supplied two specimens of breath at a police station, both of which were over the prescribed limit. The results of the analysis were observed by the police officer conducting the procedure who was called to give evidence of them at the subsequent hearing. At this hearing no printout from the device was produced, and there was no evidence that a copy had been served on the defendant or handed to him at the time.

The information was dismissed by the justices, who found that the oral evidence of the police officer was inadmissible as the printout had not been served on the defendant as provided for by the section. In the Divisional Court, the prosecutor's appeal was dismissed, as it was the clear intention of the section that the defendant was to be provided in advance of the hearing with a copy of the information recorded on the automatically produced statement. It was vital in such prosecutions that the prosecutor established that the machine was properly calibrated if it was intended to rely on the analysis produced by the device.

The above decision was followed in *Morgan* v. *Lee* [1985] RTR 409 where the results of the breath analysis were observed by the operator, but no printout was produced because the paper became entangled in the printer. As a result the defendant was required to supply an alternative sample of blood, as the police officer deemed the device to be unreliable. The defendant refused to supply a specimen of blood and was charged with that offence. The case against him was dismissed by the justices on the basis that the police officer could have given evidence of the results of the breath analysis from the screen and could further have given evidence that the machine had been operating correctly at the time. The prosecutor's appeal was dismissed. The police officer had been in a position to inform the justices of the results of the analysis and the calibration from his observations and had therefore been in error in requesting the alternative specimen, the analysis of which was inadmissible in these proceedings. The defendant had consequently not been acting unreasonably when he had refused to supply a specimen of blood.

Owen v. *Chesters* was, however, distinguished in *Hasler* v. *DPP* [1989] RTR 148. The police officer in this case did not produce the printout in court, but the justices found that there had been evidence of calibration of the device as the officer had the printout with him, despite the fact that it was not produced. The defendant's appeal against conviction was allowed on the basis that by not producing the printout, the prosecutor had failed to establish a case for the defendant to answer. The justices were in error in implying the unseen contents of the printout as having been adduced in evidence.

Where an officer does give oral evidence of the intoximeter reading and of the fact that the device produced calibration results, it is sufficient merely to give evidence that the readings showed the machine to be working properly – not to establish the actual calibration results (*Greenaway* v. *DPP* (1994) 158 JP 27 and *Thom* v. *DPP* (1994) 158 JP 414).

The section also requires that a copy of the document is either handed to the accused when the document is produced or is served on him not later than seven days before the hearing. In *Williams* v. *DPP* [1991] 3 All ER 651, it was held that 'the hearing' is not the time when the defendant first appears at court to answer the charge, but is that occasion at which the document is to be adduced in evidence.

What constitutes handing the document to the defendant is a question of fact in most cases. In *Walton* v. *Rimmer* [1986] RTR 31 the defendant was arrested after a positive screening breath test. At the police station he supplied two specimens of breath that were over the prescribed limit. Thereafter, the machine produced three statements, which were explained to the defendant by the police officer who was conducting the procedure. The documents were then placed on the police station counter for the defendant to sign. He signed two of them, but before signing the third he asked the police officer what he was signing. The police officer removed the two signed copies and left the third on the counter in front of the defendant without explaining that the copy was for the defendant in order to comply with RTOA 1988, s.16(3)(a). The justices found that the document had not been handed to the defendant by the officer leaving it on the counter and dismissed the charge against the defendant of driving whilst over the limit.

The Divisional Court, in dismissing the prosecutor's appeal, held that although RTOA 1988 could not be construed so that a defendant could render evidence inadmissible by refusing to take a document of the correct nature handed to him, it did not follow that if a defendant signed a document, it had been handed to him previously. The Divisional Court accepted that where a defendant was at a police station for the purpose of ascertaining whether he was over the prescribed limit to drive, he might well be in a state of intoxication, making it necessary that he should fully understand what was going on or, at least, it should be fully understood by a reasonable person. In this case the facts showed that the document had not been handed to the defendant at the time of production and, therefore, the justices had reached the correct conclusion.

In *McCormack* v. *DPP* [2002] RTR 355 the defendant provided two specimens of breath that were in excess of the prescribed limit. He then signed the three copies of the printout produced by the machine, but refused to accept the copy offered to him by the police officer conducting the procedure. The justices found that, notwithstanding that refusal, the printout had been 'handed to the accused when the document was produced' and convicted the defendant.

His appeal against conviction was dismissed. The requirement in RTOA 1988, s.16(3)(a) had been complied with, even though there had been no physical transfer of possession of the document to him. Accordingly, the printout had been properly admitted as evidence of the defendant's breath–alcohol level.

The requirement to serve a copy of the statement and the certificate on the defendant is a mandatory one. Thus, even where the defendant or his legal representative purports to waive service of the document, such cannot render the document admissible unless the section has been fully complied with (*Tobi* v. *Nicholas* (1987) 86 Cr App R 323). In this case the defendant had provided a specimen of blood, which had subsequently been analysed by a forensic scientist as being over the prescribed limit.

At the hearing, certificates of the doctor who took the specimen and of the analyst were served on the defendant whose counsel was constrained to waive objection to lack of timeous service. The defendant was convicted and appealed. The Divisional Court, in allowing his appeal, held that a purported waiver by counsel of objection to non-timeous service could not render the certificate admissible. The section provided for service to be effected not less than seven days before the hearing. In that the section had not been complied with, the evidence contained in the document was inadmissible. The Divisional Court did, however, leave open the question as to whether the evidence in the certificate could have been formally admitted by the defendant under the Criminal Justice Act 1967, s.10.

However, the situation is different where the certificate has been served in due time and the defendant waives the requirement for such service to be formally proved. Waiver in these circumstances produces an evidential result equivalent to the making of a formal admission of service so that a defendant cannot then argue that a certificate is inadmissible for want of service (*Louis* v. *DPP* (1998) 162 JP 287).

Even where the statement had not been served within the statutory timescale, a refusal by Justices to grant an adjournment in circumstances where neither the doctor's evidence nor the contents of the certificate were in dispute was held to be irrational by the Divisional Court (*DPP* v. *Stephens* [2006] EWHC 1860 (Admin)).

It should be noted that the requirements of RTOA 1988, s.16 do not make it necessary that the certificate is served on the defendant himself. It was held in *Penman* v. *Parker* [1986] 1 WLR 882 that service on an authorised agent in appropriate circumstances might be valid service, although much would depend on the extent of the authority given to the agent to accept service of such documents.

Thus, the wording of s.16(6) contemplates that the certificate required to be served on the defendant may be served personally or sent by registered post or recorded delivery post. In *Anderton* v. *Kinnard* [1986] RTR 11 it was held that the requirement to serve a copy of a certificate on the defendant was satisfied by serving an authorised agent of the defendant who had authority to receive and deal with documents. Furthermore, it was wholly untenable to suggest that the defendant's solicitors had no authority to receive and deal with such documents.

The section merely requires that the certificate, if not served personally, be sent by recorded delivery or registered post. There is no requirement that there be an actual delivery of the document. In *Hawkins* v. *DPP* [1988] RTR 380 the certificate of the doctor taking the sample and the analyst was served by recorded delivery post more than seven days before the hearing. This fact was proved at the hearing by a certificate endorsed in accordance with the provisions of the Magistrates' Courts Rules 1981, r.67(2). The defendant tried to prove the contrary in that he had not received the documents, but was convicted. His conviction was upheld by the Divisional Court which found that the approach taken by the justices had been 'unimpeachable'.

8.4 ERRORS ON THE FACE OF THE STATEMENT

On occasion, operator error or other unavoidable error will appear on the statement produced by the breathalyser device. The effect of such errors on the perceived reliability of the machine has already been discussed in **Chapter 7**. However, challenges have also been mounted on the back of such errors to the admissibility of the statement itself in evidence based on there having been handwritten alterations to the printout so that it can no longer be said to be a true copy, or because it has been produced by a device that is obviously unreliable.

In *Beck* v. *Scammell* [1986] RTR 162 the defendant supplied two specimens of breath that were analysed as being over the prescribed limit, and the machine produced the requisite printouts. The police officer in the case then manually altered the time shown on the printout to read one hour later than printed. The defendant was given a copy of the altered printout and left the police station. The officer then wrote on the bottom of the retained copy, 'British Summer Time not GMT'.

At his trial, the defendant objected to the admissibility of the document on the grounds that neither printout was a true document because of the handwritten amendment. He had thus not received a true copy. The justices dismissed the information on that basis and the prosecutor appealed. In allowing his appeal, it was held that albeit the officer had acted unwisely in manually altering the document, he had done no more than to indicate the substitution of BST for GMT. Therefore, the printout had not been materially altered and it remained, for the purposes of the section, a statement produced by the machine and a copy of the original document.

This approach was slightly modified in *Fawcett* v. *Gasparics* [1987] Crim LR 53 in which the printout produced by the machine was correct as to the date, but in error as to the day of the week. The Divisional Court held that in such circumstances the failure to state correctly the correct combination of day and date might go to the weight or value to be placed on what appeared on the printout, but that such an error could not undermine the admissibility in evidence of a printout purporting to be a statement relating to a specimen provided by the defendant in accordance with the section.

In an important aside, the Divisional Court also considered the effect of RTA 1988, s.7 (as to reliability of the device) on RTOA 1988, s.16. Whilst it was possible to look at s.16 for the purposes of deciding the reliability of the device under s.7, the converse did not apply. Whilst lack of reliability in the device could in some circumstances entitle a court to reject the printout evidence, it would not in all cases render it inadmissible.

The issue of whether or not the failure of the machine to recognise British Summer Time and the consequent admissibility of a printout showing a time at least 60 minutes different from the actual time of the procedure in the police station was considered by the House of Lords in *DPP* v. *McKeown*; *DPP* v. *Jones* [1997] 1 WLR 295. Although the main argument in the case turned around the effect of PACE 1984, s.69 (since repealed) and the requirement that a computer-produced document could only be admissible if accompanied by a statement showing that the computer was operating properly at all material times, the court did admit the evidence of the sergeant administering the procedure as to what he saw on the screen of the device as to the test results and the calibration. The reading from the clock incorporated in the device had no bearing whatsoever on the accuracy of the breath readings.

Whilst not in itself a case involving an error on the face of the printout, *R* v. *Brentford Magistrates' Court, ex parte Clarke* [1987] RTR 205 deserves mention. Here, the two specimens of breath provided by the defendant were both analysed as containing not less than 75 µg of alcohol in 100 ml of breath. The defendant submitted that the printout could not be adduced in evidence as it did not give details of the lower reading that the prosecutor had to rely on in the proceedings. This argument was rejected by both the justices and the Divisional Court which held that, since the purpose of the section was to give the motorist the benefit of the lower of the two readings, entitling the prosecutor to rely on only the reading more favourable to the motorist, the purpose of the section and the statute itself would be defeated by the defendant's construction.

8.5 REQUIREMENT TO SIGN THE STATEMENT

Section 16 of RTOA 1988 also requires that the certificate linking the automatically produced statement to the specimen provided by the accused be signed by a constable. However, there is no requirement that the copy to be handed to the defendant should be similarly signed. In *Chief Constable of Surrey* v. *Wickens* (1985) 149 JP 333 the police officer signed one of the three identical documents produced and the defendant signed the other two. The defendant was then handed one of the copies he had signed, but which had not been signed by the officer. It was held that the unsigned copy of the document was a copy in the true sense of the word, and that it was covered by the meaning of the word 'copy' as envisaged by the legislation.

In *Garner* v. *DPP* [1990] RTR 208 the defendant was arrested. At the police station he provided two specimens of breath above the prescribed limit. A printout was produced containing the relevant readings of his name, the date and the police station where that analysis was carried out and confirmation that the calibration test was carried out both before the test began and at the end of the final test. The printout was not signed by the police sergeant conducting the test on the copy given to the defendant or on the copy retained by the police, although the defendant signed both copies. At the hearing the unsigned printout was produced in evidence. The defendant submitted that the prosecution had to fail because the printout was inadmissible for lack of compliance with the section in that it contained no certificate signed by the sergeant relating to a specimen provided by the defendant.

In dismissing the defendant's appeal against conviction, the Divisional Court held that, as the sergeant's evidence linked the defendant to the printout, it was admissible as real evidence at common law independently of the provisions of the section requiring that it be signed. The purpose and effect of the section are to permit a printout from an approved device, together with the appropriate certificate, to be tendered at the hearing of an offence and to be capable of establishing the facts stated in it without the necessity of calling evidence to prove the document.

8.6   AUTHORISED ANALYST

Section 16 of RTOA 1988 requires that certificates of analyses of blood or urine specimens be made by an 'authorised analyst', which is defined in the Act as someone possessing the qualification prescribed for appointment under the Food Safety Act 1990 for appointment as a public analyst. In addition, the Home Secretary can authorise any other person to undertake analyses of blood or urine for the purposes of the RTOA 1988. Such authority has been given to named individuals employed in Home Office forensic laboratories. The analysis can be carried out by anyone provided that the certificate is given by the authorised analyst – although some element of control and supervision must be read into this.

If the certificate purports to be signed by someone other than an authorised analyst, it will not be admissible. Unlike the evidence of a breath analysis, the oral evidence of someone not authorised to analyse a blood or urine specimen would not be admissible as an alternative to a certificate.

Where specimens are analysed by different forensic scientists (in this case by a forensic scientist and by his assistant) it is not possible for one of them to give evidence as to the analysis of all the specimens and both would have to be called to give evidence. There is a need for the prosecutor to show 'continuity' to the extent that there should be evidence regarding the taking of the sample, its labelling and despatch to the laboratory for analysis, the analysis and its result and evidence that the sample despatched was the same as the one analysed and upon which a certificate was based (*Khatibi* v. *DPP* (2004) 168 JP 361).

CHECKLIST   Evidence of analysis

---

1. If the printout is not capable of being readily understood, what oral evidence should be called to support it?
2. Was a copy of the printout handed to the accused when produced or served on him not less than seven days before the trial hearing?
3. How was it handed to him, taking into account his demeanour at the time?
4. Have copies of the relevant statements and analyst's certificates been served on the defendant within the relevant timescale?
5. Is an adjournment necessary to allow for timeous service?
6. Can the police officer give oral evidence of the results of the breath test? If so, was there a need to request alternative specimens?
7. In what manner were the documents served on the defendant – personally, by registered or recorded post or some other method not authorised by statute?
8. Was at least one of the documents properly signed – and was a copy served on the defendant?
9. Was the certificate signed by an 'authorised analyst'?
10. Is there continuity of evidence sufficient to satisfy the court that all procedures and processes have been properly carried out?

CHAPTER 9

Using specimen evidence, post-accident consumption and back-calculation

9.1 THE LEGISLATION

Section 15 of RTOA 1988 provides:

(1) This section and section 16 of this Act apply in respect of proceedings for an offence under sections 3A, 4 or 5 of the Road Traffic Act 1988 (driving offences connected with drink or drugs); and expressions used in this section and section 16 of this Act have the same meaning as in sections 3A to 10 of that Act.

(2) Evidence of the proportion of alcohol or any drug in a specimen of breath, blood or urine provided by or taken from the accused shall, in all cases (including cases where the specimen was not provided or taken in connection with the alleged offence), be taken into account and, subject to subsection (3) below, it shall be assumed that the proportion of alcohol in the accused's breath, blood or urine at the time of the alleged offence was not less than in the specimen.

(3) That assumption shall not be made if the accused proves –

    (a) that he consumed alcohol before he provided the specimen or had it taken from him and –

        (i) in relation to an offence under section 3A, after the time of the alleged offence, and

        (ii) otherwise, after he had ceased to drive, attempt to drive or be in charge of a vehicle on a road or other public place, and

    (b) that had he not done so the proportion of alcohol in his breath, blood or urine would not have exceeded the prescribed limit and, if it is alleged that he was unfit to drive through drink, would not have been such as to impair his ability to drive properly.

(4) A specimen of blood shall be disregarded unless

    (a) it was taken from the accused with his consent and either –

        (i) in a police station by a medical practitioner or a registered health care professional; or

        (ii) elsewhere by a medical practitioner;

    or

    (b) it was taken from the accused by a medical practitioner under section 7A of the Road Traffic Act 1988 and the accused subsequently gave his permission for a laboratory test of the specimen.

(5) Where, at the time a specimen of blood or urine was provided by the accused, he asked to be provided with such a specimen, evidence of the proportion of alcohol or any drug found in the specimen is not admissible on behalf of the prosecution unless –

    (a) the specimen in which the alcohol or drug was found is one of two parts into which the specimen provided by the accused was divided at the time it was provided, and

    (b) the other part was supplied to the accused.

(5A) Where a specimen of blood was taken from the accused under section 7A of the Road Traffic Act 1988, evidence of the proportion of alcohol or any drug found in the specimen is not admissible on behalf of the prosecution unless –

    (a) the specimen in which the alcohol or drug was found is one of two parts into which the specimen taken from the accused was divided at the time it was taken; and

    (b) any request to be supplied with the other part which was made by the accused at the time when he gave his permission for a laboratory test of the specimen was complied with.

9.2 EUROPEAN CONVENTION ISSUES

The principle in Article 6(2) of the Convention for the Protection of Human Rights and Fundamental Freedoms 1950 (the European Convention) that everyone charged with a criminal offence shall be presumed innocent until proved guilty according to law was incorporated into UK legislation by the Human Rights Act 1998 (HRA 1998).

In *Beauchamp-Thompson* v. *DPP* [1989] RTR 54, a case on special reasons, the defendant sought to prove that, although he was above the prescribed limit at the time he provided the blood specimen, he had been below that level at the time of driving. However, the Divisional Court upheld the decision of the justices hearing the matter at first instance that s.15(2) created an irrebuttable presumption as to the amount of alcohol at the time of driving.

The decision in *Beauchamp-Thompson* v. *DPP* was applied in *Millard* v. *DPP* (1990) 154 JP 626 where the defendant had eaten sandwiches and consumed a bottle of wine at lunchtime between 1.15 p.m. and 3.45 p.m. On leaving his office at 5.30 p.m. he drove his car to a public house where he consumed nearly all of a large whisky soon after 5.45 p.m. At 6.10 p.m. he returned to his car and drove to another parking place and then returned to the public house where he drank most of a pint of beer. He was then spoken to by a police officer, supplied a screening test and was taken to a police station. At 7.15 p.m. he provided specimens of breath with a lower reading of

56 μg. An hour later he supplied a specimen of blood, which on analysis contained 97 mg of alcohol.

It was submitted on his behalf that expert evidence could be called by him for the purpose of calculating retrospectively the effect of the whisky drunk prior to driving as well as the beer drunk after driving. The Divisional Court held that the assumption in s.15(2) was irrebuttable subject to the exception in s.15(3). The defendant was not entitled to give evidence of his consumption of alcohol prior to driving nor evidence of a medical or scientific nature to explain the effect of that alcohol in his breath, blood or urine at the time of driving for the purpose of seeking to establish that at the time of driving the level of alcohol was below the prescribed limit. This was the case notwithstanding that at the time the specimen was provided, the proportion of alcohol in the specimen exceeded the prescribed limit.

The statutory assumption that the evidence of the specimen analysis is evidence of the amount of alcohol in the offender's breath, blood or urine at the time of driving has been the subject of a number of challenges using compatibility with HRA 1998 as the basis of the appeal.

In *Parker* v. *DPP* [2001] RTR 16, the appellant was arrested following a positive roadside breath test. Subsequent analysis of a blood sample provided at the police station showed him to be 1 mg over the legal limit. At trial he submitted that the irrebuttable assumption as to the result of the analysis of the blood specimen was incompatible with the HRA 1998, s.3 and that medical evidence should have been admitted to the effect that the appellant's blood–alcohol level at the time of driving the vehicle more than one hour before the specimen was provided was unlikely to have exceeded the statutory limit.

The Divisional Court dismissed the appeal against conviction. It was clear that the statutory language in s.15 provided for an assumption to be made. Although the presumption of innocence in Art.6(2) was a fundamental principle of the rule of law, presumptions of fact or of law did not, in principle, infringe that presumption provided that they remained within reasonable limits, depending on the importance of what was at stake (*Salabiaku* v. *France* (1988) 3 EHRR CD 379).

Since the offence of driving with excess alcohol was directed at preventing consumption of excess alcohol before driving, it did not rebut the presumption of innocence when assuming that the quantity of alcohol revealed in the specimen was the quantity the motorist had in his blood at the time of driving or being in charge of a vehicle.

Alternatively, paying due regard to the societal interest at stake, the assumption in s.15 was a reasonable one and well within normal limits. Section 15(2) could be read in accordance with its natural meaning compatibly with the rights protected by Art.6 of the European Convention.

In passing, the court also said that there may be circumstances in which the test at the police station shows a very high proportion of alcohol in the sample provided where a motorist might wish to mitigate the sentence by some form of explanation. The assumption so far as the offence was concerned would still have to be that the amount of alcohol was as shown by the sample taken at the police station, but the circumstances, if established, might provide grounds of mitigation in relation to the penalty.

Compatibility with s.15 and the European Convention was also considered in *R* v. *Drummond* [2002] Crim LR 666. In this case the appellant appealed to the Court of Appeal against his conviction for causing death by careless driving whilst over the prescribed limit. Whilst driving under the influence of alcohol, the appellant had struck a motor scooter, injuring the driver and killing the passenger. The appellant went home and telephoned the police to say he thought he had fallen asleep whilst at the wheel of his car and hit something. When he was arrested 40 minutes later, he told the police he had consumed two quarter bottles of wine before the accident and two glasses of gin at home after the accident. One hour and 20 minutes after the call to the police, he provided a breath specimen at the police station which revealed 76 µg of alcohol in 100 ml of breath. At trial the Crown called expert evidence to show that the reading could not have been caused by the amount of alcohol that had been consumed prior to and after the accident.

At the conclusion of the Crown case, the appellant argued that s.15 of the Act should be read so as to impose an evidential and not a legal burden on him. As such, the legal burden would remain with the Crown to prove that the appellant had excess alcohol in his breath at the time of driving. The appellant was convicted in the Crown Court, the trial judge ruling that s.15 imposed a reverse burden of proof that was justifiable in the context of the offence and not contrary to the presumption of innocence in Art.6(2).

The Court of Appeal dismissed the subsequent appeal. There was nothing in European Convention law that meant that all apparently legal burdens of proof on a defendant had to be read down to be merely evidential burdens. It was necessary to look at the legislation as a whole to determine whether Parliament had intended to impose a legal as opposed to an evidential burden and, if such was the case, whether such a legal burden was justifiable in the context of the particular offence under consideration. In this case the offence of driving with excess alcohol did not require the court to investigate the appellant's intention at the time of the offence. It merely required a strict scientific analysis of the content of alcohol in his body at the time of the alleged offence. If an appellant consumed alcohol after the commission of an alleged offence it was he who undermined the legitimate aim of the legislature by making the simple scientific test potentially unreliable. Furthermore, the relevant scientific evidence to set against the specimen breath result was only within the knowledge of the accused, rather than the Crown. Legislative interference with the presumption of innocence as found in s.15 was justified and was not greater than was necessary.

A further European Convention challenge to s.15 was mounted in *Griffiths* v. *DPP* (2002) 166 JP 629 where the driver of a vehicle argued that between being stopped and providing the sample, his body had continued to absorb alcohol. He called expert evidence to the effect that, when he had been stopped, he would not have been over the limit (his blood sample was taken some 99 minutes after he had been stopped). The Administrative Court dismissed his appeal against conviction. A court was not competent to receive expert evidence that undermined RTA 1988, s.15(2). Moreover, the statutory assumption was wholly proportionate and not a contravention of the Art.6 right to be presumed innocent until proved guilty.

In a further court challenge based on European Convention compatibility, it was held that the requirement in s.15(5) that the accused ask to be provided with part of the blood or urine specimen taken from him does not contravene Art.6 of the European Convention to the extent that the accused should be provided with legal advice in order to assist him in making the request. In *McClenaghan* v. *McKenna* [2001] NIECA June 19, the Court of Appeal in Northern Ireland said that it was sufficient that the suspect had been made aware of his right to request a part specimen in accordance with procedures that had developed over time to ensure this happened.

9.3   METHODS OF ANALYSIS

It is open to a defendant who has provided blood or urine under either RTA 1988, s.7 or s.7A to seek to challenge the analysis that will be relied upon by the prosecutor, by having his own part of the specimen independently analysed. Thereafter, there being no other matters that cause the justices to doubt the evidence of one or the other, it is open to the justices to decide which of the two analyses they will prefer.

In *Collins* v. *Lucking* [1983] RTR 312 the defendant provided a urine sample that was analysed and found to contain not less than 205 mg of alcohol in 100 ml of urine as well as micro-organisms capable of producing alcohol. The analyst stated that it was unlikely that the micro-organisms had significantly contributed to the alcohol found in the specimen, unless the defendant had diabetes. The justices convicted on the basis that it was not for the prosecutor to disprove that the defendant had diabetes, but for the defendant to prove that he had.

The defendant's appeal was allowed on the basis that the analyst's statement was concerned with likelihoods or probabilities and did not discount reasonable possibilities, so that the justices could not be satisfied that they were sure that an offence had been committed by the defendant.

The above case was not argued on the basis that the evidence of the analyst as regards the specimen had to be taken into account as the proportion of alcohol in the defendant's urine at the time of the alleged offence. Had that argument been put, the evidence of the micro-organisms producing alcohol would not have been relevant to the statutory assumption, although it is likely that special reasons might have been found for not disqualifying the defendant from driving. In any event the defendant was found not guilty by the court because there was a reasonable doubt raised by the analyst's statement, which should have been taken into account by the justices.

The methods used by different analysts in reaching a proper analysis of the specimen provided have also been the subject of decisions by the Divisional Court. In *Stephenson* v. *Clift* [1988] RTR 171 the defendant provided a specimen of blood that was divided into two parts and subsequently analysed by different approved analysts who acted in good faith using unimpeachable methods. The defendant's analyst used the ICMA system and the prosecutor's analyst used the more modern technique of gas chromatography. Following these analyses, the prosecutor's analysis showed a reading of 91 mg, and the defendant's analysis showed a reading of 81, both after applying the appropriate deductions of 6 mg per 100 ml.

The justices heard evidence from both analysts and found that the method used by the defence analyst was less accurate than that employed by the prosecution analyst. Therefore, they preferred the evidence of the analyst for the prosecution.

Dismissing the defendant's appeal, the Divisional Court held that the question was wholly one of fact for the justices and there was nothing in the court's reasoning that could permit the Divisional Court to interfere with their decision.

The practice among practitioners of reducing the result of the analysis by a small amount in order to allow for any error in the analysis and also of rounding down in the case of any fractions, was considered further in *Oswald* v. *DPP* [1989] RTR 360 in which the defendant supplied blood that was divided in the usual way and sent independently for analysis.

Analysis of the part retained by the police provided four results, all of which were over 86 mg of alcohol in 100 ml of blood and the average was 88.2. The part analysed on behalf of the defendant provided six results over 85 mg of alcohol and the average was 86.2. The defendant contended that there must be a doubt as to whether the analysis of his part of the specimen produced a reading that was over the prescribed limit, in view of the standard practice of deducting 6 mg to allow for error and to round down to the nearest whole number. The justices did not accept this contention and convicted the defendant.

On appeal it was held that the approach of deducting 6 mg from the analysis was not necessarily appropriate when the analysis had produced a whole range of results, all of which had been in the same range and which had produced an average above the prescribed limit. The finding that at the material time the defendant had been above the prescribed limit was unassailable and the rounding down of the decimal point was a matter of scientific practice and not an issue for the court.

9.4 DIVIDING THE SPECIMEN

Section 15 of RTOA 1988 requires that the specimen of blood or urine provided by the accused under RTA 1988, s.7 or s.7A shall be split into two parts at his request and one of the two parts given to the accused so that he can arrange for an independent analysis. There is no requirement that the specimen be split into two equal parts, merely that it be split into parts that will allow for proper analysis, using ordinary equipment and normal methods. If the part provided to the accused is incapable of analysis because of insufficient quantity or because it was not provided to the accused within a reasonable time after the specimen was taken and divided, the prosecution are precluded from using it as evidence in any subsequent proceedings.

The section requires that the person giving the specimen asks to be provided with part of it. In practice, a police officer at the police station will ask the motorist which of the two samples is wanted. In *Jones* v. *Crown Prosecution Service* (2003) 167 JP 481 the question was asked and the appellant pointed to one of the samples, but then left the police station without taking hold of it or asking to take it with her.

Her subsequent conviction was upheld. The combined effect of the offer of one of two samples and of her pointing to a sample specimen amounted to a tendering of a sample to her. If she did not then take up the offer of the sample either immediately or subsequently, it could not be said that it had not been supplied to her.

There is no requirement for the part sample to be handed directly to the driver. In *O'Connell* v. *DPP* [2006] All ER(D) 260 the appellant was in hospital following a motor cycle accident. He was undergoing treatment when required to provide a sample of blood by a police officer, but consented nevertheless. He also requested that the sample be divided and a part supplied to him. The police officer gave one part to the appellant's friend as the appellant could not receive it as his arms were incapacitated and there were no available lockers or means of keeping it safe on the ward where he was.

At trial the appellant argued that there had been no provision of the part sample to him and that the evidence of analysis should be excluded under PACE 1984, s.78 as inadmissible. His subsequent appeal against conviction was dismissed. The purpose of s.15(5) was clear; it provided the procedure, compliance with which led to the admissibility of specimens taken by the police. 'Supply' was not restricted to the physical handing over of a specimen and the word could be interpreted to mean 'make available'. There had been a supply in this case, although the meaning of the word was to be decided as a question of fact in each case.

There must be continuity of evidence to show that the sample analysed was the one taken from the driver in the police station or elsewhere. In *MacDonald* v. *Skelt* [1985] RTR 321 the blood sample retained by the police officer was sent for scientific examination, labelled by the police officer with the name of the doctor who had taken the specimen, the police officer's name, the police force, the date, the time and the police station. A scientific officer provided a written statement of receipt of a sample of blood containing the same details as that which had been analysed and shown to be above the prescribed limit.

The justices ruled that there was insufficient information to link the blood sample taken and the one analysed by the scientific officer. However, they then allowed the prosecutor to re-open his case and to call evidence that adequately proved the link. This decision was later affirmed by the Divisional Court, but provides a salutary lesson to prosecutors to ensure that, where there has been a sample provided that is required to be analysed, care should be taken to call sufficient evidence to show that the sample taken was the one divided and given to the defendant and was the one sent for analysis, and which was subsequently received and analysed.

After the sample has been divided, nothing should be said or done that will lead the defendant to believe that, for whatever reason, there is no point in having his part of the sample analysed. In *Perry* v. *McGovern* [1986] RTR 240 the defendant supplied a specimen of blood that was divided into two parts and she was given an opportunity to choose one of them for independent analysis. The defendant was given a labelled Securitainer containing the part of the sample she had chosen, together with a booklet showing a list of approved analysts. However, contrary to the normal procedure, her specimen was not put into an envelope with its flap sealed and signed by the station sergeant. Later the same day the defendant received a telephone call from the police station telling her that, as the correct procedures had not been followed, it would not be possible for her to have her specimen analysed. As a result of this call, she did not submit her specimen for analysis.

She was convicted by the justices who decided that, as there was no evidence before them to show that the specimen had been incapable of analysis, the statutory requirements had been complied with and evidence of the analysis of the part retained by the police could be admitted. Her appeal was allowed by the Divisional Court as it was the plain purpose of the section that the defendant should be able to obtain an independent analysis of the blood provided by her. The defendant had been misled by the prosecutor into thinking that she did not have a specimen for analysis and the conviction was quashed.

Where, however, the requirements of RTOA 1988, s.15 have been properly followed, but analysis does not take place because the defendant's analyst refuses to provide an analysis, no point can be taken as regards any possible non-compliance with the procedure. In *Butler* v. *DPP* [1990] RTR 377 the defendant provided a sample of blood that was divided by the doctor and placed in two identical bottles inside a sealed container. The doctor then completed the labels and inadvertently wrote on the bottle the name of the police officer in the case rather than the name of the defendant. When the defendant attempted to have his part of the specimen analysed, the analyst refused to do so because the defendant gave a different name from that on the bottle.

He was convicted by the justices as the part analysed on behalf of the police showed an alcohol concentration in excess of the permitted limit, and there had been compliance with the procedures laid down by statute. The Divisional Court dismissed the defendant's appeal as there was ample evidence to show that there had been a supply of part of the specimen to the defendant as required by RTOA 1988, s.15, and that part-specimen had been capable of analysis. The defendant had not been deterred or prevented from having his part analysed, and there had been no explanation in evidence as to why the defendant's analyst had refused to carry out an analysis. Whilst the part-specimen had been wrongly labelled, this did not mean that there was no evidence for the justices to find as a fact that the statute had not been complied with. 'The duty of the prosecution in such cases was to supply to the accused one of the two parts into which the blood or urine specimen has been divided [and,] moreover, in order to satisfy the subsection, that part must be a sample which is both capable of analysis and which the accused has not been led to believe is not capable of being analysed' – per Glidewell LJ.

The specimen taken by the medical practitioner must be a single specimen and cannot be the product of two different specimens. In *Dear* v. *DPP* [1988] RTR 148 the defendant was required to provide a specimen of blood for analysis, and the doctor attempted to take blood from the defendant's right arm. A few drops were taken by the doctor and placed in a bottle. The doctor was then able to extract from the defendant's left arm a sufficient amount, which he placed in the same bottle, after dividing the sample into two parts.

The defendant submitted that there had not been full compliance with the provisions of the section in that more than one specimen had been taken. The Divisional Court agreed with him, holding that the section referred to only one specimen, taken on a single occasion from the body of the subject, which then had to be divided and one part given to the defendant. It was for the prosecutor to establish that this procedure and no other had been followed. In this case he had been unable to do so as the part that had been given to the defendant for analysis was not one-half or one part of the single specimen taken from her body, but was, in addition, blood taken from her body on a previous occasion.

Where, because of the procedure followed at the police station, there is the possibility of contamination of a blood sample, it is for the prosecution to establish beyond reasonable doubt that the analysis and result were reliable. In *Slasor* v. *DPP* [1999] RTR 432 the defendant was required to provide a blood specimen after a Camic breathalyser device failed its final calibration check. After the blood sample had been decanted by syringe into two containers, it was noticed that one was leaking. The police surgeon, using a new syringe, transferred the blood from the damaged bottle to a new one.

Dismissing the driver's appeal against conviction the Divisional Court approved the practice adopted in this case of adducing evidence of the failed breath-test result to show it was compatible with the allegedly contaminated blood sample. However, the court warned that there had to be some relevant and clearly identified purpose for doing so. Such evidence was at least capable of tending to support the reliability of the blood-analysis result, but compatibility was not established merely by adducing evidence of the two results and the significance of the relationship had to be explained by an expert and not a police officer. The prosecution had to establish beyond reasonable doubt that the blood analysis result was reliable.

The section requires that there be a division of the specimen 'at the time it was provided' and implies that there should then be a supply to the defendant within a reasonable time of that division.

In *DPP* v. *Elstob* [1992] RTR 45 a doctor had taken a sample of blood from the defendant, following which the doctor left the room, placed the blood into two capsules and then returned some two minutes after leaving the room. The justices dismissed the charge against the defendant of driving whilst over the prescribed limit, as they were of the opinion that separation of the blood sample had not taken place at the time it was provided and had not been carried out in full view of the defendant, thus infringing a vital statutory requirement.

The prosecutor's appeal was allowed by the Divisional Court, which held that the expression 'at the time' in s.15(5)(a) meant that the taking of the specimen and its division into two had to be closely linked in time and performed as a part of the same event. However, whilst compliance required the division of the specimen to take place as a part of the same event, it did not require the defendant's presence at the division, as this was not provided for by the statute.

9.5   EVIDENCE OF THE PROPORTION OF ALCOHOL

The section provides that, provided the statutory procedure has been fully complied with, evidence obtained as a result of following that procedure may be taken into account. The assumption can then be made that the analysed proportion of alcohol in the specimen provided was the same as at the time of the alleged offence.

Failure to comply with the requirement to fulfil the statutory procedures leads to the result in *Badkin* v. *Chief Constable of South Yorkshire* [1988] RTR 401 where the police constable operating the intoximeter decided that it was unreliable as it did not produce a printout. He therefore required the defendant to supply a specimen of blood, which was analysed as being over the prescribed limit. However, before the hearing of the matter, the prosecution failed to serve notice of the analysis on the defendant.

The defendant's appeal against conviction was allowed on the basis that, as the device had been proved to be unreliable, no evidence of the readings on the screen could be admitted. Furthermore, whilst the failure to provide evidence of the blood analysis breached the requirement of the Act, that evidence of the proportion of alcohol in a specimen of blood provided by the accused had to be taken into account in all cases, the statutory requirements had not been complied with and, accordingly, the evidence of the analysis was inadmissible.

There are occasions, however, when, through no fault of anyone involved in the procedure, it is not possible to make the assumption that the proportion of alcohol in the defendant's breath, blood or urine at the time of the alleged offence was not less than in the specimen. In *R* v. *Bolton Magistrates' Court, ex parte Scally* [1991] 1 QB 537 – dealing with a number of consolidated appeals – defendants who had been convicted of offences where analysis had shown their blood–alcohol levels to be above the prescribed limit applied for judicial review to quash their convictions. Their applications followed subsequent investigations that had revealed that in the standard kits used for taking blood specimens, alcohol-free swabs, used for skin cleansing before insertion of the needle for withdrawing blood, had been replaced for the period between February 1987 and December 1988 by 'Medi-prep' swabs containing ethanol. These swabs had the effect of contaminating the blood specimen and increasing the blood–alcohol level by a small, but significant, amount. It was accepted that there had been no consultation or inquiry as to the suitability of the swabs before they had been replaced. It was further accepted that the police surgeon, the police, the Crown Prosecution Service and the justices had all acted in good faith.

In quashing the convictions it was held that the prosecution had, without dishonesty, corrupted the process, thus obtaining the convictions in a manner that was unfair and analogous to fraud, collusion or perjury. The admission in evidence of the analysts' certificates had been wrong and the assumption that the proportion of alcohol in the accused's blood at the time of the offence was not less than in the specimen could not be made in this case.

Once the prosecutor has proved that the defendant was driving or in charge of a motor vehicle at the relevant time, and that an analysis of the proportion of alcohol in his breath, blood or urine showed him to be over the prescribed limit, the burden shifts to the defendant of displacing the assumption that he was over the limit at the time that he was driving or in charge. As has been shown in **para. 9.2**, the burden on the defendant is a legal as opposed to an evidential one and does not infringe Art.6(2) of the European Convention.

In *Patterson* v. *Charlton District Council* [1986] RTR 18 the defendant and one other were seen near a parked car and arrested on suspicion of theft. At the police station the defendant said he was the owner of the vehicle and that he had driven it that day and parked it at the place where he had been arrested. The police officer had smelt alcohol on the defendant's breath and required him to supply specimens of breath, which he did and which proved positive.

The prosecutor appealed against the finding by the justices that the admission by the defendant was insufficient to raise a *prima facie* case of driving. The Divisional Court held that once the defendant had admitted to driving his car and had provided specimens of breath that showed him to be above the prescribed limit at the time when they were taken, it had to be assumed that his breath–alcohol proportion at the time of the alleged offence was not less than in the specimen and that at that stage the burden transferred to the defendant of displacing the assumption that his breath–alcohol proportion exceeded the statutory limit at the time that he drove.

The assumption that the proportion of alcohol in the accused's breath, blood or urine at the time of the alleged offence was not less than in the specimen cannot be made if the accused proves, on the balance of probabilities, that he consumed alcohol before he provided the specimen and after he had ceased to drive, attempt to drive or be in charge of the vehicle, and that had he not done so, the proportion of alcohol in his breath, blood or urine would not have exceeded the prescribed limit.

Where a defendant wishes to adduce evidence that alcohol was consumed by him after the driving ceased, it will normally be the case that he will need either the evidence of an expert or, in rare cases, evidence other than that of an expert, but which allows the justices to draw by inference the conclusion that the defendant has discharged the onus upon him.

In *DPP* v. *Singh* [1988] RTR 209 the defendant collided with another vehicle and then changed places with his passenger and proceeded to drink two plastic cups full of whisky. He was arrested and required to provide two specimens of breath, the lower of which contained 127 µg of alcohol in 100 ml of breath. At his trial, the defendant gave evidence that he had consumed one and a half pints of bitter prior to the accident and contended that the two cups of whisky consumed after he ceased to drive had caused him to exceed the limit, so that the assumption could not be made that he was over the prescribed limit when driving. He called no expert evidence to this effect. The justices made no finding about the amount of pre-accident alcohol consumption and dismissed the allegation.

In allowing the prosecutor's appeal, it was held that even assuming the justices inferentially found that the defendant had only consumed the one and a half pints of beer before the accident, the case was not one of a class where they could reliably and confidently conclude that the defendant had discharged the onus on him of establishing that the alcohol consumed after the accident accounted for the excess over the limit without there being some expert evidence to support that. The defendant could, and chose not to, call such evidence, and the justices had purported to rely on common sense. Expert evidence would not only have assisted them in deciding whether the defence had been established, but would also have provided invaluable assistance in deciding whether the evidence was true.

The question of whether expert evidence should be called in all such cases was dealt with by the House of Lords in *Cracknell* v. *Willis* [1988] AC 450. Lord Griffiths, in giving the leading judgment in this case, was of the opinion that the wording of the section did not give any support to the view that Parliament intended any challenge to the reliability of a device to be limited to a particular type of evidence. The assumption in s.15(2) was not an assumption that the device was working correctly, but an assumption that the proportion of alcohol in the relevant specimen was not less than the proportion of alcohol at the time of the offence. In the case of a breath specimen there was a presumption that the machine was reliable, but if that presumption was challenged by relevant evidence the magistrates would have to be satisfied that the machine had provided a reading upon which they could rely before making the assumption. His Lordship went on to express the hope that the realisation by the motoring public that evidential breath-testing machines were proving to be reliable, combined with the good sense of magistrates, would ensure that few defendants would seek to challenge a breath analysis by spurious evidence of their consumption of alcohol.

In *DPP* v. *Spurrier* (2000) 164 JP 369 the Divisional Court was once again required to consider whether or not expert evidence was necessary to rebut the presumption of the reliability of the reading. In this case the defendant was stopped by the police at 11.45 a.m. The police evidence was to the effect that whilst her breath smelt of intoxicants, there was no evidence of erratic driving, she was not unsteady on her feet and there were no other signs of intoxication. She gave a positive roadside specimen and subsequently at the police station, a breath specimen analysed at 143 µg.

The justices found that she had consumed a quarter bottle of whisky and two cans of lager the previous evening but had ceased drinking at 11.30 p.m. that night. They concluded, therefore, that the intoximeter reading was unreliable because the reading was incompatible with the evidence of previous consumption, because of the absence of any observable signs of intoxication and because the defendant, a person of previous good character, had displayed co-operative and rational behaviour at the police station. The justices also concluded that there was no need for her to call expert or technical evidence in such a case.

The Divisional Court upheld the prosecutor's appeal. Where lower consumption was alleged than that indicated by the intoximeter, it was not necessary for the defendant to adduce expert evidence of the reading that would have been produced had consumption been as alleged by the defendant.

There was no justification in law for such an evidential regime. In some cases, expert evidence as to the effect of consumption, coupled with the absorption rate of a particular person, it being possible for such rates to vary enormously depending upon the size, make-up and physical processes of a particular person, may be essential to reach a proper conclusion on the facts.

It was a matter for the court to look critically at the facts in each case and to decide whether such evidence was necessary. Justices should bear in mind:

1. A discrepancy between claimed consumption and a reading could point to unreliability of the device, or the unreliability of the defendant's evidence as to how much he consumed. It is essential to consider the reliability of the defendant's evidence while having in mind the presumption of reliability of the device.
2. Where there is a minimal claimed consumption, a high reading and little other evidence, the discrepancy is solely derived from the defendant's claimed consumption; rebutting the presumption of reliability in such circumstances would be likely to be difficult.
3. Where there were no observable signs of alcohol save on the breath, justices should have in mind the fact that certain people can develop a high tolerance to alcohol and have high levels of alcohol without there being observable signs. Many cases depend on the facts and it might be necessary to adjourn a hearing to obtain expert evidence.
4. In cases where claims of lower consumption are raised, signs of surprise by the defendant at the reading, or the very fact of a positive test, are to be expected. The absence of surprise would be a factor for justices to consider in the light of the defendant's caution that he was not obliged to say anything, and it is for the justices to decide what weight to give that absence.
5. Where the prosecution is given no notice that the defendant intended to claim that the device was defective, it is for the prosecution to consider whether to apply for an adjournment. Justices are likely to respond favourably to such an application. It would be within the justices' discretion to order the defendant to pay the cost of the adjournment.
6. As a general rule, there is no reason why a defendant should not be taken to be required to give notice in advance of trial that he intends to rely on the fact that the device was defective. Having regard to the presumption of reliability, the efficient administration of justice requires the prosecution to know that the defendant intends to rebut the presumption.

Whether or not expert evidence as to post-accident consumption is available to the court, there is still a requirement for there to be an evidential basis laid as to the amount actually consumed, an expert opinion based entirely on a hypothesis led to an irrational decision by magistrates to conclude that there was no case to answer on the basis solely of the expert's evidence in *DPP* v. *Chambers* (2004) 168 JP 231.

The court should not seek to take judicial notice of the likely reading in a case where no expert evidence was laid before it. In *Lonergan* v. *DPP* [2003] RTR 12 the appellant was involved in a traffic accident after which he went to a public house where he consumed alcohol for some time before walking home. He subsequently provided breath specimens at a police station which were over the limit. The justices rejected his submission that RTOA 1988, s.15(3) applied on the ground that evidence given on his behalf with regard to his alcohol consumption after the collision was not credible as it would have produced a higher reading.

His appeal was successful. There was much evidence from which the justices could have concluded that they were not satisfied that the appellant had discharged the onus on him under s.15, but they had failed to identify those particular factors and had put considerable weight on their assessment of what they would have expected to be the appropriate reading. This was not the kind of matter of which they could take judicial notice since it depended too much on the particular facts of the case and the particular nature of the appellant. An injustice would have been done by the justices focusing on their own assessment as to what they thought a proper reading would have been some two hours or so after the appellant had ceased drinking.

Note also, on this point, that in *DPP* v. *Brown*; *DPP* v. *Teixeira* (2002) 166 JP 1 the Divisional Court said that the assumption in RTOA 1988, s.15(2) is an assumption that the proportion of alcohol in the relevant specimen was not less than the proportion of alcohol at the time of the offence. When the reliability of a breath-analysis machine is challenged, justices are solely concerned with the reliability of the particular device used in the individual case: it is not part of their function to consider generally whether the device ought to have received the Secretary of State's approval. If the presumption that a device is reliable is challenged by relevant evidence then the justices, looking at such evidence with a critical eye, must be satisfied that the particular machine provided a reading upon which they can rely before making the statutory assumption (see further **para. 7.5**).

9.6 BACK-CALCULATION

Whilst the question of what sort of evidence was necessary in order to mount a realistic challenge to the statutory assumption in the section that the proportion of alcohol at the time of the alleged offence was not less than in the specimen provided was occupying the minds of the higher courts, a further gloss on the section in question was to be provided by the House of Lords in *Gumbley* v. *Cunningham* [1989] AC 281. It had been thought that the provisions of the section were such as to permit the prosecution to call evidence to show that, at the time of the commission of the offence, the defendant's alcohol level was higher than that which appeared at the subsequent analysis. This was especially the case where there had been a substantial lapse of time between the offence and the provision of the specimen.

In a case that was essentially a 'special reasons' argument, the Divisional Court gave qualified approval to the principle of 'back-calculation' or 'back-tracking', provided that there was reasonably clear, straightforward and relatively simple evidence to show the level of alcohol in the blood at the time of the alleged offence (*Smith* v. *Geraghty* [1986] RTR 222). However, it was accepted that in order to be successful in such a case, the prosecution would also have to prove that the defendant had not consumed any alcohol after the commission of the alleged offence and before the provision of the sample.

The facts of *Gumbley* v. *Cunningham* provided a real test as to whether back-calculation was permissible. The defendant had been drinking and then drove from the public house with his brother as the only passenger. The vehicle was driven erratically to the extent that eventually it collided with a wall and the passenger was killed. The defendant was arrested at the scene and taken to a police station, where he complained of illness and was taken to hospital. Some four hours and 20 minutes after the accident the doctor treating him consented to his supplying a specimen of blood, which was later analysed as containing no less than 59 mg of alcohol in 100 ml of blood.

The Crown Court found as facts that the defendant was 34 years of age, of average height and of muscular build, weighing 11 stones. They found that he would eliminate alcohol from his bloodstream at between 10 and 25 mg per hour and that the concentration in his blood at the time of the accident would have been in the region of 120–130 mg. As a result the defendant was convicted.

The House of Lords subsequently affirmed the Divisional Court's decision to uphold that conviction, agreeing with that court that those who drive whilst over the limit cannot necessarily escape punishment merely because of lapse of time. Whilst the prosecution should only seek to rely on evidence of back-calculations in cases where the evidence is both easily understood and clearly establishes the presence of excess alcohol at the time when the defendant was driving, there was nothing in the statute to show that Parliament had expressly intended to exclude evidence that was relevant to establishing the blood–alcohol concentration at the time when the defendant was driving.

Back-calculation in itself provides a whole host of problems for courts, not the least of which is the requirement to understand what are often complicated scientific calculations. These calculations take into account immediate post-consumption rises in alcohol levels, the rate of decline and the effect thereon of the defendant's physical make-up, the amount of food consumed either at the time or during the hours before and after consumption of the alcohol and the amount and relative strength of the alcohol taken. In addition the evidence laid before the justices must be such that they can be sure that the defendant had been over the prescribed limit at the time of the offence, even though the analysis had later shown him to be under at the time of providing the specimen.

Thus, in *Gould* v. *Castle* [1988] RTR 57, decided by the Divisional Court at the same time as *Gumbley* v. *Cunningham*, the defendant was successful in his appeal because the justices found only that he was 'likely' to have been over the prescribed limit at the time of the offence, which was not enough to satisfy the onus on the prosecution of proving their case beyond reasonable doubt.

The above cases approve the practice of back-calculation in order to show that whilst the defendant may have been below the prescribed limit at the time of providing the specimen, he was over the limit at the time of the offence. However, it is not similarly open to the defendant to use back-calculation to show that, whilst he was over the limit at the time of providing the specimen, he was not over, or may not have been over, at the time of the alleged offence. Ingestion of alcohol does not have an immediate effect on the alcohol level in the body, but builds up slowly for some time after ingestion as the alcohol is admitted into the bloodstream.

CHECKLIST   Post-accident consumption

---

1. Where a part-specimen of blood or urine has been provided to the defendant, were arrangements made for it to be analysed immediately?
2. Was there any possibility of contamination of the specimen caused by the procedure adopted at the police station?
3. How long did it take for the police to provide the defendant with his part-specimen? Was the specimen divided 'at the time'?
4. Have the prosecution established a sufficient link between the sample provided, sent for analysis, received and analysed?
5. Was the part-specimen supplied to the defendant sufficient in volume to be analysed?
6. Was anything said or done that led the defendant to believe that his part-specimen could not be analysed?
7. Have the prosecution proved that the defendant was driving or in charge and that he was over the prescribed limit as evidenced by the analysis of the specimen provided?
8. Did the defendant consume alcohol after he had ceased to drive or be in charge of the vehicle and before he provided the specimen?
9. What is the effect of this consumption of alcohol?
10. What evidence is available to show the effect?
11. Is the case one that does not require expert evidence to be called?
12. Are the prosecution seeking to rely on 'back-tracking' for the purposes of ascertaining the defendant's alcohol level at the relevant time?
13. Is the evidence provided by the back-calculation straightforward and obvious?
14. Is there sufficient evidence to mount a challenge to the statutory assumption that the proportion of alcohol in the specimen was that at the time of driving?
15. Is expert or technical evidence necessary to assist this challenge?

CHAPTER 10

Failure to provide a specimen

10.1 THE LEGISLATION

Section 7 of RTA 1988 provides:

(1) In the course of an investigation into whether a person has committed an offence under section 3A, 4 or 5 of this Act a constable may, subject to the following provisions of this section and section 9 of this Act, require him –

    (a) to provide two specimens of breath for analysis by means of a device of a type approved by the Secretary of State, or

    (b) to provide a specimen of blood or urine for a laboratory test.

[. . .]

(3) A requirement under this section to provide a specimen of blood or urine can only be made at a police station or at a hospital; and it cannot be made at a police station unless –

    (a) the constable making the requirement has reasonable cause to believe that for medical reasons a specimen of breath cannot be provided or should not be required, or

    (b) specimens of breath have not been provided elsewhere and at the time the requirement is made a device or a reliable device of the type mentioned in subsection (1)(a) above is not available at the police station or it is then for any other reason not practicable to use such a device there, or

    (bb) a device of the type mentioned in subsection (1)(a) above has been used (at the police station or elsewhere) but the constable who required the specimens of breath has reasonable cause to believe that the device has not produced a reliable indication of the proportion of alcohol in the breath of the person concerned, or

    (bc) as a result of the administration of a preliminary drug test, the constable making the requirement has reasonable cause to believe that the person required to provide a specimen of blood or urine has a drug in his body, or

    (c) the suspected offence is one under section 3A or 4 of this Act and the constable making the requirement has been advised by a medical practitioner that the condition of the person required to provide the specimen might be due to some drug;

but may then be made notwithstanding that the person required to provide the specimen has already provided or been required to provide two specimens of breath.

[. . .]

(6) A person who, without reasonable excuse, fails to provide a specimen when required to do so in pursuance of this section is guilty of an offence.

(7) A constable must, on requiring any person to provide a specimen in pursuance of this section, warn him that a failure to provide it may render him liable to prosecution.

Section 7A(5) and (6) of RTA 1988 (as amended by Police Reform Act 2002) provide:

(5) A constable must, on requiring a person to give his permission for the purposes of this section for a laboratory test of a specimen, warn that person that a failure to give the permission may render him liable to prosecution.

(6) A person who, without reasonable excuse, fails to give his permission for a laboratory test of a specimen of blood taken from him under this section is guilty of an offence.

10.2 COMPARISON BETWEEN SECTION 7(3) AND SECTION 7(6)/ SECTION 7A(6)

Section 7(3)(a) permits a police officer to require blood or urine where he has reasonable cause to believe that for medical reasons a specimen of breath should not or cannot be provided by the defendant. The medical reasons relied on in pursuance of this subsection are often the same or similar to medical reasons put forward by a defendant as his reasonable excuse for not providing a specimen when required to do so under s.7(6).

There is, however, no corollary between the two subsections. Cases where a medical reason has been successfully argued as to why breath cannot or should not be provided have been decided differently from cases where the same medical excuse has been put forward as the reason for not complying with the police officer's request for a specimen of breath, blood or urine.

The rationale behind this seemingly inconsistent treatment of similar situations lies in the basic requirement for both subsections to be included in s.7. A medical reason is more acceptable under s.7(3)(a) than under s.7(6) because under s.7(3)(a) acceptance merely leads the police officer to consider one of the other forms of specimen evidence in order to obtain evidence to mount a successful prosecution. Under s.7(6), however, acceptance of the medical reason provides a complete defence to the charge of failing to provide the specimen.

10.3 WARNING OF THE CONSEQUENCES OF FAILURE

Section 7(7) requires that where a police officer is about to request that specimens of breath, blood or urine be provided, he must warn the defendant that a failure to provide the specimen may render him liable to prosecution. The requirement to be given the statutory warning is a mandatory one and a failure to give it, even though no prejudice is caused to the defendant, is fatal to a prosecution. In *Murray* v. *DPP* (1994) 158 JP 261, the Divisional Court, applying *Howard* v. *Hallett* [1984] Crim LR 565 held that evidence under RTOA 1988, s.15(2) of an analysis reading was only admissible if the procedure had been properly carried out and the warning given.

In *Simpson* v. *Spalding* [1987] RTR 221 the defendant was a police officer who had been involved in an accident and was subsequently required to provide a specimen of blood for a laboratory test at a hospital where he had been taken. Knowing that the defendant was a serving police officer and therefore assuming that he had at least a working knowledge of the procedure, the officer requesting the specimen failed to warn the defendant that a failure on his part to provide the specimen would render him liable to be prosecuted. The defendant was convicted of failing without reasonable excuse to provide the specimen of blood.

His appeal to the Divisional Court was upheld. The provisions of the Act were mandatory and a requirement to provide a specimen was ineffective unless accompanied by the necessary warning:

> I am confident that many police officers – and lawyers and Judges – are not fully conversant with the police procedure of investigating offences under the Act and would not have the knowledge that failure to provide a specimen after a duly made requirement would cause a driver to be liable to prosecution.
>
> per Ralph Gibson LJ.

Where the defendant's knowledge of English is limited, the onus on the police officer to warn the defendant of the consequences of failure is extended to encompass a warning couched in simple language that can be understood by the defendant. In *Chief Constable of Avon and Somerset Constabulary* v. *Singh* [1988] RTR 107 the defendant, an Indian, could understand basic English, but not long or technical words and phrases. He was involved in an accident, and the police officer who attended the scene found that she could only make herself properly understood if she used simple English.

At the police station, the sergeant conducting the procedure did not feel that there was a language barrier and proceeded to read the various requests and warnings from the standard pro forma.

It was held by the Divisional Court, allowing the defendant's appeal against conviction for failing to supply a specimen, that it was implicit in the language of the section that the warning must have been capable of informing the

141

person to whom it was directed of the possible consequences of a failure to comply. If the alleged warning was not understood as a warning by the person to whom it was given, then it was not a warning within the meaning of the section.

10.4   EFFECT OF AN UNLAWFUL ARREST

What is the situation when an arrest is made, which subsequently turns out not to have been a lawful one, but in the meantime the defendant has refused to supply a specimen that has been requested at the police station?

Provided the requirement for the breath specimen is made in good faith, the circumstances leading up to the request would appear to be immaterial provided there is a *bona fide* investigation of the question of whether the suspect has committed an offence under RTA 1988, s.4 or s.5. Thus, in *Hawes* v. *DPP* [1993] RTR 116, the fact that the defendant was seen and arrested whilst on land that was not a road or other public place was not relevant to a subsequent charge of failing to provide a breath specimen at the police station, as the officers in the case had been genuinely concerned to discover whether the defendant had been guilty of a s.4 offence.

In *McGrath* v. *Vipas* [1984] RTR 58, an accident occurred and the defendant was arrested. The defendant genuinely, but mistakenly, believed that the arresting police officer was not acting *bona fide* and that he had no reasonable cause to believe that the defendant had been driving or attempting to drive the vehicle involved in the accident; accordingly, he refused, when requested, to supply specimens of breath for a breath test.

It was held that his belief at the time the request was made that the request was invalid, immaterial and, in view of the wording of the statute, the defendant could not rely on the common law principle that an honest and reasonable belief in the existence of circumstances that, if true, would make the act innocent, would provide a defence.

In *Gull* v. *Scarborough* [1987] RTR 261, the Divisional Court held that a requirement to supply a specimen of blood at a police station was lawful, even in circumstances where the defendant had been unlawfully arrested at the outset. Similarly, in *Hartland* v. *Alden* [1987] RTR 253 the defendant was observed by a police officer to be driving erratically. He was followed and then unlawfully arrested at his home. At the police station he was required to provide specimens of breath for analysis and refused to do so on the grounds that his arrest had been unlawful. He conceded that, throughout, the police had acted in good faith, but submitted that the wrongfulness of his arrest vitiated the subsequent police procedures and provided a reasonable excuse for his refusal.

It was held that the procedure adopted prior to the defendant's arrival at the police station was immaterial and that the breath specimen required there had been required during the course of an investigation into whether the defendant had committed an offence. Therefore, the specimens of breath had been lawfully required. In addition, since the defendant could not rely on the unlawful arrest to vitiate the procedure at the police station, he similarly could not use it as a reasonable excuse for not providing the required specimen.

This approach was followed in *Thomas* v. *DPP* [1991] RTR 292 where it was held that an unlawful arrest without more would not vitiate subsequent procedures carried out at a police station. However, it was open to a defendant to argue that the procedures at the police station had been so tainted by the previous conduct of the police at the roadside as to give rise to the possibility of the exercise of discretion under PACE 1984, s.78. These circumstances would exclude the evidence of what happened at the police station. It was not open to the defendant to argue that there had been *mala fides* on the part of the police officer, as this had been expressly negated by the findings of the justices in the case. Additionally, it was held that a previous unlawful arrest was irrelevant to subsequent procedures at the police station and could not amount to a reasonable excuse under RTA 1988.

10.5 'FAILS' AND 'REFUSES'

By virtue of RTA 1988, s.11(2) the word 'fail' includes the word 'refuses'.

In *Smyth* v. *DPP* [1996] RTR 59 a motorist initially refused to provide two specimens of breath for analysis. However, within five seconds he then asked whether he could change his mind and followed this with a definite statement that he had changed his mind. He was convicted of failing to provide on the basis that his original response had been clear and unequivocal. His appeal was allowed. Whether the defendant's words and conduct amounted to a refusal was a matter of fact for decision by the tribunal. The defendant's secondary responses were clearly relevant words and conduct to be taken into account. The justices had been wrong to ignore those words and had clearly not applied their minds to all the relevant words and conduct of the defendant.

For further commentary on the similarity of these words and for case law on the subject, see **para. 2.8**.

10.6 CONSULTING A DOCTOR OR SOLICITOR

It is well established that whether the defendant has a reasonable excuse for failing or refusing to provide the specimen is a question of fact for the justices and the court has to be satisfied beyond reasonable doubt that the defendant did not have a reasonable excuse before a conviction can be recorded.

However, whether or not the facts amount to a reasonable excuse is a question of law, and the court must be careful when dealing with such cases to ensure that it first decides whether the facts are, indeed, capable of amounting to a reasonable excuse. Secondly, the court must then decide whether, in the particular case, there was a reasonable excuse and whether the prosecutor has discharged the burden on him of negating it.

Other than *Billington* which is dealt with below, the cases which appeared in the first edition of this book on whether or not it is permissible to delay procedures in the police station pending the taking of advice from a solicitor or reading the relevant PACE Codes of Practice have been removed. A number of cases on these points have been decided since publication of the first edition and the principles determined in these new cases, based as they are on issues arising from a consideration of European Convention principles, are considered to be more germane to this issue than those previously digested.

There would appear to be a conflict between the approved procedure in the police station and the requirements of PACE 1984, s.58 and s.66, and the Codes of Practice drawn thereon. The latter allow a suspect an opportunity to consult a solicitor or to contact others prior to any interviews or before making any admissions. It is worth considering these cases in isolation from others that deal with the question of what is or is not a reasonable excuse for failing to provide a specimen of breath, blood or urine, if only from the point of view of practitioners who are called in the middle of the night by clients who wish to discuss the finer points of the police station procedure before consenting to supply specimens.

In *DPP* v. *Billington* (1988) 152 JP 1 the Divisional Court dealt with four appeals by motorists who, having been required to provide specimens of breath for analysis at a police station, refused to provide them until they had consulted a solicitor. In support of this they contended that PACE 1984, s.58 entitled them to consult a solicitor as soon as practicable, and the Codes of Practice made under that Act required that, if interviews were commenced after a suspect had requested a solicitor and before he had had access to one, a record of such should be made in the interview record to that effect.

The Divisional Court dismissed this argument by saying that nothing in PACE 1984, either expressly or by implication, required the police to delay the taking of a specimen under RTA 1988, and the statutory right to consult a solicitor did not furnish a defendant with a reasonable excuse for failing to provide a specimen. The court did, however, leave open the question of whether there might be a reasonable excuse in circumstances where a defendant was told affirmatively that he would not have to provide a specimen until after he had consulted a solicitor.

In *Kennedy* v. *DPP* [2004] RTR 6, (a case decided in November 2002) the defendant was arrested after providing a positive roadside sample and taken to a police station, arriving there at 3 a.m. At 3.20 a.m. he was taken to the custody desk where he asked for a solicitor. He was given a notice, which he chose not to read, stating that the right to legal advice did not entitle a person in his position to delay procedures under RTA 1988. During the period from 3.30 a.m. to about 10 minutes thereafter, he refused to take part in the usual procedures to obtain specimens. At 3.41 a.m. the police contacted a duty solicitor, whose representative arrived at 4.40 a.m. He subsequently appealed against his conviction for failing to provide a specimen.

The Divisional Court said that although the right to a fair trial enshrined in Art.6 of the European Convention was in play from the outset of a police investigation, that right did not spell out a right to legal advice at any particular stage. A driver, in the circumstances of the particular case, must be permitted to consult a solicitor as soon as is practicable as provided for by PACE 1984, s.58 which fully satisfied the requirements of Art.6. It was a question of fact and degree in any case whether the custody officer had acted without delay to secure the provision of legal advice and whether the person held in custody had been permitted to consult a solicitor as soon as practicable. Where the matter under investigation was a suspected offence under RTA 1988, s.5, the public interest required that the obtaining of breath specimens part of the investigation could not be delayed to any significant extent in order to enable a suspect to take legal advice. In the present case, the suspect had done no more than indicate a general desire to have legal advice and there was no reason why the custody officer should not have simply continued to take details and alert the solicitor's call centre at the earliest opportunity. The breach of the statutory requirement in s.58 was neither significant nor substantial and could not have led to the exclusion of evidence under PACE 1984, s.78.

This decision was followed in *Kirkup* v. *DPP* (2004) 168 JP 255. In this case the duty solicitor was called immediately after the driver's request for legal advice, but did not arrive until nine minutes after there had been a refusal to provide a specimen. The justices found that there had been a breach of PACE 1984, s.58 and paragraph 6.5 of the relevant Code of Practice (Code C), but that it was neither significant nor substantial and thus exercised their discretion not to exclude the police officer's evidence concerning the requests for breath specimens.

In dismissing the driver's appeal, the Divisional Court said that the justices' finding that there had been a breach of s.58 and the Code had to be weighed against the public interest which requires that the obtaining of breath specimens cannot be delayed to any significant extent in order to enable a suspect to take legal advice. Article 6 does not confer a right to legal advice at any particular stage and if there is good cause to do so which is proportionate in the circumstances, there will be no ground for appeal.

In *Whitley* v. *DPP* (2004) 168 JP 350 the driver arrived at the police station some two hours after a traffic accident, having been detained in hospital during the intervening period. On being booked in at the police station he requested that he be allowed to speak to a solicitor at the earliest opportunity. A police officer was already standing by, prepared to administer a breath test and the driver was informed that the procedure would not be delayed to wait for legal advice. The request for a duty solicitor to attend was not made until three minutes after the breath test procedure was terminated on the driver's refusal to provide specimens.

The Divisional Court said that whether a custody officer had acted without delay to secure the provision of legal advice and whether the person held in custody had been permitted to consult a solicitor as soon as is practicable is a question of fact and degree. Given the enormous variety of circumstances that could face a custody officer, it was important that he should be given the flexibility to respond to the demands of a particular case. In this case the procedure had already been seriously delayed and the police were right to have made arrangements to ensure that the evidential breath specimens could be recorded as soon as possible.

A similar result ensued in *Myles* v. *DPP* [2005] RTR 1 in which the driver first of all indicated that he did not need the services of a solicitor, but later changed his mind when he was required to provide a specimen of blood. His appeal against conviction for failing to provide the specimen was dismissed on the grounds that no one in the defendant's position had the right to delay the procedure under s.7 in order to obtain advice since it was obvious that specimens had to be taken as close to the time of the alleged offence as possible. The suggestion that it should be permissible to hold up the sample-taking process for some defined short period of, say, 15 minutes, ran counter to the clear views of the Divisional Court that the process should not be delayed to any significant extent.

In an effort to bring this particular line of cases to an end, 'I would not expect, in the foreseeable future, to see appeals in which the principles to be applied in these particular cases are raised, save in exceptional circumstances', the Divisional Court further reviewed the authorities in *Causey* v. *DPP* (2005) 169 JP 331 and came to the following conclusions:

1. There was no general duty on the police to delay taking a specimen at the police station until a detainee had obtained legal advice.
2. It was a question of fact and degree, depending on the circumstances of the case, whether the custody officer had acted without delay and had permitted the appellant to consult a solicitor as soon as was practicable.
3. A custody officer could not know how long it would take to receive a response from a legal representative.
4. If a custody officer knew a solicitor was immediately available, the appellant should be allowed to consult with his lawyer before deciding whether or not to provide specimens. Specimens must, however, be taken as close to the time of an alleged offence as possible.

5. A short and unwarranted delay in contacting a solicitor when requested might constitute a breach of PACE 1984, s.58 such as not to merit excluding the evidence of the detainee's refusal.

The court had been correct to conclude that the fairness test laid down in PACE 1984, s.78 did not require the exclusion of the evidence of the refusal to provide a breath test at the police station. Nothing that occurred was causative of any unfairness. This was not a case where a protection to which the appellant was entitled and which, if afforded, might have made a real difference to the outcome, had been denied. A solicitor could not have added anything of significance to the information already given to the appellant both orally and in the form with which he was provided. There was no substance in the complaint that the evidence had been obtained during an unfairly conducted procedure or that there was any material breach of the appellant's Art.6 rights.

Just as there is no right to consult a solicitor or to read relevant Codes of Practice before providing a specimen at the police station, so, similarly, there is no right to consult a legal text book before doing so. In *DPP* v. *Noe* [2000] RTR 351 it was held that the fact that a defendant wished to consult a solicitor before providing a specimen was incapable in law of amounting to a reasonable excuse and a defendant was not entitled to impose a condition before providing a specimen by refusing to do so until he had read the Codes of Practice or until he had had the opportunity to check a law book to verify the legality of the police request to provide specimens of breath.

10.7 MAKING EVERY EFFORT

Section 11(3) of RTA 1988 states that a person does not co-operate with a preliminary test or provide a specimen of breath for analysis unless his co-operation or the specimen:

(a) is sufficient to enable the test or analysis to be carried out; and
(b) is provided in such a way as to enable the objective of the test or analysis to be satisfactorily achieved.

In *R* v. *Lennard* [1973] 1 WLR 483 it was decided that a reasonable excuse had to arise out of a physical or mental inability to provide a specimen or where its provision would constitute a substantial risk to health. All approved devices require that a certain amount of breath at a certain pressure and over a certain length of time is necessary if the device is to operate properly. What, then, is the situation where the defendant asserts that he had made every effort to provide the specimen of breath, but because of some physical incapacity at the time, he was unable to do so?

In *Anderton* v. *Waring* [1986] RTR 74 the defendant placed the mouthpiece to his mouth and blew and the machine registered 'no sample'. At his trial for failing to provide a specimen, evidence was given that the defendant had blown around rather than into the mouthpiece. The justices found that the defendant had made a proper attempt to blow, and that the machine would have displayed the word 'aborted' in the circumstances described by the officer, so that the device must have been defective. Therefore, the defendant had not failed to provide the specimen.

The Divisional Court allowed the prosecutor's appeal saying that, in the light of the wording of RTA 1988, s.11(3), there was no evidence upon which to find that the defendant had a reasonable excuse for not supplying the specimen. In any event, the approved device had to be presumed to be in good working order unless there was evidence to the contrary upon which the court could rely. Furthermore, it was wrong for justices to rely on their previous experience of similar devices to found inferences about the visual display on the device.

The decision in *R* v. *Lennard* was the basis for the decision in *Cotgrove* v. *Cooney* (1987) 151 JP 736 where the defendant was given four (prosecution case) or nine (defence case) attempts to blow into the Lion Intoximeter. The justices found that he had tried as hard as he could to provide a specimen and that there had been no wilful refusal on his part. In addition, whilst there was no medical reason for the failure, the fact of being stopped late at night by the police and taken to a police station might have induced a stressful state, which caused an inability to provide the specimen.

The prosecution appealed on the basis that a defendant should be required to raise a specific cause for the failure if he is to be successful in such cases. To hold otherwise would be to provide a blanket defence whereby a defendant would be able to argue that he had tried as hard as he could, but had not been able to supply the specimen. This argument was dismissed by the Divisional Court, which held that it was a question of fact for the justices and that, whilst extra care should always be taken in such cases to ensure that there was a genuine attempt by the defendant to provide the specimens, a defendant should not be convicted in a case where he had tried as hard as possible, but had been unable to do so.

The above was considered by the Divisional Court in *Grady* v. *Pollard* [1988] RTR 316 in which the defendant was unable properly to inflate a road-side screening device and where, on appeal, the defendant asserted that he had tried as hard as he could to inflate the device, but was unable to do so. His appeal against conviction was dismissed as there was no evidence that the defendant was physically or mentally unable to provide a specimen of breath and therefore there was no question of there being a reasonable excuse for failure to provide the specimen. Whilst such evidence would normally be provided by a medical practitioner, that need not be necessary in all such cases, and there might be cases where that evidence could come from the defendant himself as well as from other sources.

The distinction between *Cotgrove* v. *Cooney* and *Grady* v. *Pollard* seems to be that in *Cooney* the court found that the defendant had tried as hard as he could and had therefore satisfied the requirements of s.11 whereas in *Grady* the defendant sought to rely on his perceived inability to provide the specimen as a reasonable excuse for not so providing. The court was therefore prepared to allow the former, but could not allow the latter as to do so would negate the decision in *R* v. *Lennard*.

This rather thin dividing line was considered further in *DPP* v. *Eddowes* [1991] RTR 35 in which Watkins LJ, whilst not going so far as to overrule the decision in *Cotgrove* v. *Cooney*, said that the observations in *R* v. *Lennard* were to be preferred as a point of guidance.

In *DPP* v. *Eddowes* the defendant was arrested and required to supply two specimens of breath for analysis. He supplied the first sample, which resulted in a reading of 126 µg of alcohol in 100 ml of breath and then attempted, but failed, to provide the second specimen. He was charged with failing to supply specimens of breath and the justices, being of the opinion that he had been ready and willing to provide a second specimen and had tried as hard as he could to supply it, dismissed the charge as they found there to be a reasonable excuse for his failure on the basis of the decision in *Cotgrove* v. *Cooney*.

In allowing the prosecutor's appeal, the Divisional Court found that the justices were wholly wrong in their approach to the case and should have concluded that there was no excuse and certainly not a reasonable one for the defendant's failure to provide a second specimen of breath. The case was remitted to the justices with a direction to convict.

It would appear, therefore, that the decision in *Cotgrove* v. *Cooney* is to be treated as a decision very much on its own peculiar facts. The reasoning in *R* v. *Lennard* is to be preferred, so that a reasonable excuse must arise out of a physical or mental inability to provide a specimen or create a substantial risk to health in its provision. Where the defendant is able to show that he has tried as hard as he is able to supply the specimen, but is unable to do so, then unless he can call evidence to show lack of lung capacity or physical incapacity, he will stand to be convicted of a charge of failing to provide a specimen.

Mention should also be made of *Stepniewski* v. *Commissioner of Police of the Metropolis* [1985] RTR 330 where the defendant provided the first specimen of breath, which was seen by the police officer in the case, but not by the defendant, as being 34 µg of alcohol in 100 ml of breath. Thereafter he refused to supply the second specimen, giving no reason for this refusal. He was charged and convicted of failing to supply two specimens of breath as required.

His appeal against conviction was dismissed, as clearly he had been required to provide two specimens of breath and had failed to do so in the absence of any defence of reasonable excuse or special circumstances. However, the court went on to say that in such cases there was little point in prosecuting and that, if the same circumstances were to apply in the future, prosecuting authorities should consider very carefully whether it was appropriate to prosecute.

The situation was different in *DPP* v. *Thomas (Elwyn Kenneth)* (1993) 157 JP 480 in which the defendant provided a first specimen of breath, which was over the limit. He then argued that a second was unnecessary because the first was over the limit. Because the machine did not have time to complete its cycle, it aborted and the defendant was charged with the offence of failing to supply specimens of breath without reasonable excuse.

The defendant was acquitted by the justices, who found that the police officer gave no clear indication to the defendant that he would have to provide a second specimen within three minutes of the first. The Divisional Court upheld the prosecutor's appeal on the basis that the failure to provide the specimen was due to the respondent's arguing that there was no point in supplying the second specimen, rather than the failure of the police officer to explain the procedure. The defendant had not argued that he had a reasonable excuse for failing to supply the second specimen and the justices had been wrong to acquit him on that basis.

The question of whether a refusal to provide a second specimen of breath after already supplying a positive first specimen constituted an offence under s.7(6) also arose in *May* v. *DPP* [2000] RTR 7. At the police station the defendant provided a first specimen of breath, which was over the prescribed limit. He then indicated to a police officer that the reading related not to alcohol, but to medication that he had been prescribed. He declined to give a second specimen of breath, but offered to provide a blood specimen, which was taken.

His conviction for failing to supply specimens of breath as required was overturned by the Divisional Court. It was plain that the matter had not ended with the defendant's refusal to provide a second specimen of breath. The power to require the taking of blood samples was strictly regulated and there was no evidence before the court to suggest that the police officer had formed the opinion that, for medical reasons, a specimen of breath should not be required.

It would therefore appear that the statutory procedure must be adhered to whether or not the first sample of breath is under or over the prescribed limit. It is not for a driver to choose after the first sample whether to give a second sample and a failure to do so will, without more, lead to a prosecution for failing to provide.

In determining whether or not a driver has made every effort to provide a specimen, regard can be had to expert medical evidence that shows that if a person can sufficiently inflate a roadside hand-held device, then they should be able to provide a sufficient sample for the purposes of an evidential device at a police station. Similarly, where a driver provides a first sample of breath at a police station, but then states that he is unable to provide a second, the court should be slow to make a finding that there was a reasonable excuse for not doing so in the absence of any medical or other evidence on the point (*DPP* v. *Radford* [1995] RTR 86).

Finally, it should be noted that a driver does not have an infinite amount of time in which to provide a specimen. In *DPP* v. *Coyle* [1996] RTR 287 the prosecutor's appeal against the magistrate's decision to acquit was allowed where the approved device concluded its cycle before the defendant could provide a second sample of breath. It was not a reasonable excuse that the motorist was doing his best, or trying as hard as he could, without succeeding. Nor was the fact that the police officer did not tell the defendant that the machine operated on a three-minute cycle a reasonable excuse. Only if the defendant could lay down some evidential basis for the proposition would a failure to inform about a mechanical limit on the device be open to consideration as a reasonable excuse.

Applying the above principle in *Cosgrove* v. *DPP* [1997] RTR 153 the Divisional Court also said that if the administering officer concludes that the person required to give a breath sample is not making proper attempts to do so, then he can terminate the procedure halfway through the cycle and treat the defendant as if he had failed to provide a sample. In this particular case the officer took such a view when only one minute had elapsed. It was held that, on the evidence before the court, he was entitled to do so.

10.8 REASONABLE EXCUSE

What is and what is not a reasonable excuse is primarily a question of fact for the justices who are, nevertheless, constrained in making such decisions by the requirement that they must act according to law. First, the justices must decide whether the facts in the present case amount to a reasonable excuse; second, they must decide whether as a matter of fact and degree such is the case in the matter they are hearing. In *R* v. *Lennard* [1973] RTR 252 it was said that a reasonable excuse must arise out of a physical or mental inability to provide a specimen or a substantial risk to health in the provision of one.

Once the defence of reasonable excuse has been put forward the onus is then on the prosecution to disprove it and the court must be satisfied beyond reasonable doubt that the defendant had no reasonable excuse before a conviction can ensue.

In deciding whether a driver has a reasonable excuse for not providing a specimen, the court has to make findings about what would, or was likely to happen if the driver had been required to provide the specimen in question. In *DPP* v. *Mukandiwa* (2006) 170 JP 17, the respondent, a spirit medium, would not consent to the provision of blood for analysis for 'spiritual reasons'. His evidence and that of his expert that the sight of blood might cause him to go into a trance and become violent was accepted by the court as a health concern and he was acquitted.

The prosecutor's appeal was allowed. If the court had addressed the issue of what would have happened if the respondent had been required to provide a blood specimen, it would have identified that it was the sight of blood that was the problem. On the face of it, that problem could easily have been avoided by the respondent shutting his eyes or looking away as the blood was taken. The court had made no finding that a trance would have necessarily followed the sight of blood and no real analysis had been conducted of the likely consequences. The finding that there was a substantial risk to the respondent's health was not open to the court on the facts.

In *Sykes* v. *White* [1983] RTR 419 the defendant refused to supply blood and gave no reason, after which he was given the opportunity to supply urine, to which he responded that he did not believe in it. At his trial he claimed for the first time that he became light-headed and had to sit down at the sight of blood, and he had been apprehensive that if this had happened, the police would have suspected him of excessive consumption.

The Divisional Court, in allowing the prosecutor's subsequent appeal against the dismissal of the charge by the justices, held that the mere dislike of the sight of blood, causing the observer to become light-headed, did not amount to a phobia causing physical incapacity to provide a blood specimen. Furthermore, an irrational belief that the manifestation of that light-headedness would cause the police to assume excessive consumption could not amount to a reasonable excuse for refusing to supply a specimen of blood.

In *Palmer* v. *Killion* [1983] RTR 138 the justices accepted the defendant's contention that he had been unable to supply blood because he was a haemophiliac, but convicted him of failing to supply urine as they did not accept that the defendant's embarrassment at having to supply a specimen of urine was capable of amounting to a reasonable excuse. This decision was upheld on appeal by the Divisional Court who left open the question whether embarrassment that caused a state of hysteria would be sufficient to constitute a reasonable excuse.

There would appear to be a duty on a motorist who knows that his medical condition prevents him from providing sufficient breath as is required to fulfil the conditions of s.7 to inform the police officer requiring the specimen of that medical condition. In *Teape* v. *Godfrey* [1986] RTR 213 the defendant was required to supply two specimens of breath for analysis and deliberately failed to provide them. At his trial he sought to raise a reasonable excuse in that he suffered from asthma, information that was not given to the police officer in the case either at the roadside or at the police station. His appeal against conviction was dismissed as the defendant had not done his best on either occasion to provide the specimen, so that he had not laid the factual basis that would allow him to invoke the defence of reasonable excuse.

The effect of an asthma attack on a defendant's ability to provide specimens of breath was the point under consideration in *DPP* v. *Curtis* [1993] RTR 72 where the defendant was arrested and taken to a police station after supplying a positive screening breath sample. At the police station she was required to provide two specimens of breath for analysis, at which point she told the officer that she had a cold, but did not complain of any other medical condition. It was noticed that she was nervous and upset. She provided one specimen, but was unable to provide a second.

At her trial for failing to supply specimens of breath, a doctor gave evidence that she had a very low anxiety threshold and had suffered from asthma in the past. The justices, who all had experience or knowledge of asthma, concluded that she had suffered an asthma attack as a result of the stress and anxiety of the occasion and had been physically incapable, therefore, of providing the specimen. They dismissed the charge. The prosecutor's appeal was allowed. Justices were not to act upon material that was additional to the evidence before them, and whilst they could, where appropriate, use their knowledge of a particular subject, they should be wary of using knowledge of a physical or mental condition that was not supported by evidence in deciding why a specimen of breath had not been supplied.

The later discovery of a physical reason for not being able to provide a specimen cannot be used to make out a reasonable excuse if it was not known about at the time of being asked to provide the specimen. In *DPP* v. *Furby* [2000] RTR 181 the defendant was asked to provide two specimens of breath at a police station. He failed to comply by blowing around, rather than into the mouthpiece and tried to obstruct the view of the police officer by covering the mouthpiece with his hand.

At trial a consultant chest physician gave evidence of reduced lung capacity, which would have rendered the defendant incapable of providing a suitable breath specimen for analysis. The court found this to be a reasonable excuse for the failure to provide.

The prosecutor successfully appealed. The wording of s.7(6) in the present tense was such as to make it clear that there had to be a direct relationship between the excuse relied on and the failure to provide a sample. A motorist who was unaware of an impairment could not rely on it as an excuse unless he made a genuine attempt to provide the specimen. If the driver was unaware of his incapacity and had made no genuine attempt, he could not have had, at the time of his failure, a reasonable excuse for it. The fact that it was subsequently discovered that had he made a genuine attempt he would not have been able to provide a specimen is irrelevant for the purposes of the statute. If the condition had been known and had the officer in the case been aware of it, this would have triggered an inquiry by the officer under RTA 1988, s.7(3) which might have led to an alternate specimen being requested.

In this case there was no causative link between the physical condition and the failure to provide a specimen.

Even where the physical condition is known at the time, details of it must be provided to the officer carrying out the investigation at the police station who has the power to require specimens of breath or alternative specimens.

Thus, in *DPP* v. *Lonsdale* [2001] RTR 29, CA the driver told the constable at the roadside that he suffered from bronchitis, but was still able to provide a sufficient screening sample. At the police station the custody sergeant was not told about the bronchitis and required two specimens of breath. The defendant was acquitted of the offence of failing to provide on the basis that the breath-test procedure had been flawed by the arresting officer's failure to communicate the information about the bronchitis to the custody sergeant.

The prosecutor's appeal was allowed. No objective observer could have said that the custody sergeant had reasonable cause to believe that for medical reasons a specimen of breath should not be required. If a constable required a motorist to take a breath test in a police station and the motorist made no effort at all to blow into the device, the motorist could not subsequently contend that he had a reasonable excuse for failing to do so if he did not give details of that excuse at the time the procedure was being carried out.

In *Kemp* v. *Chief Constable of Kent* [1987] RTR 66 the defendant was at a hospital following a road traffic accident and provided a specimen of blood for the purposes of his examination and treatment by the hospital. He was later required to provide a further specimen of blood to ascertain whether or not he was over the prescribed limit for driving but he refused, as he had provided blood earlier.

Although it was accepted that he was in pain and discomfort, he was convicted of the offence, as he had understood the requirement and because his reason for refusal did not amount to a physical or mental incapacity. The defendant was not physically incapable of providing the sample and there was no medical objection to its provision. The defendant's appeal to the Divisional Court was dismissed, as the justices had been plainly entitled to reach the decision they had reached.

In *DPP* v. *Fountain* [1988] RTR 385 the defendant was required to supply a sample of blood and replied, 'In view of the danger of AIDS, I would rather not give blood'. The justices were of the opinion that, had the defendant been given a proper explanation of the procedure for taking samples of blood, he would have supplied it. If his answer constituted a refusal, in law he had a reasonable excuse because of his fear of AIDS. Therefore, they dismissed the allegation.

The prosecutor's appeal was allowed. The burden was on the prosecutor to disprove to the ordinary criminal standard that there was a reasonable excuse. Whether the facts before the court constituted a reasonable excuse was a matter of law, and the defendant's belief in relation to AIDS was not capable of constituting a reasonable excuse.

By way of contrast, the Divisional Court held in *De Freitas* v. *DPP* [1992] Crim LR 894 that a genuine phobia of catching AIDS did amount to a reasonable excuse for failing to provide two specimens of breath for analysis. In this case the Crown Court found that the defendant had a long-standing obsession with his health and a genuine, but unreasonable, fear of contracting AIDS. He was nevertheless convicted of failing to supply the specimens. The Divisional Court allowed his appeal in that the Crown Court had made findings both as to the medical evidence, showing there to be a phobia, and as to the genuineness of it, but had sought to negate those findings by holding that the phobia was an obstinate and absurd belief that could not amount in law to a reasonable excuse.

The distinction between the two cases seems to be that in *Fountain* the defendant was merely expressing a concern about AIDS as his reason, whereas in *De Freitas* there was not only hard evidence as to the existence of a medical condition amounting to a phobia, but also evidence showing the defendant's genuine belief in it. Extreme conditions such as a phobia have been accepted as capable of amounting to a reasonable excuse in the past, although it would appear that something other than the word of the defendant alone is necessary to plead reasonable excuse successfully in such circumstances.

A situation that occurs frequently, especially in view of the nature of the offences involved, is where the defendant puts forward as a reasonable excuse that at the time the requirement is made of him to supply specimens, he is too drunk to understand the requirement. In *DPP* v. *Beech* [1992] RTR 239 the defendant refused to supply a breath specimen as he was too drunk to understand the procedure. The justices accepted this as a reasonable excuse for failing to provide the required specimen and dismissed the allegation. The prosecutor successfully appealed to the Divisional Court. As it was the defendant's self-induced intoxication that rendered him incapable of understanding what was said to him by the police officer, it would defeat the object of the legislation to hold that the fact that the defendant was too drunk to understand what was said to him could provide him with a reasonable excuse. The matter was remitted to the justices with a direction to convict.

However, in *Young (Paula Anne)* v. *DPP* (1993) 157 JP 606 it was held that a state of intoxication could be regarded as a medical reason within the meaning of RTA 1988, s.7(3)(a) so that, following a breath-specimen failure, a police officer was entitled to proceed to require a specimen of blood or urine. Whilst voluntary intoxication could not be a reasonable excuse under s.7(6), it could be a medical reason under s.7(3).

Whether or not a condition amounts to a reasonable excuse will often depend on the evidence before the court. Whilst this evidence need not necessarily be of a medical nature, it was said in *DPP* v. *Ambrose* [1992] RTR 285 that the finding of a physical or mental inability to supply a specimen was a finding only achievable on evidence that would, in almost all imaginable cases, be evidence of a medical nature, and it was not possible to make such a finding on an assumptive basis.

There are, however, some cases where the court has been able to make a finding of reasonable excuse for medical reasons, even though there has been no medical evidence before the court. In *DPP* v. *Pearman* (1993) 157 JP 883 the defendant was terrorised into driving after a party by persons who were rowdy, intoxicated and violent. She was arrested and provided a first breath specimen at the police station. She then lost composure, appeared to be suffering from shock and sobbed continuously. She told the police officers that she felt short of breath and could not provide a further breath sample. She offered to supply blood instead. It was held by the Divisional Court that it was open to the justices, on the facts, to find that she was physically incapable of supplying a breath specimen.

In *DPP* v. *Crofton* [1994] RTR 279 the defendant gave evidence that he had been suffering from depression and that, when depressed, he experienced breathlessness. No medical evidence was called on his behalf. The justices found him to be an honest witness whose evidence was wholly convincing, that he had come close to providing the requisite amount of breath, but it was insufficient each time and that his evidence on important factual issues was supported by police officers present at the police station. They concluded that breathlessness caused by pre-existing depression that was not self-precipitated had caused his failure to provide two specimens of breath. The absence of medical evidence notwithstanding, the justices accepted the defendant had a reasonable excuse for the failure to provide which had not been negated by the prosecutor beyond reasonable doubt.

The Divisional Court declined to overturn a decision made on such unimpeachable findings of fact. The important matters for consideration by the justices were the need for evidence of physical or mental incapability to provide the specimen, that medical evidence would normally be required to support such a claim and the existence of a necessary causative link between the physical or mental conditions and the failure to provide the specimen.

In *DPP* v. *Falzarano* (2001) 165 JP 201 the respondent was required to provide two specimens of breath at a police station. She failed to do so and, at trial, produced medical evidence from her general practitioner that she had been prescribed medication to alleviate panic attacks to which she had a predisposition, and that if she failed to take the medication, she would be more prone to panic attacks, but that such an attack would neither prevent her from understanding what was being said to her, nor would there be anything physical or mental to prevent her providing a specimen. The justices concluded that she had suffered a panic attack that had prevented her from providing a specimen and that she had a reasonable excuse for failing to do so.

The prosecutor's appeal was dismissed. The justices had correctly applied their minds to the need for evidence of physical or mental incapability to provide a specimen; had had in mind that medical evidence would normally be required to support the defence and had carefully considered the evidence of the defendant's general practitioner in the light of legal advice given to them. The justices' findings that the defendant had done her best to provide a breath specimen and that shortness of breath brought on by a panic attack had prevented her from so doing disclosed a causative link between the physical and mental condition of the defendant and the failure on her part to provide a specimen. The justices had been entitled to make those findings of fact on the evidence, and, accordingly, the defendant had a reasonable excuse for failure to provide two specimens of breath for analysis.

Justices should only make a decision on reasonable excuse where it has been raised by the defendant and should not embark on an investigation of their own.

10.9 'DRIVING' OR 'IN CHARGE': EFFECT ON SENTENCE

Where a defendant fails to convince the court that he had a reasonable excuse for refusing or failing to supply the specimen, the sentence for the offence will depend, at least as far as the disqualification provisions provide, on whether the defendant was arrested as being the driver of the vehicle in question or being merely in charge of it.

In *Gardner* v. *DPP* (1989) 153 JP 357 a police officer required the defendant to provide two specimens of breath for analysis during the course of an investigation into an offence of being in charge of a motor vehicle whilst over the prescribed limit. Even though there was ample evidence to show that the defendant was driving at the time of the offence, it was held that the offence attracted only the discretionary disqualification provisions, as the offence of being in charge of the vehicle had been specified by the police officer.

Similarly, in *George* v. *DPP* [1989] RTR 217 the defendant admitted that he had been driving a vehicle on a road, but pleaded guilty to an offence of failing to supply specimens of breath on the basis that it would be presented in court as if he had been in charge of the vehicle. The justices felt that as he had admitted that he had been driving the vehicle, disqualification was obligatory and he was fined and disqualified for three years.

His appeal against sentence was allowed by the Divisional Court. Even though there was just enough evidence for the justices to find that he had been driving rather than in charge of the vehicle, it was wholly contrary to the justice of the prosecution, which had been conducted on an 'in charge' basis and which should therefore have attracted the discretionary disqualification provisions.

These issues formed the basis of the decision in *DPP* v. *Corcoran* [1992] RTR 289 which, for a short period during the course of 1992, provided a glimmer of hope for many motorists that a legal technicality would serve to have their driving licences returned before the end of their disqualification periods.

In *Corcoran* it was held that, because of the difference in maximum punishment specified in Schedule 2 to RTOA 1988 depending upon whether the offence of failing to provide a specimen had been committed after the defendant had been driving or attempting to drive, or in charge of the vehicle, s.7(6) created two offences. Thus, an information alleging that the defendant failed to provide a specimen during the course of an investigation into a s.4 or s.5 offence was bad for duplicity and could not be cured retrospectively; therefore, the justices had been right to dismiss the information for this reason.

Five months later the Divisional Court was able to nullify the effects of *Corcoran* in a number of consolidated appeals nominally headed by *Shaw* v. *DPP* [1993] RTR 45. The leading judgment was given by Watkins LJ who said that in the course of an investigation into an offence under RTA 1988, s.4 or s.5 a police officer could require the provision by the defendant of a specimen for analysis. Provided that specimen had been lawfully required, RTA 1988, s.7(6) then created an offence that was, of itself, the product of a single course of conduct, namely the refusal without reasonable excuse to provide that specimen. On that basis, a charge could not be bad for duplicity.

He concluded that *Corcoran* must have been decided *per incuriam* although conceding at the same time that if that view was wrong, the court would still have taken the rare course in this case of departing from a previous decision on the basis that it was erroneous. He added that it would be of use in similar cases in the future if the defendant were to be informed, at an early stage of the proceedings, of the circumstances that were to be relied on by the prosecution in order to maintain procedural fairness.

The decision in *Shaw* v. *DPP* did not, however, conclude the matter. The issue arose again in *Crampsie* v. *DPP* [1993] RTR 383 in which the Divisional Court opined that:

> it would be helpful if justices would make it clear on which basis they are sentencing. It would be sufficient to say, 'we find you guilty of the offence and, furthermore, we are also satisfied that you were driving, or attempting to drive' or 'we find you guilty of the offence, but we are not satisfied that you were driving or attempting to drive, but only that you were in charge'.

The matter finally came to the attention of the House of Lords in *DPP* v. *Butterworth* [1995] 1 AC 381. The Divisional Court had posed three questions for the House to determine:

1. Does s.7(6) create more than one offence?
2. Does an information which merely alleges that the accused failed to provide a breath sample for analysis comply with the Magistrates' Courts Rules 1981, r.12(1)?

3. In order to comply with the Magistrates' Courts Rules 1981, r.12 and r.100, must an information alleging an offence give sufficient information so that it is manifest what is the maximum penalty for the offence?

The House of Lords held, overruling *DPP* v. *Corcoran* and approving *Shaw* v. *DPP*, that s.7(6) contained a single course of conduct, namely the failure to provide a specimen without reasonable excuse. The constable was carrying out a general investigation into whether a person had committed any offence under RTA 1988, ss.4 or 5. It was not necessary to specify which offence in the charge. The punishment issue was a matter for sentence only if necessary by means of a Newton hearing (*R* v. *Newton* (1983) 77 Cr App R 13). The charge was not bad for duplicity and there was no failure to comply with r.12(1) or r.100 of the 1981 Rules.

The rule therefore is that it is the circumstances of the offence specified by the investigating officer that determine the appropriate maximum sentence in cases where the defendant is charged with an offence of failing to provide a specimen of breath, although there is nothing wrong in the charge specifying both ss.4 and 5 as the reason for requiring the specimen.

CHECKLIST Failing to supply a specimen

1. Was the driver given an adequate warning of the consequences of failing or refusing to provide a specimen?
2. Was the warning couched in terms that the defendant could understand?
3. Does the defendant believe he has been unlawfully arrested? Should he still be advised to comply with the request for a specimen and to argue about the lawfulness of the arrest at a later stage?
4. Does the defendant wish to consult his solicitor or his doctor before complying with the request? Are there circumstances that make this a reasonable excuse?
5. Did the police officer expressly consent to the defendant's discussing the situation with his solicitor or his doctor, thus providing a reasonable excuse?
6. Has the defendant been given a pro forma that makes him believe he is entitled to consult a solicitor before supplying a specimen? Is the form worded in such a way that the court may exercise its discretion under PACE 1984, s.78 to exclude evidence gained in the proceedings?
7. Does the reasonable excuse put forward by the defendant arise from a physical or mental inability to provide the specimen, or would provision constitute a substantial risk to health?
8. If the defendant asserts that he did his best to provide the specimen, why was he unable to do so?
9. Does the defendant have a physical or mental condition that would prevent a specimen being provided?
10. Can medical evidence of this be obtained?
11. Has the defence of reasonable excuse been made out on the balance of probabilities?
12. Has the prosecution negated it beyond reasonable doubt?

159

13. At the time of attempting to provide the specimen, did the defendant inform the police of any medical condition that was likely to prevent or that was preventing him from supplying the specimen?
14. Did the defendant nevertheless try as hard as he was able to supply the required specimen?
15. Does the defendant have a phobia, supported by medical evidence, for failing to provide the specimen?
16. Was the initial investigation on the basis of driving or attempting to drive, or in charge? What is the effect, therefore, on the appropriate maximum penalty?

CHAPTER 11

Causing death whilst under the influence of drink or drugs

11.1 THE LEGISLATION

The Road Traffic Act 1991 inserted a new s.3A into RTA 1988:

(1) If a person causes the death of another person by driving a mechanically propelled vehicle on a road or other public place without due care and attention, or without reasonable consideration for other persons using the road or place, and –

    (a) he is, at the time when he is driving, unfit to drive through drink or drugs, or

    (b) he has consumed so much alcohol that the proportion of it in his breath, blood or urine at the time exceeds the prescribed limit, or

    (c) he is, within 18 hours after that time, required to provide a specimen in pursuance of section 7 of this Act, but without reasonable excuse fails to provide it,

    he is guilty of an offence.

(2) For the purposes of this section a person shall be taken to be unfit to drive at any time when his ability to drive properly is impaired.

(3) Subsection (1)(b) and (c) above shall not apply in relation to a person driving a mechanically propelled vehicle other than a motor vehicle.

11.2 THE OFFENCE

The Road Traffic Law Review Committee, under the chairmanship of Dr Peter North, published its Report in April 1988 making a number of recommendations designed to influence future legislation and to ensure public confidence in road safety. During the course of the committee's deliberations, evidence was tendered by a number of organisations concerned about the increasing number of incidents that led to the death of road users where the driver of a motor vehicle had combined poor driving with excessive consumption of alcohol.

The result of these deliberations is now to be found in RTA 1988, s.3A, which created an offence of causing death by careless driving when under the influence of drink or drugs. The offence requires that it must be the driving of a mechanically propelled vehicle on a road or other public place that causes the death of another person. The offence can be committed, therefore, not only on a road, but also in other places to which the public has access, such as a car park or a caravan site.

The driving must also be without due care and attention or without reasonable consideration for other road users. The driving need not be dangerous and need not fall far below the standard of the reasonably prudent and competent driver doing his best in all the circumstances in order to determine culpability under the section. The words used in the section are the same as those in RTA 1988, s.3 and it can be assumed that case law applicable to the offences of driving without due care and attention and without reasonable consideration for other road users will just as equally apply to this part of the s.3A offence. Whilst this may seem somewhat harsh in the circumstances, it should be remembered that the purpose of the section is to catch those drivers whose driving is poor and whose poor driving is exacerbated by the excessive consumption of alcohol or ingestion of drugs.

The final and most important element of the offence relates to the condition of the driver and the fact that, whilst driving, he has consumed alcohol or drugs in such quantities as to allow the prosecution to prove beyond reasonable doubt that he was unfit to drive through drink or drugs; that the proportion of alcohol in his breath, blood or urine exceeded the prescribed limit or that within 18 hours of the driving taking place he was required to provide a specimen of breath, blood or urine for analysis and failed without reasonable excuse to do so. Case law on the provision of blood or other samples will be just as germane to this issue as to prosecutions under RTA 1988, ss.4, 5 or 7. See, for example, *R* v. *Boyd* [2004] RTR 7 for a case where an evidential sample relied on by the Crown was held to be inadmissible where the prosecution had behaved with 'complete incompetence' so far as the preservation of the blood sample was concerned.

In *R* v. *Millington* (1996) 160 JP 39 the appellant appealed against his conviction for an offence under RTA 1988, s.3A. Whilst driving his vehicle at almost twice the legal limit of alcohol for driving, he failed to see, collided with and killed a pedestrian. He admitted having consumed six vodkas and two pints of beer, but denied that he had been adversely affected by the drink. The issue in the case was whether he had driven without due care and attention and the judge invited the jury to draw inferences from their own experience as to the likelihood that he had been adversely affected by the alcohol and had been driving without due care and attention.

The Court of Appeal said that as the appellant had almost double the permitted level of alcohol in his body, there was evidence of likely effect to put before the jury relevant to carelessness. Expert evidence was not necessary. The court was entitled to consider all the circumstances, including evidence that a driver was adversely affected by drink or that the amount of drink taken was such as would adversely affect a driver.

The offence is triable only on indictment and the maximum penalty on conviction is 14 years' imprisonment or an unlimited fine or both. Until implementation of Criminal Justice Act 2003, s.285 on 27 February 2004 the maximum period of imprisonment was 10 years and practitioners will need to be aware of the impact of this change when advising clients. The offence is subject to a period of mandatory disqualification for a minimum period of two years and compulsory endorsement of the offender's driving licence with between 3 and 11 penalty points. Since 31 January 2002, the Driving Licences (Disqualification until Test Passed) (Prescribed Offence) Order 2001 also requires a court disqualifying anyone for an offence under s.3A (committed on or after that date) to order that the driver must pass an extended driving test before obtaining a full driving licence at the end of any period of disqualification. In addition, the offence is added to the category of drink-driving offences for which a further offence committed within a period of 10 years of a similar matter increases the minimum period of disqualification to three years.

The first case to consider the sentencing implications of s.3A was *Attorney-General's References (nos. 14 and 24 of 1993)* [1994] 1 WLR 530 in the course of which judgment, the Lord Chief Justice, Lord Taylor, said:

> These reforms show an intention by Parliament to strengthen the criminal law, to reduce death on the roads by increasing the punishment available to the courts, and by specifically targeting those who cause death whilst driving with excess alcohol. The five-year maximum sentence for causing death by dangerous driving has been doubled. In tandem with that, causing death by the less serious form of culpable driving, characterised as careless, carries the same maximum sentence if coupled with driving whilst unfit through drink or over the limit. The latter offences do not require proof of a causal connection between the drink and the death. Thus, under section 3A, whoever drives with excess alcohol does so at his or her peril, and even if the driving is merely careless but death results, the courts' powers to punish are the same as for causing death by dangerous driving.

The offence under s.3A, although requiring proof only of careless driving rather than dangerous driving, also has built into it the aggravating feature of consumption of alcohol or drugs. Thus, where a driver is over the limit, and kills someone as a result of his careless driving a prison sentence will ordinarily be appropriate. The length of sentence will, of course, depend upon the aggravating and mitigating circumstances in the particular case, but especially on the extent of the carelessness and the amount the defendant is over the limit. In an exceptional case, if the alcohol level at the time of the offence is just over the border line, the carelessness is momentary, and there is strong mitigation, a non-custodial sentence may be possible. But in other cases a prison sentence is required to punish the offender, to deter others from drinking and driving, and to reflect the public's abhorrence of deaths being caused by drivers with excess alcohol.

The main guideline case on causing death by dangerous driving and careless driving whilst under the influence of drink or drugs is *R* v. *Cooksley* [2004] 1 Cr App Rep (S) 1. The Court of Appeal identified a number of aggravating and mitigating factors for courts to take into account when sentencing such offences, but made it clear that it did not consider the list to be exhaustive:

1. It will usually be obvious to the offender that the driving was dangerous and therefore deserves to be punished accordingly.
2. Parliament regarded the consequences of dangerous driving as being a relevant consideration so that if death does result, this in itself can justify a heavier sentence than could be imposed for a case where death does not result.
3. The impact on the family (where death results) is a matter that the courts can and should take into account.
4. In determining sentence, it is important for courts to stress the message as to the dangers that can result from dangerous driving on the road. Motor vehicles can be lethal if not driven properly and, this being so, drivers must know that if as a result of their driving dangerously, a person is killed, no matter what the mitigating circumstances, normally only a custodial sentence will be imposed. This is because of the need to deter other drivers from driving in a dangerous manner and because of the gravity of the offence.

The court said that the following factors indicated a highly culpable standard of driving at the time of the offence:

*   the consumption of drugs (including legal medication known to cause drowsiness) or of alcohol, ranging from a couple of drinks to a motorised pub crawl;
*   greatly excessive speed; racing; competitive driving against another vehicle; 'showing-off';
*   disregard of warnings from fellow passengers;
*   a prolonged, persistent and deliberate course of very bad driving;
*   aggressive driving (such as driving much too close to the vehicle in front, persistent inappropriate attempts to overtake or cutting in after overtaking);
*   driving whilst the driver's attention is avoidably distracted, for example, by reading or by use of a mobile phone (especially if hand-held);
*   driving when knowingly suffering from a medical condition that significantly impairs the offender's driving skills;
*   driving when knowingly deprived of adequate sleep or rest;

- driving a poorly maintained or dangerously loaded vehicle, especially where this has been motivated by commercial concerns;
- other offences committed at the same time which tend to show driving habitually below an acceptable standard such as driving without ever having held a driving licence, driving whilst disqualified, without insurance, whilst a learner under supervision; taking a vehicle without consent or driving a stolen vehicle;
- having previous convictions for motoring offences particularly offences that involve bad driving or the consumption of excessive alcohol before driving;
- more than one person killed as a result of the offence (especially if the offender knowingly put more than one person at risk or the occurrence of multiple deaths was foreseeable);
- serious injury to one or more victims, in addition to the death(s);
- irresponsible behaviour at the time of the offence, such as failing to stop, falsely claiming that one of the victims was responsible for the crash, or trying to throw the victim off the bonnet of the car by swerving in order to escape;
- causing death in the course of dangerous driving in an attempt to avoid detection or apprehension;
- the fact the offence was committed whilst on bail for other offences will always be an aggravating factor.

The court identified mitigating factors as follows:

- a good driving record;
- the absence of previous convictions;
- a timely plea of guilty;
- genuine shock or remorse (which may be greater if the victim is either a close relation or a friend);
- the offender's age (but only in cases where lack of driving experience has contributed to the commission of the offence); and
- the fact that the offender has also been seriously injured as a result of the accident caused by the dangerous driving.

Where there are no identified aggravating factors, the court was of the view that, after a trial, a custodial sentence of 12–18 months was appropriate for adult offenders. Offences of intermediate culpability where the dangerous driving was momentary or there was an error of judgement or a short period of bad driving would merit a custodial sentence of 2–3 years rising to 5 years where there were a number of aggravating factors present. A starting point of 4–5 years would be appropriate where the standard of the offender's driving disclosed one or two aggravating factors and culpability was high.

Disqualifications of up to 2 years would be appropriate where the offender had a good driving record and the offence was a momentary error of judgement. Where the offence and the offender's record show a tendency to disregard the rules of the road or drive carelessly or inappropriately, a disqualification of 3–5 years was merited. Disqualifications of 5–10 years would be appropriate where the offence and the offender's record represent a real and continuing danger to other road users.

In *R* v. *Gray* [2006] 1 Cr App Rep (S) 126 the Court of Appeal considered the impact of the increase in maximum sentence from 10 to 14 years on the guidelines in *Cooksley*. Maurice Kay LJ said:

> It seems to us that, since *Cooksley*, Parliament, reflecting public concern, particularly about the gravest cases, has increased the maximum sentence by 40%. That, we apprehend, was mainly to cater for the worst of cases such as that of *Noble* [2002] EWCA Crim 1713 which contained so many aggravating features and no mitigating ones whatsoever. . . We must have regard to the increase in the statutory maximum, but that does not mean that sentences at every point of the scale and in every case must be uplifted schematically by 40% since *Cooksley*.

The court went on to reduce a sentence of 30 months' custody to one of 21 months.

CHAPTER 12

Sentencing

12.1 PENALTIES FOR THE OFFENCES

Other than the s.3A offence of causing death by careless driving when under the influence of drink or drugs, which is an indictable offence, the offences of drinking and driving and related matters contained in RTA 1988, ss. 4–7 are triable on a summary basis only in the magistrates' court.

Unless there are aggravating factors present to make the offence so serious that only a custodial sentence can be justified, the usual sentence in the magistrates' court will either be a financial penalty or, if the offence is seen as more serious having regard to the way in which it was committed, a community sentence with requirements.

In 2000 a working party consisting of lay magistrates, district judges, justices' clerks and others involved in the criminal justice system at the magistrates' courts level produced the Magistrates' Courts Sentencing Guidelines, which set a 'starting point' for consideration of a number of common offences in the magistrates' courts. (The Guidelines, which were last substantially amended in January 2004, are now part of the Adult Court Bench Book issued by the Judicial Studies Board.) The Guidelines were originally published with the approval of the Lord Chief Justice and the Lord Chancellor who said:

> They are of course only guidelines – they do not curtail your independent discretion to impose the sentences you think are right, case by case. But they exist to help you in that process. To give you a starting point. To give you more information in reaching your decisions. And, importantly, they help to assist the magistracy to maintain an overall consistency of approach.

In determining the amount of a fine to be imposed on any offender, Criminal Justice Act 2003 (CJA 2003), s.164 requires the court to take into account, *inter alia*, the financial circumstances of the offender so far as they are known to the court (s.164(1)) and to ensure that the amount of the fine reflects the seriousness of the offence (s.164(2)). The guidelines contained in the Adult Court Bench Book reflect this legal position to the extent that offences are divided into three grades of seriousness – 'A', 'B' and 'C' – and then applied to the financial means of the offender whereby a 'grade A' level fine equates to 50 per cent of weekly net income, 'grade B' to 100 per cent and 'grade C' to 150 per cent.

There are three other factors which the court must consider when determining the appropriate sentence for a drink-driving offence under CJA 2003:

- s.143(2) requires the court to determine the seriousness of an offence by taking account of any previous convictions of the offender or any failure to respond to previous sentences;
- s.144 requires the court to have regard to the fact that the offender has pleaded guilty to the offence and the circumstances in which and the stage in the proceedings at which that plea was entered; and
- s.172 places a duty on all courts when sentencing an offender to have regard to any guidelines issued by the Sentencing Guidelines Council which are relevant to the offender's case.

It should be noted that the requirement in s.143, when applied generally to road traffic offences, can lead to a situation of double jeopardy, where points from previous offences on the licence accumulate leading to a 'totting' disqualification before any consideration is given to the aggravating seriousness of the offence to reflect those same previous endorsements.

In the past there has been little opportunity for the Court of Appeal or Divisional Court to offer guidance to magistrates on the appropriate circumstances that would lead to a custodial sentence for offences involving drinking and driving.

In *R* v. *Cook* [1996] RTR 304 an offender of previous good character was sentenced to two months' imprisonment and disqualified for four years (and until a driving test was passed) for a drink-driving offence where the alcohol level was found to be 140 µg in 100 ml of breath.

On appeal, the Court of Appeal said that it could never be appropriate to imprison a man for this sort of criminality, which was at the lower end of the scale. The sentence of imprisonment was quashed and the disqualification period reduced to two years.

At the time the guidelines used by the Magistrates' Association suggested consideration of custody at the 100 µg plus level. The decision in *R* v. *Cook* therefore, led to justifiable concerns. However, the Lord Chief Justice, having consulted the judges constituting the court in *R* v. *Cook* was able to announce in *R* v. *Shoult* [1996] RTR 298 that the decision in *Cook* had been based on a 'misunderstanding about the effect of the figure as to the alcohol content in the breath sample'. He went on to approve the sentencing guidelines, saying that the penalties in that document were 'sound and appropriate' although each case was to be considered individually on its own merits.

As part of the sentence on conviction of an offence under RTA 1988, ss.4(1), 5(1) and 7(6), the court is obliged to impose on the offender a mandatory disqualification from driving for a period of at least 12 months, unless there are special reasons (see **para. 12.4**) for not doing so.

Where an offender has been convicted of one of these offences and has, within the 10 years immediately preceding the commission of the offence, been convicted of a similar offence, then the minimum period of 12 months is increased to three years (RTOA 1988, s.34(3)).

The guidelines in the Adult Court Bench Book link the length of the disqualification to the amount by which the alcohol level of the offender exceeds the prescribed limit. This is in line with previous decisions of the Court of Appeal where the courts have sought to differentiate between offenders who are only just over the prescribed limit and those who are far in excess – and where other features of the offence may aggravate the situation.

Other than in exceptional circumstances it has been the policy of the Court of Appeal to avoid excessively lengthy periods of disqualification on the basis that to impose such a long disqualification only leads to the offender's continuing to drive and eventually facing imprisonment for driving whilst disqualified. In *R* v. *Rivano* (1994) 158 JP 288 the appellant was sentenced to six months' imprisonment and disqualified from driving for life following his conviction in the Crown Court for driving whilst disqualified and driving with excess alcohol where his lower reading was 120 µg in 100 ml of breath. He was already subject to a disqualification imposed for 10 years on a previous occasion.

The Court of Appeal reduced the period of disqualification to one of 10 years. There were no very exceptional circumstances, such as psychiatric evidence, to indicate that the appellant would be a danger to the public indefinitely which required disqualification for life.

It is *not* a consideration to be taken into account when determining the length of a disqualification that the offender will be able to apply to the magistrates' court to remove the disqualification under RTOA 1988, s.42. This section provides that:

(1) Subject to the provisions of this section a person who, by an order of a court is disqualified may apply to the court by which the order was made to remove the disqualification.

(2) On any such application, the court may, as it thinks proper having regard to –

    (a) the character of the person disqualified and his conduct subsequent to the order,

    (b) the nature of the offence, and

    (c) any other circumstances of the case,

    either by order remove the disqualification as from such date as may be specified in the order or refuse the application.

(3) No application shall be made under subsection (1) above for the removal of a disqualification before the expiration of whichever is relevant of the following periods from the date of the order by which the disqualification was imposed, that is –

(a) two years, if the disqualification is for less than four years,
(b) one half of the period of disqualification, if it is for less than ten years, but not less than four years,
(c) five years in any other case;

and in determining the expiration of the period after which under this subsection a person may apply for the removal of a disqualification, any time after the conviction during which the disqualification was suspended or he was not disqualified shall be disregarded.

(4) Where an application under subsection (1) above is refused, a further application under that subsection shall not be entertained if made within three months after the date of the refusal.

In *Corner* v. *Southend Crown Court* (2006) 170 JP 6 the claimant appealed to the Crown Court against a disqualification imposed by magistrates for four years with a requirement to undergo an extended driving test. The appeal was dismissed, but the court commented that the claimant could apply to the magistrates' court after two years to remove the disqualification. The Divisional Court said that it was quite wrong for the judge to have made such a reference. If a proper disqualification is imposed then there could be no reference properly made to any possible reduction. The court exercised its jurisdiction to reduce the disqualification to two years.

Examples taken from the Adult Court Bench Book Guidelines are shown on the following pages (see **Table 12.1**).

12.2 INTERIM DISQUALIFICATION

Once a motorist has pleaded guilty to or been convicted of an offence which, at the sentencing stage, will carry a period of mandatory disqualification there is no reason why the motorist should not be removed from the road after the conviction has been recorded but before sentence where, for example, there had been an adjournment for reports. Section 26 of the RTOA 1988 provides for the court to impose an interim disqualification in the following circumstances:

(1) Where a magistrates' court –

(a) commits an offender to the Crown Court under section 6 of the Powers of Criminal Courts (Sentencing) Act 2000, or any enactment mentioned in subs (4) of that section, or any enactment to which that section applies, or
(b) remits an offender to another magistrates' court under section 10 of that Act,

to be dealt with for an offence involving obligatory or discretionary disqualification, it may order him to be disqualified until he has been dealt with in respect of the offence.

(2) Where a court in England and Wales –

(a) defers passing sentence on an offender under section 1 of that Act in respect of an offence involving obligatory or discretionary disqualification, or

(b) adjourns after convicting an offender of such an offence, but before dealing with him for the offence,

it may order the defendant to be disqualified until he has been dealt with in respect of the offence.

(3) [*Relates to Scotland*]

(4) Subject to subsection (5) below, an order under this section shall cease to have effect at the end of the period of six months beginning with the day on which it is made, if it has not ceased to have effect before that time.

(5) [*Relates to Scotland*]

(6) Where a court orders a person to be disqualified under this section ('the first order'), no court shall make a further order under this section in respect of the same offence or any offence in respect of which an order could have been made under this section at the time the first order was made.

This interim power of disqualification has been seen by sentencers as a useful tool when it has been necessary to adjourn a case after an unequivocal guilty plea. Theoretically, the power can be exercised at any time after a guilty plea has been entered or a conviction recorded, although practitioners should be alert to challenge such an order where, for example, the adjournment is to consider special reasons, sentence after a contested trial (especially where there has been an argument on a point of law) and where the conviction has been recorded in the absence of the defendant.

Once the defendant has been sentenced, the period of the final disqualification will be reduced by the period of any interim disqualification imposed upon the defendant. In effect, any disqualification imposed as part of the sentence is deemed to run from the date the interim disqualification was imposed. The record will show the length of the disqualification in full with the relevant start date shown as the date of the interim disqualification.

It should be noted that only one interim disqualification may be imposed for a set of offences, up to a maximum of six months, prompting many courts to word such disqualifications as 'disqualified until sentence has been passed and in any case for not longer than six months'.

12.3 MAXIMUM PENALTIES

Whilst the offence under RTA 1988, s.3A (causing death by careless driving whilst under the influence of drink or drugs) is triable only on indictment, all other offences under those parts of RTA 1988 dealt with in this book are purely summary offences.

A table showing the various maximum penalties for offences contained in the drinking and driving legislation follows (**Table 12.2**).

171

12.4   SPECIAL REASONS

The legislation

Section 34 of RTOA 1988 provides:

(1)   Where a person is convicted of an offence involving obligatory disqualification, the court must order him to be disqualified for such period not less than twelve months as the court thinks fit unless the court for special reasons thinks fit to order him to be disqualified for a shorter period or not to order him to be disqualified.

[. . .]

(3)   Where a person convicted of an offence under any of the following provisions of the Road Traffic Act 1988, that is –

(a)   section 4(1) (driving or attempting to drive while unfit),

(aa) section 3A (causing death by careless driving when under the influence of drink or drugs),

(b)   section 5(1)(a) (driving or attempting to drive with excess alcohol), and

(c)   section 7(6) (failing to provide a specimen) where that is an offence involving obligatory disqualification,

(d)   section 7A(6) (failing to allow a specimen to be subjected to a laboratory test) where that is an offence involving obligatory disqualification,

has within the ten years immediately preceding the commission of the offence been convicted of any such offence, subsection (1) above shall apply in relation to him as if the reference to twelve months were a reference to three years.

The basic law relating to the requirements to be fulfilled before a finding can be made that special reasons exist is to be found in *R* v. *Wickens* (1958) 42 Cr App R 236 where the Court of Criminal Appeal prescribed four criteria that must exist in order to raise the issue of special reasons:

(a)   it must be a mitigating or extenuating circumstance;

(b)   it must not amount in law to a defence to the charge;

(c)   it must be directly connected with the commission of the offence; and

(d)   the matter must be one that the court ought properly to take into consideration when imposing punishment.

However, in *Jarvis* v. *DPP* (2001) 165 JP 15 the Court of Appeal said that in breathalyser (and dangerous driving) cases, the appropriate authority to refer to is not *R* v. *Wickens*, but *R* v. *Jackson*, *R* v. *Hart* (1970) 53 Cr App R 431. The facts of *Jarvis* are that the appellant pleaded guilty at a magistrates' court to an offence of dangerous driving. It was submitted on her behalf, however, that because at the time of the offence she was suffering from hypoglycaemia brought on by diabetes, the offence had been committed through no fault of her own and the magistrates were therefore entitled to find that a special reason existed for not disqualifying her from driving. The magistrates rejected this contention and disqualified the appellant for 12 months. Her appeal against the justices' decision to the Crown Court on the existence of special reasons was dismissed. She appealed by way of case stated.

The considerations that apply to both breathalyser and dangerous driving offences are different from those that were perceived to apply in *Wickens*. The special reasons put forward in the instant case only related to the offence of dangerous driving in the sense that it was part of the context of the offence. In so far as it was a circumstance peculiar to the offender, as distinguished from the offence, it plainly fell outside the ambit of permissible special reasons as formulated by Lord Goddard CJ in *Whittall* v. *Kirby* [1947] 1 KB 194:

> A 'special reason' within the exception is one which is special to the facts of the particular case, that is, special to the facts which constitute the offence. It is, in other words, a mitigating or extenuating circumstance, not amounting in law to a defence to the charge, yet directly connected with the commission of the offence, and one which the court ought properly to take into consideration when imposing punishment. A circumstance peculiar to the offender as distinguished from the offence is not a 'special reason' within the exception.

The facts in *Jackson* were that the defendant suffered from a liver complaint, which interfered with his blood pressure and caused the duration of retention of alcohol in his blood and therefore his vulnerability to being over the limit on a breathalyser test to be longer than usual. It was found that the defendant was not aware of that condition. Sachs LJ, in giving the judgment of the court, set out the passage from *Whittall* v. *Kirby* previously cited, including the last sentence of that passage in the judgment of Lord Goddard CJ. He described that statement as to the distinction between matters relating to the offence and matters relating to the offender as a vital principle of general application. But he went on to say that the special reasons that the court may take into account may differ according to the nature of the offence charged.

It was these two considerations that led the Court of Appeal (Criminal Division) in *Jackson* and *Hart* to hold that *Wickens* was not authority in relation to cases under the Road Safety Act 1967 – that is to say, putting it globally, breathalyser cases. That was because the test under those provisions is purely objective: whether the blood is over the limit. The physical condition of the accused that leads to the reading – whether a liver complaint as in *Jackson* or a physical disability as in *Stewart* – is a condition special to the offender, not the offence. The court expressed the view that in breathalyser cases the appropriate authority to refer to is not now *Wickens* but rather *Jackson* and *Hart*. The reason for that is the reason given in *Jackson* and *Hart* – that the considerations to apply in respect of a breathalyser offence are different from those that were perceived in *Wickens* to apply in a case of being incapable of control of a vehicle.

That consideration and approach in my judgment is, *a fortiori*, when, as here, the charge is dangerous driving. There the offence is the mode of driving whatsoever may be the reason for it. Mrs Jarvis' condition was special to her. It formed no part of the content of the offence. It only related to the offence in the sense that it was part of the context in which the offence was committed; but applying the test formulated by Lord Goddard CJ, that matter plainly falls outside the ambit of permissible special reasons.

In *Lodwick* v. *Brow* [1984] RTR 394 it was argued that a special reason for not imposing a mandatory disqualification existed in circumstances where, after a road traffic accident, the defendant had provided a sample of blood at a hospital, which had been properly divided, but which had been lost because the defendant suffered post-traumatic amnesia after the accident and therefore could not have his own part tested. The prosecutor's appeal against the decision not to impose a disqualification was allowed by the Divisional Court. Special reasons had to relate to the commission of the offence and as the blood-test procedures had taken place after the offence had been completed, the loss of the specimen could not be a special reason that related to the commission of the offence.

It is not necessary that the defendant give an explanation at the time of the offence of any reason for refusing to comply with a reasonable request by a police officer, but if subsequently he wishes to argue that special reasons exist for not disqualifying him this is a factor to be taken into account by the court.

In *DPP* v. *Kinnersley* [1993] RTR 105 the defendant raised as a reasonable excuse for not providing specimens of breath his fear of contracting HIV and the possibility of AIDS. He did not tell the police at the time of his fears, and the justices convicted him of the offence as they did not believe that he had a reasonable excuse. The defendant then submitted that there were special reasons for not disqualifying him using the same argument. The justices acceded to this request and did not impose a disqualification when sentencing.

The prosecutor unsuccessfully appealed. The Divisional Court held that a motorist's failure to give an explanation at the time of refusal did not exclude a future finding that special reasons existed, although it would be an important factor in the court's deliberations. A police officer was under no legal duty to explain to the defendant that the mouthpiece was sterile, although this would be a factor to be taken into consideration when deciding whether a special reason existed.

A good example of a case where the criteria in *R* v. *Wickens* were held to be applicable was *Bobin* v. *DPP* [1999] RTR 375. The defendant, having had the breathalyser procedure explained to him, then asked the police officer whether failure to provide a specimen was 'a definite disqualification'. The officer replied that it wasn't! This inaccurate information fulfilled all the requirements for a special reason in that:

- it was a mitigating or extenuating circumstance;

- it did not amount in law to a defence to a charge of failing to provide;
- the inaccurate information affected the driver's decision whether or not to provide a specimen and accordingly it was directly connected with the offence; and
- it was a matter the court ought properly to take into account when sentencing.

In *Woolfe* v. *DPP* [2006] All ER(D) 261 the court considered whether the *Wickens* criterion that the special reason 'must not amount in law to a defence to the charge' was to be interpreted as meaning that if a defence failed at trial, it was not then available as a special reason pertinent to sentence. The appellant suffered from a medical condition of regurgitation of stomach content into the oesophagus and was convicted after running a defence to the allegation of driving whilst over the prescribed limit that the breathalyser reading had wrongly taken into account alcohol in his mouth at the time of the provision of the specimen. The justices then refused to allow him to plead the same matter as a special reason relevant to whether or not he should be disqualified.

The Divisional Court said that the justices had been in error in excluding special reasons on the basis that as previous case law on the point had precluded the reason from being a defence, so it similarly precluded it as a possible basis of special reasons. The two are to be treated as separate issues and can form the basis of separate pleadings before the court.

Ignorance of the effects of alcohol

There is an assumption by the courts that motorists have more knowledge than is actually the case about the more scientific aspects of the effect of alcohol on the body. In *DPP* v. *White* [1988] RTR 267 the defendant was stopped and breathalysed at the roadside – the test was negative. He drove on and was stopped again, at which time he provided a positive roadside test and was arrested. He was taken to a police station where analysis of his breath showed him to be above the prescribed limit.

In declining to find there was a special reason because of the defendant's reasonable and honest belief that he was fit to drive, the Divisional Court said every person should know that after consuming alcohol, there was a gradual build-up of alcohol in the bloodstream rather than an immediate release. Therefore, any person who consumed alcohol and then drove ran the risk of being over the prescribed limit at some stage of that driving.

Ignorance of the effects of alcohol was also considered in *DPP* v. *O'Meara* [1989] RTR 24 where the defendant, a bus driver, drank six or seven pints of beer over a period of four hours, slept for eight hours, consumed a meal and then drove a vehicle on a road. He was subsequently breathalysed and pleaded guilty to driving whilst over the prescribed limit. He pleaded as a special reason that his ignorance of the long-term effects of alcohol and their dispersal rates was such that a disqualification should not be imposed.

The Divisional Court rejected this approach. Whilst the facts could amount to a mitigating or extenuating circumstance, they did not amount to a defence and ought properly to be taken into account when sentence was imposed, the fact that the defendant did not believe himself to be over the prescribed limit was connected not directly with the commission of the offence, but to the offender and, therefore, ignorance of the long-term effects of alcohol could not constitute a special reason.

Consumption of other products containing an alcohol base does not provide a special reason even if the defendant is unaware of the whole effect of the consumption. In *DPP* v. *Jowle* (1999) 163 JP 85 a motorist provided breath samples which, on analysis, proved to contain 94 µg of alcohol per 100 ml of breath. The defendant argued that his addiction to a popular brand of mouthwash, which had led to this reading, should be treated as a special reason. The reading was consistent with his having consumed 800 ml of mouthwash. The Divisional Court said that the magistrates' finding of there being special reasons was perverse. Over a period of a considerable amount of time the respondent had known that if he drank mouthwash, it gave him a lift. On the day of the offence he took mouthwash and drove a motor vehicle erratically. It was impossible to conclude that he could not have realised that he was not in a fit state to drive.

Emergency situations

Whilst it has been accepted that an emergency situation is capable of being a special reason, courts have been slow to find such where there has been an alternative course of action available. In *DPP* v. *Waller* [1989] RTR 112 the defendant had received a telephone call from his fiancée, who told him that she had just received a threatening telephone call from her former husband and requested the defendant to collect her immediately. The justices found that there was a special reason, as the defendant was genuine in his view that an emergency existed and no course of action was open to him other than to drive in order to remove his distressed fiancée from the threat.

The Divisional Court held that no special reason existed. There must have been means, other than driving away from the scene, of removing his fiancée from the perceived threat and the defendant must have known that he was over the prescribed limit at the time that he set out to drive. The defendant had a duty in this sort of case to consider whether any other means existed of concealing her from her momentarily expected ex-husband, other than taking her away in his motor vehicle. The emergency had ceased at the time that the defendant collected his fiancée from the restaurant, and a special reason could not exist after that time that would prevent the defendant from being disqualified.

The test for deciding whether or not an emergency situation requires a drinking motorist to drive in order to remedy the situation was set out by the Divisional Court in *DPP* v. *Bristow* [1998] RTR 100. In this case the defendant, who had been drinking at home, was informed that his children had been assaulted and were being held, against their will, in a nearby house. The magistrates found that although there were other friends with him who could have driven, he had to take immediate action without time to make reasonable inquiries into alternative ways of resolving the problem. He had, therefore, driven a short distance across a housing estate on quiet roads and in a well-maintained vehicle. The court found these facts to constitute special reasons for exercising their discretion not to disqualify.

The prosecutor's appeal was allowed. The key question to be asked in such cases was what would a sober, reasonable and responsible friend of the defendant present at the time, but himself a non-driver and thus unable to help, have advised in the circumstances: drive or do not drive? Justices could only properly find special reasons and exercise discretion not to disqualify if they thought it a real possibility rather than merely an off-chance that such a person would have advised the defendant to drive.

The most critical factors which will influence that advice will be how much the defendant had had to drink, what threat he would pose to others when driving in that condition given the distance proposed, the likely state of the roads and condition of the vehicle, how acute was the problem that existed and what, if any, alternatives were open to the defendant. These four matters should be taken as complementing the seven listed in *Chatters* v. *Burke* [1986] 1 WLR 1321 (see below), which focus more narrowly on cases where the defendant has driven only the very shortest distance. Applying those considerations to the facts of *Bristow* should have led to a finding that the only advice a sober, responsible friend could have given would be not to drive.

Duress

The availability of the defence of duress in a motoring case was first alluded to in *R* v. *Willer* [1987] RTR 22, a case of reckless driving, and extended to cases of driving with excess alcohol in *DPP* v. *Bell* [1992] Crim LR 176 where it was held that the defendant had to act out of fear of death or personal injury as would a sober person of reasonable firmness sharing the same characteristics as the driver.

A developing theme of duress is whether necessity or duress of circumstances can be used to base a special reason not to disqualify in cases of drinking and driving. There is an obvious inter-relationship between special reasons and the complete defence of necessity or duress of circumstances and, in appropriate circumstances, a genuine emergency may give rise to a complete defence.

In *DPP* v. *Goddard* [1998] RTR 463 the defendant, who had been assaulted in a public house the previous evening, went back to the premises the following day. Having had a drink, he went to get his belongings from his car, not intending to drive. He was then further assaulted and, in order to escape, got into his car and drove eight miles to his sister's house. His special reasons plea failed. There had been an emergency at the time of driving away from the car park, but once in a position of relative safety, he should have ceased driving.

In similar circumstances, the Divisional Court considered whether duress could be open as an absolute defence to a motorist. In *Tomkinson* v. *DPP* [2001] RTR 38 the defendant was violently assaulted by her husband after a New Year's Eve party. The husband also inflicted injuries upon himself and left for the hospital warning his wife to be gone by the time he returned. Having only recently moved to the area she decided to drive to her former home where her children would be. After driving for 72 miles she was stopped and positively breathalysed.

She was acquitted by justices of the drink-drive offence on the basis that she believed the threat of death or serious injury to be an ongoing one if she were to remain at home. The prosecutor's appeal was allowed. Although, in extreme circumstances, English law recognised a defence of duress by circumstances where the accused could be said to be acting reasonably and proportionately in order to avoid the threat of injury, this was not the case at the time of her arrest, as she was no longer subject to any effective threat at the hands of her husband. There was no basis for the conclusion by the justices that a sober woman of reasonable firmness would or might have responded to the situation as the defendant did.

Similarly, in *DPP* v. *Hicks* (2002) 166 JPN 594 the Court of Appeal refused to allow a defence of necessity to be established in circumstances where alternative courses of action, other than driving, had been open to the father of a small child taken ill who had been on his way to an all-night chemists to purchase an over-the-counter remedy. Had the illness been a serious one, a reasonable person would have asked neighbours to call a doctor or would have used a public callbox.

Shortness of distance

A reason often put forward as a possible ground for finding that the mandatory disqualification provisions of RTOA 1988 should not be invoked is the shortness of the distance driven by the defendant prior to being stopped and breathalysed. In *De Munthe* v. *Stewart* [1982] RTR 27 the defendant was asked by a police officer who had just seen him park his car to move it as it was causing an obstruction. Whilst he was re-parking it, the police officer formed a reasonable suspicion that the defendant had consumed alcohol and required him to provide a specimen of breath. Subsequently, the defendant was convicted of driving whilst over the prescribed limit. Before sentence, the defendant put forward special reasons to avoid disqualification based on the fact that the driving complained of was undertaken at the police officer's request. This argument was rejected by the stipendiary magistrate dealing with the case and, on appeal, by the Divisional Court, which held that account had to be taken not only of the driving having been done at the constable's request, but also that the defendant had, until that time, been driving voluntarily, thus negating any special reasons that might have existed because of the officer's request.

In *Redmond* v. *Parry* [1986] RTR 146 the defendant had driven his car into a hotel car park where he was attending a function with his wife. They had agreed previously that the wife would be driving home after the event. On returning to the car the wife requested that the defendant back the car out from the parking space: he did so and collided with another car.

The defendant submitted that the shortness of the distance he drove in the car park, coupled with his intention not to drive further that night and the absence of pedestrians in the vicinity, were sufficient to constitute a special reason for not disqualifying him from driving. This argument was not accepted by the justices who disqualified him. In allowing his subsequent appeal, the Divisional Court held that the fact that the defendant had only driven a short distance in these particular circumstances was capable of amounting to a special reason. The case was remitted to the justices with a direction to consider the case in the light of this finding.

In *Chatters* v. *Burke* [1986] 1 WLR 1321 the Divisional Court laid down seven criteria that the court must take into account when considering whether special reasons were to be found in cases such as these. The defendant, who had been drinking, asked a friend to drive him home. On the way, the driver lost control of the vehicle and rolled on to a field adjacent to the highway. The defendant then drove the car from the field and on to the highway where he waited for the police.

On appeal by the prosecutor against the justices' decision to find that the shortness of the distance driven was a special reason for not disqualifying, the Divisional Court identified seven criteria to be taken into account in deciding whether or not a special reason existed:

- the distance driven;
- the manner of the driving;
- the state of the vehicle;
- the intention of the driver about driving further;
- the prevailing conditions of the road and traffic on it;
- the possibility of danger by contact with other users on the road; and
- the reason why the vehicle was driven.

The court went on to say that, of these criteria, by far the most important was the question of contact causing danger with other road users. The distance travelled was not, in itself, sufficient for a finding to be made that special reasons existed. Where this was the only factor put forward to justify a finding of special reasons, courts should be slow to make such a finding. Similarly, in *DPP* v. *Conroy* (2003) 167 JP 418, where the principal reason put forward was that there was no original intention to drive after consuming alcohol, it was said that the court should be very slow to find that a special reason exists.

These criteria were germane to the issue in *DPP* v. *Corcoran* (1991) 155 JP 597 in which the defendant had left his car outside a theatre in Bristol. After the show, and having consumed alcohol, he drove a short distance of 40 yards to a car park where he intended to leave it for the night. There were pedestrians in the area, but no other cars and it was accepted that no danger was caused to other road users. It was held by the Divisional Court that the shortness of the distance driven, coupled with the absence of any danger to the public were capable of amounting to a special reason for not imposing a mandatory disqualification on the defendant.

Another important factor in these circumstances is the intention of the driver at the time of driving. In *DPP* v. *Humphreys* (2000) 164 JP 502 the defendant was seen late at night in the driver's seat of a car, with a friend trying to push the car from a parking bay on to the main road. The police were called and found the defendant trying to 'hot-wire' the vehicle. At trial the magistrates found special reasons not to disqualify him because of the shortness of the distance driven.

The Divisional Court said that it was not the fact that the vehicle was only driven for six feet that mattered, it was the fact that the driver intended to drive it on the public highway in order to get home with all the attendant danger that entailed, given that he was unfit to drive, which was germane.

Laced drinks

If the question of distance travelled has provided a number of arguments over special reasons in recent years, then that of 'laced drinks' has proved to be just as contentious.

In *Pridige* v. *Grant* [1985] RTR 196 the defendant pleaded guilty to driving a motor vehicle whilst the proportion of alcohol in his blood was 180 mg of alcohol in 100 ml of blood. He gave evidence that he had abstained from drinking alcohol for a number of years for medical reasons and drank only non-alcoholic lager. He had been to a party where, without his knowledge, his drink had been laced with vodka and he had then driven home. Apart from feeling tired, which he attributed to a long day at the office, he was unaware that he had consumed alcohol.

The Divisional Court held that, in considering whether or not a special reason existed in these circumstances, the court had to decide whether the defendant should have realised that he was not fit to drive by reason of the presence of alcohol in his body. Where a defendant had no reason to think that he had consumed alcohol, a court could find that there was a special reason for not disqualifying, subject to the defendant's inferred knowledge that his condition must be due to consumption of alcohol.

The question of what weight should be given to the defendant's own perceptions of his fitness or otherwise to drive was considered further in *DPP* v. *Barker* [1990] RTR 1. The defendant, an infrequent drinker, consumed two or three glasses of wine at a restaurant and then, at a party, consumed a tumbler full of what she thought to be orange juice, but which was in reality one-third vodka and two-thirds orange juice. She could remember nothing after the first drink. She was arrested and supplied a breath specimen at a police station, which contained 109 µg of alcohol in 100 ml of breath. The justices found that special reasons existed in that she would not have been over the limit were it not for the laced drink. As she had suffered a total loss of knowledge of her actions, she could not have been aware that her condition was influenced by consumption of alcohol.

The Divisional Court dismissed the prosecutor's appeal. The justices had considered the defendant's mental and physical condition on the day, that she was an infrequent drinker and had never consumed spirits, the quantity of alcohol consumed, the effect of alcohol on her, the fact that the effect was sudden rather than gradual, that she could not detect the vodka, that she had suffered a total loss of knowledge of her actions and was not aware her condition was influenced by consumption of alcohol. The justices' finding that she could not have been aware of her actions or appreciate that she was unfit to drive were sufficient to contribute towards the finding that a special reason existed.

In *Smith* v. *Geraghty* [1986] RTR 222 the Divisional Court said that in cases where it was alleged that the defendant's drink had been laced, it was important to ascertain the blood–alcohol concentration at the time when the offence was committed and any difference there would have been if the drink suspected of being laced had not been consumed. The burden of proving that the excess of the blood–alcohol reading was caused by the doctored drink was on the defendant and had to be proved to the civil standard of balance of probabilities. Justices should not be drawn into detailed scientific calculation regarding the rate of dispersal of alcohol in the body and should only take such evidence into account in cases where it was relatively clear and straightforward.

In such cases, therefore, what evidence is expected from the defendant to show the effect of the laced drink and what can be inferred by the court from its own knowledge of such matters? In *Smith* v. *DPP* [1990] RTR 17 the defendant pleaded special reasons where he admitted the consumption of one and a half pints of ordinary strength lager and a non-alcoholic fruit juice, which he had consumed not knowing that it contained a single measure of vodka. Later analysis showed 86 mg of alcohol in 100 ml of his blood. It was held by the Divisional Court that it was unnecessary for medical evidence to be called in support in such cases where it should have been obvious to the court that it was the alcohol that the defendant had unknowingly consumed that was responsible for his being above the prescribed limit.

Comprehensive guidance was given to justices when considering special reasons arguments in the context of laced drinks (*DPP* v. *O'Connor* (1992) 13 Cr App R (S) 189). In such cases there is a two-stage process to be gone through by the courts that involves initially determining whether special reasons exist and then determining whether the court is prepared to exercise its discretion not to disqualify or to disqualify for a shorter period. The onus of establishing special reasons was on the motorist, who had to prove his case on the balance of probabilities. Thus, when seeking to establish a special reason in a laced drinks case, the motorist would have to establish by relevant and admissible evidence that his drink had been laced; that he did not know or suspect that his drink had been laced; and that, if he had not consumed the laced drink, he would not have exceeded the prescribed limit.

In order to establish that the motorist's drink has been laced, expert evidence will normally be called to indicate whether the amount that the motorist admitted drinking would in any event have taken him above the prescribed limit and to examine critically the contentions put forward by the motorist as to the amount of drink consumed. However, where it is obvious to a layman that the laced drink has taken the defendant over the limit, as the reading was only just over the prescribed limit, then it will not be necessary to call expert evidence, subject to the caveat that it will never be possible to define those cases where it might be 'obvious' to a layman.

In *DPP* v. *Sharma* [2005] RTR 27 the defendant motorist went for a drink with friends after work. Believing that she would be travelling home by taxi and would appreciate a stronger drink, a friend added vodka to two Smirnoff Ice drinks bought for her. An evidential breath test subsequently showed her to be twice the prescribed limit.

The justices found that she was unaware that extra vodka had been added to her drinks; that she did not display any signs of impairment as a result; that there had been nothing unusual about her manner of driving and that, but for the added vodka, she would not have been over the prescribed limit. Despite evidence provided by experts that, given the level of alcohol in the defendant's breath they would have expected her to have been aware of being affected by alcohol, the court found special reasons not to disqualify her.

Whilst pointing to the fact that it was for a defendant motorist to prove, often by expert evidence, that drinks had been laced, that he did not know this to be the case and that without the additional alcohol he would not have exceeded the prescribed limit, the Divisional Court accepted that cases turned on their own facts. Whilst it might seem surprising that the justices had found that the driver had felt no effect of the additional alcohol, such a finding was not, in the circumstances, perverse or wrong in law.

In addition to the tests laid down in *O'Connor*, there is also considerable force in the proposition that where a drink an appellant has been offered may contain alcohol, there is a duty on that person to inquire what he is drinking. Any driver, attending a function at which alcohol is being consumed, who assumes that a particular drink contains no alcohol is taking a risk. The purpose of the road traffic legislation is to ensure, in the public interest, that people do not drive when they have taken alcohol in excess of the prescribed limit. Therefore, if the penalty of disqualification is to be mitigated, a driver must be able to show that he has done all that could reasonably be expected of him to avoid the commission of an offence (*Robinson* v. *DPP* (2004) 168 JP 522).

In cases where the motorist intends to call evidence to prove facts or medical opinion in support of a plea of special reasons, it is desirable that notice of the evidence to be called be given to the prosecution in sufficient time to enable them to deal with the evidence. Even where special reasons have been established it does not follow that disqualification is automatically avoided. Where the motorist drives erratically or is substantially over the prescribed limit, the court will need to take into account whether he should have appreciated that he was not in a condition to drive.

The complexity of 'laced drinks' cases and the need to establish medical support for the contentions of the driver led the Divisional Court in *R* v. *Gravesend Magistrates' Court, ex parte Baker* (1997) 161 JP 765 to say that in cases where it was necessary to call a scientific expert to give evidence whether the applicant's explanation was consistent with the scientific facts and to say whether the amount of alcohol that the applicant admitted consuming would have resulted in any event in his being over the prescribed limit, legal aid (or a grant of representation) should be granted. The assistance of a solicitor would be required to find witnesses of fact, to take proper proofs and to extract the story in the witness box from those witnesses and from the applicant. These cases were clearly cases where the court itself would benefit from the driver having legal representation.

It is also possible in such cases for the prosecution to bring proceedings against the person responsible for lacing the drink if he was aware that the person whose drink he was lacing was later going to drive. In cases where evidence is going to be called that drinks have been laced it would appear therefore that the court should first warn the perpetrator that he need not answer any question that may tend to incriminate him at a later stage.

No intention of driving

Where a defendant has been charged under RTA 1988, s.7(6) with failing to provide a specimen in circumstances where it is alleged that the defendant was in charge of the vehicle and not driving or attempting to drive, then in *McCormick* v. *Hitchins* [1988] RTR 182 it was held that, if it were proved to the satisfaction of the court that the defendant had no intention of driving the vehicle and could not have been a danger on the road, there may be special reasons for not endorsing the defendant's licence with the penalty points appropriate to that offence. However, the decision whether or not to endorse the licence is one to be taken in the exercise of the normal discretion in such cases, and even where the defendant proves that he would not have driven or been a danger on the road, the court may still find that special reasons exist, but endorse the licence.

12.5 ALTERNATIVE VERDICTS

Section 24 of RTOA 1988 provides that a magistrates' court dealing with the trial of certain offences can convict a defendant of an alternative offence where the allegations made amount to or include an allegation of an offence set out in the section as being an alternative. The section provides that alternative findings of guilt can be made in the circumstances described in **Table 12.3**. The section expressly precludes an alternative finding of being 'in charge' of a vehicle where the original charge is one under RTA 1988, s.3A.

12.6 DRINK-DRIVE REHABILITATION COURSES

The North Committee Review of Road Traffic Law recommended the setting up of courses designed to rehabilitate offenders who commit offences involving drinking and driving. The aims of the committee were given legislative effect by RTA 1991, which inserted a new RTOA 1988, s.34A after s.34:

  (1) This section applies where –

      (a) a person is convicted of an offence under section 3A (causing death by careless driving when under the influence of drink or drugs), 4 (driving or being in charge when under influence of drink or drugs), 5 (driving or being in charge with excess alcohol) or 7 (failing to provide a specimen) of the Road Traffic Act 1988, and

      (b) the court makes an order under section 34 of this Act disqualifying him for a period of not less than twelve months.

  (2) Where this section applies, the court may make an order that the period of disqualification imposed under section 34 shall be reduced if, by a date specified in the order under this section, the offender satisfactorily completes a course approved by the Secretary of State for the purposes of this section and specified in the order.

  (3) The reduction made by an order under this section in a period of disqualification imposed under section 34 shall be a period specified in the order of not less than three months and not more than one quarter of the unreduced period (and accordingly where the period imposed under section 34 is twelve months, the reduced period shall be nine months).

(4) The court shall not make an order under this section unless –

(a) it is satisfied that a place on the course specified in the order will be available for the offender,

(b) the offender appears to the court to be of or over the age of 17,

(c) the court has explained the effect of the order to the offender in ordinary language, and has informed him of the amount of the fees for the course and of the requirement that he must pay them before beginning the course, and

(d) the offender has agreed that the order should be made.

(5) The date specified in an order under this section as the latest date for completion of a course must be at least two months before the last day of the period of disqualification as reduced by the order.

(6) An order under this section shall name the petty sessions area (or in Scotland the sheriff court district or, where an order has been made under this section by a stipendiary magistrate, the commission area) in which the offender resides or will reside.

The introduction of the scheme throughout Great Britain followed a six-year experimental period during which the Transport Research Laboratory carried out a programme of research to assess the re-offending rates of those who attended the courses. The results of the monitoring showed that the scheme was effective in reducing the re-offending rates of those who attended courses by nearly 60 per cent. As a result the scheme was made permanent from 31 December 1999 and made available to all courts.

The primary objective of such courses for alcohol-impaired drivers is to reduce the incidence of drinking and driving and repeated offences. The Department of Transport sets minimum requirements for such courses to cover:

• information about alcohol and its effects on the body, including concepts of tolerance and dependence, physical effects, disease and sensible drinking;

• the effect of alcohol consumption on performance;

• an analysis of the offender's behaviour;

• alternatives to drinking and driving;

• future action and sources of help.

Drink-drive rehabilitation courses have been available to all courts in England and Wales since 1 January 2000 as a consequence of the Courses for Drink-Drive Offenders (Experimental Period) (Termination of Restrictions) Order 1999. Whilst practices may vary, the majority of courts see the scheme as a useful antidote to the punitive effects of mandatory disqualification and are, therefore, prepared to offer the scheme to most, if not all, convicted offenders.

Once the offender has consented to the scheme and agreed to pay the relevant fees (some organisers offer pre-payment by regular weekly or monthly part-payment) he must attend the course regularly and in a sober condition.

On satisfactory completion, the course organiser notifies the court which, in turn, notifies the Driver and Vehicle Licensing Agency so that the offender's driver record is amended. A decision not to issue a completion certificate can be appealed to the supervising court, which can give a declaration that the organiser's decision was contrary to the requirements of the statute.

12.7   HIGH RISK OFFENDERS

Special arrangements came into existence from May 1983 whereby those offenders who are perceived to have a continuing alcohol problem are required to convince the Department for Transport that there is no longer such a problem before they can apply to have their driving licences returned after the end of their disqualification period.

Since June 1990, 'high risk offenders', as defined by reg.74 of the Motor Vehicles (Driving Licences) Regulations 1999 (SI 1999/2864) (the '1999 Regulations') for the purposes of RTA 1988, s.94(4) are:

(a)   those disqualified for driving whilst two and half times or more over the prescribed limit;

(b)   those disqualified for failure, without reasonable excuse, to supply a specimen for analysis pursuant to RTA 1988, s.7; and

(c)   those disqualified on two or more occasions within 10 years for either exceeding the legal limit of alcohol in their breath, blood or urine, or being unfit to drive through drink.

Offenders who fit these criteria will be notified by the DVLA after conviction that when their disqualification expires, any application for renewal of their licence may be deferred pending consideration of whether the conviction indicates a medical disability and, if so, whether the person concerned has managed to bring the drinking problem under control during the time when he has been disqualified from driving. The driver is advised by letter to seek help and advice during the period of the disqualification.

Four months before the end of the period of disqualification the Medical Advisory Branch of the Department for Transport will send the driver an application form to renew the licence together with a further letter explaining that the licence will not be renewed unless the Secretary of State can be satisfied that there is no longer an alcohol problem.

If the driver makes an application to renew, he will be asked to attend an assessment centre for interview and medical examination. In addition, he will be required to provide a blood sample at a local hospital for analysis. The result of the analysis together with the interview will then determine the Secretary of State's decision. Borderline cases can be referred to a consultant psychiatrist who deals with alcohol problems.

12.8 SENTENCING GUIDELINE TABLES

Table 12.1(a) Magistrates' courts sentencing guidelines – excess alcohol

Excess alcohol (drive or attempt to drive)	Road Traffic Act 1988 s.5(1)(a) Penalty: Level 5 and/or 6 months Triable only summarily Must endorse and disqualify *at least* 12 months: disqualify at least 36 months for a further offence within 10 years

CONSIDER THE SERIOUSNESS OF THE OFFENCE
THE LEVEL OF SERIOUSNESS AND GUIDELINE SENTENCE ARE RELATED TO THE BREATH/BLOOD/URINE LEVEL

 ### CONSIDER AGGRAVATING AND MITIGATING FACTORS AND THE WEIGHT TO ATTACH TO EACH

for example	for example
Ability to drive seriously impaired Caused injury/fear/damage Police pursuit Evidence of nature of the driving Type of vehicle, eg carrying passengers for reward/large goods vehicle High reading (and in combination with above) *This list is not exhaustive*	Emergency Moving a vehicle a very short distance Spiked drinks *This list is not exhaustive*

If offender is on bail, this offence is more serious
If offender has previous convictions, their relevance and any failure to respond to previous sentences should be considered – they may increase the seriousness. The court should make it clear, when passing sentence, that this was the approach adopted.

TAKE A PRELIMINARY VIEW OF SERIOUSNESS, THEN CONSIDER OFFENDER MITIGATION

for example
  Co-operation with police

CONSIDER YOUR SENTENCE

Offer a rehabilitation course.
Compare your decision with the suggested guideline level of sentence and reconsider your reasons carefully if you have chosen a sentence at a different level.
Consider a reduction for a timely guilty plea.

DECIDE YOUR SENTENCE

BREATH	BLOOD	URINE	DISQUALIFY NOT LESS THAN	GUIDELINE
36-55	80-125	107-170	12 months	B
56-70	126-160	171-214	16 months	C
71-85	161-195	215-260	20 months	C
86-100	196-229	261-308	24 months	CONSIDER COMMUNITY PENALTY
101-115	230-264	309-354	28 months	
116-130	265-300	355-400	32 months	CONSIDER CUSTODY
131+	301+	401+	36 months	

Table 12.1(b) Magistrates' courts sentencing guidelines – refuse evidential specimen

Refuse evidential specimen (Drive or attempt to drive)	Road Traffic Act 1988 s.7(6) Penalty: Level 5 and/or 6 months: Triable only summarily` Must endorse and disqualify at least 12 months: disqualify at least 36 months for a further offence within 10 years

CONSIDER THE SERIOUSNESS OF THE OFFENCE

IS DISCHARGE OR FINE APPROPRIATE?
GUIDELINE: → **IS IT SERIOUS ENOUGH FOR A COMMUNITY PENALTY?**
IS IT SO SERIOUS THAT ONLY CUSTODY IS APPROPRIATE?

THIS IS A GUIDELINE FOR A FIRST-TIME OFFENDER PLEADING NOT GUILTY

 ## CONSIDER AGGRAVATING AND MITIGATING FACTORS AND THE WEIGHT TO ATTACH TO EACH

for example 　Ability to drive seriously impaired 　Caused injury/fear/damage 　Evidence of nature of the driving 　Police pursuit 　Type of vehicle, eg carrying passengers for 　　reward/large goods vehicle 　*This list is not exhaustive*	for example 　Not the driver

If offender is on bail, this offence is more serious
If offender has previous convictions, their relevance and any failure to respond to previous sentences should be considered – they may increase the seriousness. The court should make it clear, when passing sentence, that this was the approach adopted.

TAKE A PRELIMINARY VIEW OF SERIOUSNESS, THEN CONSIDER OFFENDER MITIGATION

for example
　Evidence of genuine remorse
　Voluntary completion of alcohol impaired driver course (if available)

CONSIDER YOUR SENTENCE

Offer a rehabilitation course.
Endorse licence. DISQUALIFY – a minimum period of 24 months is suggested.
Examine carefully aggravating/mitigating factors disclosed – do these justify any variation in period of disqualification suggested? If substantial aggravating factors, consider higher fine/community penalty/custody
Compare it with the suggested guideline level of sentence and reconsider your reasons carefully if you have chosen a sentence at a different level.
Consider a reduction for a timely guilty plea.

DECIDE YOUR SENTENCE

Table 12.2 Maximum penalties for offences

Section	Offence	Disqualification	Penalty Points	Fine	Imprisonment
3A	Causing death through careless driving whilst unfit	Obligatory (2 years) and mandatory re-test	3–11	Unlimited	14 years
4(1)	Driving or attempting to drive whilst unfit through drink or drugs	Obligatory	3–11	Level 5	6 months
4(2)	In charge whilst unfit	Discretionary	10	Level 4	3 months
5(1)(a)	Driving whilst over the prescribed limit	Obligatory	3–11	Level 5	6 months
5(1)(b)	In charge whilst over the prescribed limit	Discretionary	10	Level 4	3 months
6(4)	Refusal of screening breath test	Discretionary	4	Level 3	
7(6)	Fail to provide specimen when driving	Obligatory	3–11	Level 5	6 months
7(6)	Fail to provide specimen when in charge	Discretionary	10	Level 4	3 months
7A(6)	Failing to allow specimen of blood to be subjected to laboratory test (driving)	Obligatory	3–11	Level 5	6 months
7A(6)	Failing to allow specimen of blood to be subjected to laboratory test (in charge)	Discretionary	10	Level 4	3 months

Table 12.3 Alternative offences

Offence charged	Alternative
Causing death by careless driving when under the influence of drink or drugs.	Careless and inconsiderate driving Driving when unfit to drive through drink or drugs Driving with excess alcohol in blood, breath or urine Failing to provide a specimen
Driving or attempting to drive whilst unfit through drink or drugs	Being in charge of a vehicle whilst unfit through drink or drugs
Driving or attempting to drive with excess alcohol in breath, blood or urine	Being in charge of a vehicle with excess alcohol in breath, blood or urine

CHAPTER 13

Road Safety Act 2006

13.1 BACKGROUND

In 2000 the Prime Minister launched the Road Safety Strategy 'Tomorrow's Roads – Safer for Everyone', which set out the Government's framework for improving road safety, integral to which was the achievement of casualty reduction targets of 40 per cent of those killed and seriously injured (50 per cent for children) by 2010. In 2004 the Government published the first three-year review of the strategy, which evaluated the effectiveness of the strategy and the likelihood of delivering the 2010 targets. The Road Safety Act gives effect to several elements of the Government's wider road safety strategy to reduce casualties and it supports the push towards achieving the casualty reduction targets.

The Act consists of 63 sections and 7 Schedules and makes wide-ranging changes to road traffic law with a view to introducing measures designed to address the consequences of bad driving and to give those guilty of such offences the opportunity for further training to assist in ensuring that they do not commit similar offences when allowed back on the roads. The following sections have relevance to the drinking and driving provisions already outlined in this book.

13.2 SECTIONS

Section 13: High risk offenders: medical inquiries following disqualification

This section prevents high risk offenders (as defined in the relevant Regulations – see below) from having entitlement to drive by virtue of RTA 1988, s.88 whilst awaiting the outcome of medical inquiries relevant to an application for the return of a licence following a period of disqualification. This will ensure that those who, by the nature of their offending, have been identified as presenting a greater risk of being medically unfit to drive are prevented from driving until the Secretary of State is satisfied that they are fit to do so.

'High risk offenders' are defined by reg.74 of the Motor Vehicles (Driving Licences) Regulations 1999 (SI 1999/2864) for the purposes of RTA 1988, s.94(4) as:

(a) those disqualified for driving whilst two and half times or more over the prescribed limit;
(b) those disqualified for failure, without reasonable excuse, to supply a specimen for analysis pursuant to RTA 1988, s.7; and
(c) those disqualified on two or more occasions within 10 years for either exceeding the legal limit of alcohol in their breath, blood or urine, or being unfit to drive through drink.

Section 88 of RTA 1988 sets out exceptions to the general requirement for anyone wishing to drive a motor vehicle on a road to have the appropriate licence authorising him to do so. These include, under s.88(1)(a)(i), where the driver has held a licence to drive that class of vehicle and, under s.88(1)(b)(i), where the Secretary of State has received a qualifying application by the driver for a licence to drive that class of vehicle.

Section 14: Period of endorsement for failure to allow specimen to be tested

Section 45(7) of RTOA 1988 provides that the period of effectiveness of an endorsement in respect of specified driving offences connected with drink or drugs or failing to provide a specimen is 11 years from the conviction. This section amends s.45(7) by adding the offence of failing to allow a specimen to be subjected to a laboratory test (RTA 1988, s.7A(6)), so that where a person is guilty of an offence under RTA 1988, s.7A(6) the endorsement will remain effective for a period of 11 years from the conviction.

This corrects a consequential amendment missed in the Police Reform Act 2002 which inserted s.7A (specimens of blood taken from persons incapable of consenting).

Section 15: Alcohol ignition interlocks

This section inserts into RTOA 1988 new ss.34D, 34E, 34F, 34G and 41B.

Its effect is to give courts the power in certain circumstances to offer offenders the opportunity to participate, at their own expense, in an 'alcohol ignition interlock programme'. Where an offender agrees to this his overall period of disqualification may be reduced. The provision applies to a person who is convicted of a relevant drink driving offence on a second occasion in a period of 10 years and is to be disqualified for no less than two years. The period on the programme must be at least 12 months but must not exceed a half of the original unreduced disqualification period. This programme may not be offered to someone for whom an order is made under s.34A (drink drive offenders rehabilitation order).

The programme requires the offender to comply with certain conditions. These include elements of education and counselling but a central feature is that the offender may only drive a motor vehicle that is fitted with an alcohol interlock device that is designed to prevent the vehicle being driven until a specimen of breath has been given in which the proportion of alcohol does not exceed a specified amount. If a person interferes with the device to try to prevent it working he commits a new offence, as does someone other than the offender who gives a specimen of breath to enable the offender to drive the vehicle.

Any failure on the part of the offender to comply with the conditions of the programme will result in restoration of the full original disqualification period. The interlock device will be type approved by the Secretary of State and will be set at 9 µg of alcohol in 100 ml of breath.

Provision is made for a 'certificate of failing fully to participate' in a programme. In the event of such a certificate being issued the offender must be notified and given an opportunity to appeal to the supervising court. If he does appeal the court may allow him to continue on the programme until the outcome of the appeal is known.

The Secretary of State may vary by regulations the period of 10 years that determines whether a previous offence is relevant, the minimum disqualification period before an offender becomes eligible for the programme, the minimum period of the programme and the maximum proportion of the original disqualification period that may be served on a programme.

Section 16: Experimental period for section 15

This section provides for an experimental period for the alcohol ignition interlock programme described in section 15. The experiment may continue until the end of 2010 but the Secretary of State may specify a later date by order. He may also terminate the restrictions specified for the experimental period. The section provides for the Secretary of State to designate certain court areas for the purpose of the experiment. During the experimental period the programme would not be offered to persons convicted under RTA 1988, s.3A (causing death by careless driving when under influence of drink or drugs).

Section 31: Extension of offence in section 3A of Road Traffic Act 1988

Subsection (2) of this section extends the offence in RTA 1988, s.3A (causing death by careless driving when under the influence of drink or drugs) to allow for a person whose blood has been taken under s.7A (specimens of blood taken from persons incapable of consenting) to be prosecuted for the s.3A offence where, without reasonable excuse, that person does not (when he is later able to) consent to his blood being subjected to a laboratory test.

The effect of subs.(3) of this section is that a prosecution for the s.3A offence on the basis of a refusal of consent under s.7A would only be possible where the offence was committed with a motor vehicle, as opposed to any other kind of mechanically propelled vehicle. This is consistent with the limitation already in RTA 1988, s.3A(3).

Subsection (4) amends RTOA 1988, s.24(1) to provide that conviction of an offence under s.7A(6) (failing to give permission for laboratory test) may be an alternative verdict to conviction of an offence under s.3A.

Section 35: Reduced disqualification period for attendance on course

This section substitutes RTOA 1988, ss.34A, 34B and 34C replacing these with new subsections.

The amended versions of these sections extend the principle of the drink drive rehabilitation scheme to certain other offences. Courts will have the power to offer offenders the opportunity to pay for and undertake a retraining course, successful completion of which will reduce the period of the offender's disqualification by an amount specified in the court order. In addition to those for whom this option is currently available, it will also be available for those persons who are disqualified for 12 months or more on conviction of failing to allow a specimen to be subjected to a laboratory test in the course of an investigation into certain offences: careless, and inconsiderate driving, failing to comply with traffic signs or speeding. The option will *not* be available to any person who has committed one of the offences mentioned in the section in the previous three years and success-fully completed an approved course pursuant to an order under RTOA 1988, ss.34A or 30A on conviction of the offence, nor to a person who is within his probationary period under the Road Traffic (New Drivers) Act 1995.

The effect of the substituted provisions also means that the court in which the conviction is registered will administer the case (the 'supervising court'). If the offender appeals against a course provider's decision not to give a certificate of completion of a course or seeks a declaration that the course provider is in default, he may apply to either the supervising court or a rele-vant local court in the area in which the offender resides. This replaces the previous system whereby in all cases where the offender lived outside the petty sessional area of the court where the conviction was heard, a super-vising court was appointed in the petty sessional area in which the offender resided or was about to reside.

The Secretary of State may vary by regulations those specified offences in respect of training course orders that may be made under s.34A. The Secretary of State may also vary by regulations the minimum period for which a person must be disqualified to be eligible for such an order, the minimum reduction in the disqualification period, the fraction of the disqualification period that may be the reduction, and the period over which a previous conviction and successful completion of a previous training course would make the offender ineligible for a course under s.34A.

Index

Accidents 19
  'reasonable belief' after 17–9
Acetone 79
Admission of evidence 100–1
Aiding and abetting 52
AIDS 154–5
Alcohol
  ignorance of effects of 175–6
  laced drinks 180–3
  prescribed limit 67–8
Alcohol ignition interlocks 192–3
Alternative verdicts 184, 189
Arrest 29–30
  checklist 37–8
  driving or in charge whilst unfit 61
  effect of unlawful arrest 142–3
  legislation 27–9
  protection of hospital patients 37, 41
  trespass and 31–5
Asthma 153
Attempting to drive
  definition 52–3

Back-calculation 135–7
Blood tests 2–4, 28
  authorised analyst of blood 119–20
  dividing the specimen 127–30
  driver preference 101–4
  failure to provide specimen *see*
    Failure to provide specimen
  hospital patients 39–40, 42, 43–7
  human rights issues 122–5
  methods of analysis 125–7
  obligation and option to provide
    specimen 95–108
  option where evidence of drug
    impairment 58–61
  provision of specimens for analysis
    69, 97–100

results of test *see* Statement of
  measurement of alcohol
specimen taken from person incapable
  of consenting 45–7
Breath tests 2, 3, 28
  achieving objective of test 11
  arrest after *see* Arrest
  carrying out of breath test by
    constable in uniform 11–2
  checklist 24–5
  devices *see* Devices for breath tests
  failure to provide specimen *see*
    Failure to provide specimen
  hospital patients 41, 44–5, 71
  place for administration of test
    20
  power to require preliminary tests
    5–8
  provision of specimens for analysis
    68–77
  random testing 12–4
  reasonable belief 17–9
  reasonable suspicion of offence 12–7,
    30
  record printout 112–3
  results of test *see* Statement of
    measurement of alcohol
Bronchitis 154
Burden of proof 124, 131

Campaigns against drink driving 15
Car *see* Motor vehicle
Car parks 54–6, 71
Caravan parks 54–5
**Causing death whilst under the influence
  of drink/drugs**
  legislation 161
  offence 161–6
  Road Traffic Bill 2006 and 193–4

Challenges to approved devices 84–94
  challenging approval following post-
    approval testing 92–4
  general unreliability 84–7
  reliability in individual cases 87–92
Community sentences 167
Custodial sentences 163, 165, 168

Death *see* Causing death whilst under
  the influence of drink/drugs
Defences
  'in charge' statutory defence 63–6
  see also Special reasons
Depression 156
Detention of persons affected by alcohol
  or drugs 36–7
Devices for breath tests 8–11
  approval of devices 83–4
  approved 8–9, 80
  challenges to approved devices 84–94
  manufacturer's instructions 9–11
  record printout 112–3
  reliable device not available for use
    77–9
  unreliable 80–2, 84–92
Diabetes 49–50, 125, 172
Disqualification from driving 163, 165–6,
  168–9
  failure to provide specimen and 157
  high risk offenders 186, 191–2
  interim 170–1
  removal of 169–70
  special reasons for not disqualifying
    see Special reasons
Distance driven 178–80
Dividing the specimen 127–30
Doctor
  consultation with 143–7
Double jeopardy 168
Drink drive rehabilitation courses 184–6,
  194–5
Driving
  definition 50–3
Driving or in charge whilst unfit
  arrest provisions 61
  blood/urine option where evidence of
    drug impairment 58–61
  checklist 61–2
  definitions 49–58
  'in charge' 53
  'in charge' statutory defence 63–6
  legislation 49

  'unfitness to drive' 57–8
Driving whilst over prescribed limit
  approval of test devices 83–4
  challenges to approved test devices
    84–94
  checklist 108–9
  'in charge' statutory defence 63–6
  legislation 67
  obligation and option to provide
    blood/urine 95–108
  prescribed limit 67–8
  provision of specimens for analysis
    68–82
Drugs 82
  blood/urine option where evidence of
    drug impairment 58–61
  definition 49–50
  impairment tests 23–4
Duress 177–8

Embarrassment 152
Emergency situations 176–7
Entry
  by force 33
  by implied licence 35–6
  trespass 31–5
Errors on face of the statement 117–8
Evidence
  admission of 100–1
  authorised analyst of blood 119–20
  back-calculation 135–7
  checklist 120
  dividing the specimen 127–30
  errors on face of the statement 117–8
  human rights issues 122–5
  legislation 111–2
  of proportion of alcohol 130–5
  service of statement 113–7
  signing statement 118–9
  status of the statement 112–3
  using specimen evidence 121–2

Failure to provide specimen
  blood tests 45
  breath tests 20–2, 30
  checklist 159–60
  consultation with doctor or solicitor
    143–7
  effect of unlawful arrest 142–3
  effect on sentence 157–9, 188, 192
  'failure' and 'refusal' 143
  legislation 139–40

making every effort 147–51
medical reasons for not providing
    specimen 72–7, 104–8, 140,
    152–7
reasonable excuse 22–3, 143–4, 147,
    151–7
trespass and 31, 32
warning of consequences 141–2
Fines 167–8

Gastric reflux 80, 81

Health professionals
taking blood specimens 97
see also Doctor
High risk offenders 186, 191–2
HIV/AIDS 154–5
Hospitals
breath tests at 41, 44–5, 71
checklist 47
definitions 41–3
protection of hospital patients 37,
    39–41
providing blood/urine specimen at
    2–4, 44–7, 69–70, 71
treatment in 43–4
Human rights issues 122–5

Ignition interlocks 192–3
Ignorance of effects of alcohol 175–6
Impairment tests 23–4
Imprisonment 163, 165, 168
'In charge of motor vehicle'
definition 53
no intention of driving 183–4
statutory defence 63–6
Informants 15–6
Innocence
presumption of 122, 123
Insulin 49–50
Intention
no intention of driving 183–4
Interim disqualification from driving
170–1

Laced drinks 180–3
Language problems 141
Learner drivers 52–3
Legal advice 143–7
Liver conditions 173

Maximum penalties 171, 189

**Medical inquiries following
    disqualification** 186, 191–2
**Medical reasons for not providing
    specimens**
blood specimen 104–8, 154–5
breath specimen 72–7, 140, 152–4,
    156–7
Methods of analysis 125–7
Mobile telephones 79
Motor vehicle
definition 56–7

Overview of procedure 1

Panic attacks 156–7
Phobias 74, 105, 152, 155
Points on licences 168
Police officers
carrying out of breath test by
    constable in uniform 11–2
requirement to sign statement of
    measurement of alcohol 118–9
trespass by 31–5
Police station
detention of persons affected by
    alcohol or drugs 36–7
place for administration of
    preliminary test 20
providing blood/urine specimen at
    2–4, 28, 69–70, 71–2
Post-accident consumption
checklist 137
Preliminary tests
breath tests *see* Breath tests
impairment tests 23–4
Presumption of innocence 122, 123
Prison sentences 163, 165, 168
Proof
burden of 124, 131

Radio interference with test devices 79
Random testing 12–4
Reasonable belief 17–9
**Reasonable excuse for failure to provide
    specimen** 22–3, 143–4, 147, 151–7
medical reasons 72–7, 104–8, 140,
    152–7
Reasonable suspicion of offence 12–7, 30
after vehicle stopped 14–5
information provided by another 15–6
offence committed while vehicle in
    motion 17

Reasonable suspicion of offence *cont.*
random testing 12–4
Reflux 80, 81
Refusal *see* Failure to provide specimen
Rehabilitation courses 184–6, 194–5
Results of test *see* Statement of
measurement of alcohol
Road Safety Act (2006) 191–5
Roads
definition 54–6

Sentencing 167–70
alternative verdicts 184, 189
causing death whilst under the
influence of drink/drugs 163
community sentences 167
custodial sentences 163, 165, 168
failure to provide specimen and
157–9, 188, 192
fines 167–8
guideline tables 187–9
maximum penalties 171, 189
rehabilitation courses 184–6, 194–5
special reasons *see* Special reasons
see also Disqualification from driving
Shortness of distance driven 178–80
Solicitor
consultation with 143–7
Special reasons 172–84
duress 177–8
emergency situations 176–7
ignorance of effects of alcohol 175–6
laced drinks 180–3

legislation 172–5
no intention of driving 183–4
shortness of distance 178–80
Statement of measurement of alcohol
errors on face of 117–8
requirement to serve 113–7
requirement to sign 118–9
status of 112–3
Suspicion *see* Reasonable suspicion of
offence
Swabs 131

Tests *see* Blood tests; Breath tests;
Impairment tests; Urine tests
Trespass 31–5

'Unfitness to drive'
definition 57–8
Urine tests 2–4, 28
authorised analyst of urine
119–20
dividing the specimen 127–30
driver preference 101–4
hospital patients 45
methods of analysis 125–7
obligation and option to provide
specimen 95–108
option where evidence of drug
impairment 58–61
provision of specimens for analysis
69, 97–100
results of test *see* Statement of
measurement of alcohol

Key Criminal Cases 2006

Edited by Andrew Keogh

Fully updated, this excellent collection provides you with a quick and easy way to access the key criminal cases from 2006 and bring yourself up to date with the latest in criminal litigation.

Key cases include:

- *R.* v. *Ashton* (procedural failures)
- *R.* v. *O'Brien and others* (dangerous offenders)
- *R.* v. *Card* (bad character)

The cases are organised alphabetically within subject areas for swift navigation, enabling the reader to quickly find the most up to date cases. Each case contains a concise digest of the essential ruling and is supported by electronic updates via Crimeline (www.crimeline.info).

Available from Law Society Publishing:
Email marketing@lawsociety.org.uk for order details

1 85328 579 X
Approx: 176 pages
£29.95
February 2007

The Law Society

Immigration Advice at the Police Station

3rd Edition

Rosie Brennan

Providing essential coverage of both immigration and criminal practice it takes the reader through the situations that clients may face, offering advice on practice and conduct, illustrated using case studies.

Key revisions and new material includes:

- updated information on the system of immigration enforcement action
- chapter on criminal offences introduced by the Asylum and Immigration (Treatment of Claimants) Act 2004, updated information on other immigration offences and discussion of the immigration aspects of these criminal cases
- the amended immigration appeal system
- updates on detention and bail in the police station
- changes to the funding regime.

Available from Law Society Publishing:
Email marketing@lawsociety.org.uk for order details

1 85328 948 5
408 pages
£34.95
January 2006

The Law Society